THE
POLITICS OF
AUTHENTICITY

STUDIES IN POLITICAL THEORY

Michael Walzer, General Editor

THE
POLITICS OF
AUTHENTICITY

Radical Individualism
and the Emergence
of Modern Society

MARSHALL BERMAN

ATHENEUM   New York

1970

To my mother and sister
and to the memory of my father

The nakedest, savagest reality, I say, is preferable to any semblance, however dignified. . . . Given the living man, there will be found *clothes* for him; he will find himself clothes. But the suit-of-clothes pretending that *it* is both clothes and man! . . . Semblance, I assert, must actually *not* divorce itself from Reality. If Semblance do— why then, there must be men found to rebel against Semblance, for it has become a lie!

THOMAS CARLYLE
The French Revolution

"Know Thyself" was written over the portal of the antique world. Over the portal of the new world, "Be Thyself" shall be written.

OSCAR WILDE
The Soul of Man Under Socialism

Preface

T HE IDEA THAT I have called "the politics of authenticity" is a dream of an ideal community in which
individuality will not be subsumed and sacrificed, but fully
developed and expressed. This dream is at once old and
new. "New," first of all, in that it is *modern:* it presupposes
the sort of fluid, highly mobile, urban society, and the sort
of dynamic, expansive economy, which we experience as
distinctively modern, and which nearly everyone in the West
lives in today. But it is "old" too: it has been a leitmotif in
Western culture since early in the eighteenth century, when
men began to feel modernization as an irreversible historical
force, and to think systematically about its human potentialities. This ideal was one of the deepest and most pervasive themes of the Romantic Age, the years roughly from
1789 to 1848. It is central to the work of Blake and Carlyle,
of Chateaubriand and Stendhal, of Schiller and Novalis.

and Hegel. Marx and Engels invoke it in the *Communist Manifesto:* "In place of bourgeois society, with its classes and class conflicts, we will have an association in which the free development of each will be the condition of the free development of all."

The *Manifesto* appeared in 1848, on the eve of the revolutions that would bring to a climax a century of romantic dreams. But this climax turned out to be a catastrophe: the defeats of 1848–1851 generated a disenchantment and despair so deep that the very memory of the dream was lost, wiped out, submerged; for a whole century, the politics of authenticity virtually disappeared from the Western imagination. Thus, from the start of the 1850's to the end of the 1950's, in nearly all arguments between radicals and their opponents, both parties identified the capitalist economy and the liberal state with "individualism," and equated radical aims with a "collectivism" that negated individuality. Political thought was frozen into this dualism until the cultural explosion of the 1960's redefined the terms. The New Left's complaint against democratic capitalism was not that it was too individualistic, but rather that it wasn't individualistic enough: it forced every individual into competitive and aggressive impasses ("zero-sum games") which prevented any individual feelings, needs, ideas, energies from being expressed. The moral basis of this political critique was an ideal of authenticity. This outlook was new and yet old, radical yet traditional. Thus the New Left's lasting cultural achievement—one that may outlive the New Left itself—has been to bring about a return of the repressed, to bring radicalism back to its romantic roots.

When I first thought of writing a book on "the politics of authenticity," American culture had come very close to those roots. But the road was murky and tortuous, and no one knew how close we all were. I was just coming of age then, and the 1950's were beginning to turn into the 1960's. The teachers who were teaching me most, in the fervidly genial atmosphere of Columbia College, were thinking very intensely and deeply about "the self" as an intellectual and cultural problem. They had good reasons of their own for thinking this way. They had been burned badly by the radical politics of the 1930's, a politics that had led them to the verge of a monstrous self-betrayal, or of a nightmarish self-dissolution. Now, shaken but intact, reincarnate as academic humanists and cultural critics, they were hoping to salvage whatever elements of decency and beauty they could find in a wrecked, bleak world, and to put together fragmented but honest lives for themselves. Their concern with personal authenticity grew out of a loss of political faith, hope and love. And yet, even though they had cut themselves off from all radical movements, there was something unmistakably radical in the way they moved. Although they denounced every romantic hope, we could feel something vividly and beautifully romantic about the very intensity of their despair. Even as they spurned and cursed Marxism for its spiritual emptiness, they themselves embodied a different kind of Marxism, a Marxism with soul. The vibrations they unconsciously gave off were far more powerful than the ideology (or, as they would have said, anti-ideology) they tried so hard to transmit. Ironically, then, so many of the great teachers of that time opened doors for their students which they had closed on themselves; they turned us on to currents of desire and hope, of feeling and thought, which they hoped to turn off forever. Thus the same sensibility and awareness which led them away from politics and from radicalism in the 1940's and 1950's led us back to politics and into a new kind of radicalism in the 1960's. The upheavals of these last years have generated a bitter conflict of generations in American intellectual life. In trying to clarify the political consequences of the search for personal authenticity, I have focused on an ultimate concern which I believe both generations share. If we all come to understand what is involved in the desire to be ourselves, it may bring us closer together than we have been.

When I began to write this book, I envisioned it as a comprehensive interpretation of the political and social thought of the Romantic Age. I intended to begin with the decade of the French Revolution, and to explore its spiritual and political impact on the youth of France, England and Germany. I would discuss Montesquieu and Rousseau—and Diderot along with them, so I thought—but only briefly, as a sort of prelude. Before long, however, I found that pre-romantic and pre-revolutionary thought about "the politics of authenticity" was far richer, more complex and exciting than I had imagined; Rousseau, in particular, turned out to be a gold mine—or else, as I sometimes felt, a bottomless pit. I decided then that, instead of trying to "cover" many men and ideas, it would be more fruitful to fix on a few, and to follow them as far as they could lead me. As a result, the book has emerged with a rather peculiar structure. Its focus is at once very narrow and very wide. On one hand, it confines itself to eighteenth-century history, to the lives and ideas of Montesquieu and Rousseau. On the other hand, it opens outward toward a general theory of the structure of personal, social and political life in the modern world. I am not sure what it ultimately "is," history or theory, but I think it is relevant and should be helpful to both.

This book has developed over the years, out of my own search for authenticity. To acknowledge properly all the friends and colleagues who have helped me with the book would require a full confession. Instead, for now, I will thank only those who have figured in the history of the manuscript itself. First of all, Michael Walzer has read it all, in all of its many phases, scrutinized it lengthily and incisively, and kept up a critical but friendly dialogue between us; without him this book could never have come into being. Louis Hartz, Harvey Mansfield, Jr., and Judith Shklar encouraged me to work out some of my romantic dreams in a doctoral dissertation, out of which this book has grown. My friends Morris Dickstein, Richard Locke, Arnold Birenbaum, Shaya Izenberg, Franz Nauen, Ellen Stark, Erika Weinfeld and Martin Wenglinsky read various sections of the manuscript in various stages of development, and their responses helped me to develop it further. The members of the New Collegiate Division of the University of Chicago, and of the Columbia University Seminar in Political and Social Thought, and my colleagues in the Department of Political Science, City College of New York, were receptive and appreciative when I presented fragments of this work before them. The Graduate School of Arts and Sciences of the City University of New York gave me a Faculty Research Grant, which provided time and money at a time when I had little of either and needed lots of both. Robert Zenowich and Laura Johnson of Atheneum helped teach me what a book was, and what I would have to do in order to write one. Michel Radomisli convinced me that I could afford finally to let the manuscript go, that I would not be empty without it. My students at City College listened and talked to me with an avidity and intensity that both opened my mind and eased my soul. My mother and sister, Betty and Diane Berman, labored long and lovingly as editors, typists and spiritual guides. Finally, Carole Greenman Berman, my wife, came into my life at a moment when the thought —and, even more, the feeling—of authenticity were far away; her love for me, like Sophie's for Emile, has "given me all the more reason to be myself," and brought me back into touch with the sources of strength and vision from which any politics of authenticity must arise.

New York City
May 1970   M.B.

Introduction:
The Personal is Political

The problem is you. No scholar to be
found far and wide.

FRANZ KAFKA

My ideas had been broadened by the
study of the history of morals. I had come
to believe that everything is rooted in
politics. . . .

JEAN-JACQUES ROUSSEAU,
Confessions

I HAVE USED the word "authenticity" to designate a
whole family of aspirations and ideals which are central to the cultural life of our age. But my choice of the
word was rather arbitrary; so many others might have done
as well. "Identity," "autonomy," "individuality," "self-
development," "self-realization," "your own thing": our vocabulary overflows with expressions which express a persistent and intense concern with *being oneself*.[1]

[1] This sense of the word "authenticity" has been popularized in the
twentieth century by writers in the tradition of Existentialism. It is
one of the key words in Martin Heidegger's *Being and Time,* trans-
lated from the German by John Macquarie and Edward Robinson
(London: SCM Press, 1962) and in Jean-Paul Sartre's *Being and Noth-
ingness,* translated from the French by Hazel Barnes (New York:
Philosophical Library, 1956). Cf. also J. F. Bugental, *The Search for
Authenticity: An Existential-Analytic Approach to Psychotherapy*
(New York: Holt, Rinehart and Winston, 1965); Amitai Etzioni, *The
Active Society: A Theory of Societal and Political Processes* (New
York: The Free Press, 1968), especially Epilogue, "Alienation, Inauthen-

There is something strange about such a concern. It seems to violate the most basic principle of logic, the law of identity, that A is A. After all, isn't everyone himself already? How can he help being himself? Who or what else could he be? To pursue authenticity as an ideal, as something that must be achieved, is to be self-consciously paradoxical. But those who seek authenticity insist that this paradox is built into the structure of the world they live in. This world, they say, represses, alienates, divides, denies, destroys the self. To be oneself in such a world is not a tautology, but a *problem*.

There have been many times in the history of the West when thinking men have experienced authenticity as a problem. But it is only in modern times that men have come to think of the self as a distinctly *political* problem. In the past two centuries, a radical form of individualism has embedded itself deeply in all Western political cultures;

ticity and their Reduction," 617–667, which includes a discussion of recent uses of the word; Albert Syzmanski, "The Inauthentic Sociology: A Critique of *The Active Society,*" *The Human Factor,* IX. 2 (Spring, 1970), 53–63.

Here is a sampling of the vast literature on "being oneself": Erich Fromm, *Man for Himself* (New York: Rinehart, 1947); Rollo May, *Man's Search for Himself* (New York: Norton, 1956); R. D. Laing: *The Divided Self: An Existential Study in Sanity and Madness* (London: Tavistock, 1956); Alan Wheelis, *The Quest for Identity* (New York: Norton, 1958); Helen M. Lynd, *On Shame and the Search for Identity* (New York: Harcourt, Brace, 1958); Erik H. Erikson, *Identity and the Life Cycle* (New York: International Universities Press, 1959), and Introduction by David Rapaport, "A Historical Survey of Psychoanalytic Ego Psychology"; Erikson, *Identity: Youth and Crisis* (New York: Norton, 1967); Abraham H. Maslow, *Toward a Psychology of Being,* second edition (New York: Van Nostrand, 1968). Many valuable shorter pieces are collected in Maurice R. Stein, Arthur J. Vidich and David Manning White, editors, *Identity and Anxiety: Survival of the Person in Mass Society* (Glencoe, Ill.: The Free Press, 1960), and Eric and Mary Josephson, editors, *Man Alone* (New York: Dell, 1962).

On the theoretical problems that underlie these ideas, cf. Peter Berger and Stanley Pullberg, "Reification and the Sociological Critique of Consciousness," in *History and Theory,* IV, 2 (1965), 196–211.

indeed, as modernization has spread farther and farther beyond the West, this individualism has made itself felt as a political force all over the world.

In the nineteenth century the desire for authenticity became a point of departure for both liberal and socialist thought. Thus, according to John Stuart Mill, "in things that do not primarily concern others, individuality should assert itself"; the freest expression should be given to "experiments in living," "varieties of character" and "different modes of life." Mill insists that, "Where not the person's own character, but the traditions and customs of other people are the rule of conduct are the rule of character, there is wanting one of the principal ingredients of human happiness." [2] The same values underlay Marx's radical indictment of liberalism: liberal economics and politics, he argued, generated "a contradiction between the individuality of each separate proletarian and the condition of life forced upon him, . . . labor." Thus "the proletarians, if they are to assert themselves as individuals, have to abolish the very condition of their existence up to now—which has, moreover, been the condition of all society up to now—namely, labor." Because the modern state, whether liberal or authoritarian, only reinforced and legitimized that condition, it followed that "In order to assert themselves as individuals," the workers would have to "overthrow the state." [3]

The desire for personal authenticity has reasserted itself powerfully in the political culture of our own time. The New Left of the 1960s "appeal to . . . men's unrealized potentiality for self-cultivation, self-direction, self-under-

[2] *On Liberty,* Chapter III, in Marshall Cohen, editor, *The Philosophy of John Stuart Mill* (New York: Modern Library, 1961), 249–50. Cf. also Mill's long citation from Wilhelm von Humbolt, 251.
[3] *The German Ideology,* Part I, translated by Roy Pascal (New York: International Publishers, 1947), 78.

standing and creativity," and seeks to build a society in which every man can find or create "a meaning in life that is personally authentic." [4] The far Right appeals to ideals not so far from these: "Every man, both for his own individual good and for the good of society, is responsible for his own development. The choices that govern his life are choices he must make: they cannot be made by any other human being, or by a collectivity of human beings." [5] Our most vivid and powerful black voices, too, speak to all of us in the name of the self: "I had to find out who I am and who I want to be, what kind of man I should be, and what I could do to become the best of which I was capable. I understood that what had happened to me had also happened to countless other blacks, and it would happen to many, many more." With this need and this understanding, a man experiences a turning point in his life: his personal anger and anguish will develop into political consciousness; he will transform himself from a rapist into a revolutionary.[6] Finally, the emerging movement for women's liberation asserts "women's need for identity, for self-esteem, for achievement, and finally for expression of her own unique individuality." [7] Its most immediate aim is to make it clear to oppressed women everywhere—and to the men who, intentionally or inadvertently, oppress them—that "the personal is political." [8]

[4] Port Huron Statement, 1962, first manifesto of the SDS, in Paul Jacobs and Saul Landau, editors, *The New Radicals* (New York: Vintage Books, 1963), 149–62.

[5] Barry Goldwater, *The Conscience of a Conservative* (Shepherdsville, Kentucky: Victor Publishing Company, 1960), 11.

[6] Eldridge Cleaver, *Soul on Ice* (New York: Delta Books, 1968), 15.

[7] Betty Friedan, *The Feminine Mystique* (New York: Dell, 1964), 304. Cf. especially Chapter 13, "The Forfeited Self," 299–325.

[8] Carol Hanisch "The Personal is Political," in Shulamith Firestone and Anne Koedt, editors, *Notes from the Second Year: Major Writings of the Radical Feminists* (New York, 1970), 76–8.

The search for authenticity, nearly everywhere we find it in modern times, is bound up with a radical rejection of things as they are. It begins with an insistence that the social and political structures men live in are keeping the self stifled, chained down, locked up. It argues that only if the old structure is renovated, or if a new one is built from the ground up—or if the old one is wrecked and nothing put in its place, so that men may live without any structure at all—only then can the self come into its own. It asks what is to be done, and tries to do it. Thus the desire for authenticity has emerged in modern society as one of the most politically explosive of human impulses. I want to examine this impulse in an especially fruitful phase, in the years before the French Revolution, when its political implications were first becoming clear and its disruptive and constructive potentialities were opening up.

In order to bring the problem of authenticity into clear focus, we should imagine a type of social experience in which authenticity is *not* a problem. In a closed, static society governed by fixed norms and traditions which are accepted by all its members, authenticity has no place in the vocabulary of human ideals. Here men are satisfied with the life options which their social system provides for them: they conceive of their highest good as Emile Durkheim defines it, as "the fulfillment of a determinate social function." (*Division of Labor,* 43) [9] They experience themselves as pegs, and aspire only to fill the holes that fit them best. This conception of the self is unfolded concisely in Plato's *Republic*. Plato envisions a social function predestined for

---

[9] *The Division of Labor in Society,* translated by George Simpson (Glencoe, Ill.: The Free Press, 1964). This is Durkheim's reformulation—in effect, his "socialization"—of the Kantian categorical imperative.

every man: once he has arrived there his nature is at one with itself, and he comes to rest in a static equilibrium. The Guardians must "assign [each man] the station proper to his nature." (370, 415) Once a man is fitted into the niche he was born for—whether laborer, soldier or philosopher—the loose ends in his character fall away, "each part of his nature is exercising its proper function," and he takes on that perfect balance which Plato calls justice. (442) If all citizens are "set to the tasks for which their natures are fitted, one man to one work, [then] each one of them, fulfilling his own function, [will] be not many men, but one. . . ." (423) [10] Thus it is the filling of a niche in society that gives a man his identity, that makes him the particular man he is. Violent class struggles may go on; but they concern only the allocation of particular holes to particular pegs. The board itself, the closely knit but rigidly stratified social system of the Greek *polis,* which defines men precisely by their functions, remains unquestioned and intact.

It was only long after the disintegration of this ancient *polis* that the basis of personal identity was questioned systematically and a search for authenticity was formally begun. The Stoics of Nero's age found themselves in a world governed by chance, contingency and arbitrary power; they could find nothing in it that a man might count on, nothing he could call his own. Personal identity had to be fought for and wrested from such a world; thus the Stoics depicted life as a combat (sometimes athletic, sometimes military) for which their philosophical and moral discipline kept a man in training. Thus, Epictetus said, although we might at any

---

[10] *Republic,* translated by F. M. Cornford (New York: Oxford University Press, 1956). Arabic numbers designate pages in the Stephanus (1578) edition, standard for references to Plato.

moment be stretched out on the rack by a tyrant's whim, a man's "true self . . . is not flesh or bones or sinews, but the faculty which uses them, and which also governs the impressions and understands them." If physical things were irrelevant to the self, so equally were social phenomena: "It's not my place [in society] that makes me well off, but my judgments, and these I can carry with me, . . . these alone are my own and can't be taken away." (*Discourses,* IV. 3) [11] The Stoics' idea of how man fitted into the world was expressed most vividly in Epictetus' metaphor of the world as a theater—a metaphor which would appear as a central symbol throughout the history of the search for authenticity.

> Remember that you are an actor in a play, and that the Author has chosen the character of it. If he wants the play to be short, it's short; if he wants it long, it's long. If he wants you to play the part of a poor man, you must act the part with all your powers; similarly if your role be that of a cripple, a magistrate or a layman. For your business is to play the role assigned you and play it well; but the choice or the cast is an Other's. [*Enchiridion,* 17]

The whole social system, then, was nothing more than a great stage, a platform for performance and role-playing. The world could offer men no opportunity for genuine action, but only for acting out; moreover, they were conscripted into their roles.

This image of man's true self appeared in radical opposition to the existing social order. And yet, it was not an

11 Citations of Epictetus are from G. M. Oates, editor, *The Stoic and Epicurean Philosophers* (New York: Modern Library, 1947). For the *Discourses,* Roman numbers designate the Book, Arabic numbers the Chapter. For the *Enchiridion,* Arabic numbers designate the Maxim.

opposition which in any practical way threatened that order. The Stoics opposed themselves not to any particular ordering of the world, but to the world *per se*. If they felt man's true self to be alienated *from* the world, they found the self at home in a transcendent realm *beyond* the world. They tried to disregard the chaos and absurdity immediately around them, and to contemplate instead the ultimate "harmony of the universe." (*Discourses* I, 12) Ironically, their prescription for immediate action was quite similar to Plato's: each man should "fulfill his own function"— with the understanding, however, that this function was not *really* "his own" at all. Men were asked to stay in place, not because it mattered where they were or what they did, but precisely because it *didn't* matter. "What place shall I have in the state?" Epictetus was asked. "Whatever place you can hold while you maintain the . . . fidelity and self-respect that is within you." (*Enchiridion*, 24) The world was such that one had to play *some* role; but to discriminate among roles, renouncing some, selecting or creating others, would be to attach more importance to the world outside than it deserved. The world beyond and the world within (ultimately these two were one) were where the authentic action was. Thus the search for authenticity began with a negative interpretation of the world, but initiated no positive attempt to change it. In this form, as an ethic of disengaged conformity and internal liberation, it passed into the mainstream of Western culture.

In modern times, however, the ideal of authenticity suddenly emerged as a politically explosive and revolutionary force. We can observe the change very clearly by citing one of its most avid opponents, Edmund Burke. Burke was writing in 1790, at a time when it was clear a Revolution was taking place in France, but not at all clear how far or in what direction it would go. His lurid, apocalyptic imagination brought to the surface all the most radical undercurrents of eighteenth-century thought that were feeding the revolutionary stream. He understood, better than the revolutionaries themselves, that the critical thought of the Age of Enlightenment had destroyed a structure of experience that no counter-revolution could ever put back together. He wrote that a multitude of "sophisters, economists and calculators" had seized the historical initiative, and that "the glory of Europe" was "extinguished forever":

> now all is to be changed. All the pleasing illusions which made power gentle and obedience liberal, which harmonized the different shades of life, and which, by a bland assimilation, incorporated into politics all the sentiments that beautify and soften private society, are to be dissolved by the new conquering empire of light and reason. All the decent drapery of life is to be rudely torn off. All the superadded ideas, furnished from the wardrobe of a moral imagination, which the heart owns, and the understanding ratifies as necessary to cover the defects of our naked, shivering nature, and to raise it to dignity in our own estimation, are to be exploded as a ridiculous, absurd and antiquated fashion. [*Reflections*, 348–49] [12]

Burke was willing to admit in a time of crisis what the defenders of the established order had never been willing (or perhaps able) to face in times of peace: that the whole social system of Europe was essentially a system of lies. The

[12] *Reflections on the Revolution in France.* Arabic numbers designate the page in *Works* (12 volumes, London: Bohn's British Classics, 1855), Volume II.

basic fact of social life, Burke conceded almost offhandedly, was repression: the "power" of some, the "obedience" of the rest. But the fact of repression had itself been systematically repressed. Thus life became a great masquerade, in which disagreeable social roles were embellished with "pleasing illusions" and "superadded ideas." These fictions and forms, "furnished from the wardrobe of a moral imagination," had closed a repressive social system with an illusory dignity and beauty—and so, subtly, had strait-jacketed the self-expression of the men within it.

The primary symbol of society, as Burke saw it, was clothing. It was only fitting, then, that the primary aim of critical thought should have been to strip the clothes away. Thus "All the decent drapery of life is to be rudely torn off." Men had stripped themselves down to their "naked, shivering nature." What Burke called "the new conquering empire of light and reason" had finally exposed man as he really was.

But why the sudden violence? "All the decent drapery of life is to be rudely torn off." The Stoics felt no need to tear off the costumes and masks; to see through them was enough. Why should the ideal of authenticity, which had co-existed for so long with real repression in society and the state, now suddenly help to generate a revolutionary upheaval against it? How did men's self-consciousness become political consciousness? In the following pages we shall examine the thought of Montesquieu and Rousseau in order to explore some of the ways in which this great change came about.

Contents

I

The Subjugated Self
in Revolt

Montesquieu's
Persian Letters

A<small>T FIRST GLANCE</small>, the whole issue of authenticity seems alien to the sensibility of the Enlightenment. The intellectual energy of the age seems to flow outward rather than inward, through the world rather than into the self. Thus the *philosophes* shun Descartes's method of introspective doubt and reconstruction; they no longer look for truth in his "clear and distinct ideas" perceptible to the unmediated mind. Instead, as Ernst Cassirer explains their method:

> One should not seek order, law and "reason" as a rule that may be grasped prior to the phenomena, as their *a priori:* one should rather discover such regularity in the phenomena themselves, as the form of their immanent connection. . . . The mind must *abandon itself to the abundance of phenomena and gauge itself constantly by them.* For it may be sure that it will not get lost, but that instead it will find here its real truth and standard. Only in this way can the genuine correlation of subject and object, of truth and actuality, be achieved. . . . [9][1]

[1] *The Philosophy of the Enlightenment,* translated by Fritz C. A. Koelin and James P. Pettegrove (Boston: Beacon Press, 1955). Emphases here, as throughout unless otherwise indicated, are mine.

Accordingly, the *philosophes'* practical activity in science, art and politics is inseparable from the scientific, aesthetic, and political theories they developed. "The power of reason" for them, Cassirer says, "does not consist in enabling us to transcend the empirical world, but rather in teaching us to feel at home in it." (13) When the thought and action of the *philosophes* are examined in any breadth or depth, it is precisely "their craving for reality and their flexible sense of the real" (267) that strikes us as the heart of their whole intellectual enterprise.

But it was just this craving for reality that forced the most creative thinkers of the Age of Enlightenment to perceive authenticity as a problem. Precisely by extending human interest and reason into every sphere of the world, the Enlightenment had generated the ideal of a man who could engage the world with an immediacy and fullness of being, and thus fulfill its newly discovered potentialities. It soon became clear, however, that the possibilities for human activity and happiness, which had been opened up by the modern world, were stifled by the traditional political and social systems that ruled this world. Burke understood that once men's "light and reason" were free to explore and analyze the world around them, "all the decent drapery of life" would soon be torn away, and men would come face to face with themselves behind the curtain, in their "naked, shivering nature," as they really were. He knew that although the work of unmasking might begin in the realm of "private society," it would inevitably extend to the false political order which the illusions of private life reinforced. Moreover, once men confronted themselves and each other in their "naked, shivering nature," they would not shiver for long: it was only a matter of time before they would warm themselves by committing to the flames the whole

4

system whose rigidity had frozen their self-expression. In this section I want to show, by analyzing one seminal work, Montesquieu's *Persian Letters,* how the problem of authenticity emerged and developed out of problems central to the Enlightenment, and how its political implications crystallized gradually, and made themselves more and more deeply felt.

The Persian Letters *and the Dilemma of Individualism*

The Persian Letters, Montesquieu's first book, appeared in 1721, when he was thirty-two. It has never received any extensive or intense critical scrutiny. This is unfortunate, for it is one of those rare works which contain within themselves the whole history of an epoch. Its internal development prefigures the course of European history in the eighteenth century: it begins in exoticism and ends with revolution. On the way, all the main ideas of the century come into play; interacting with one another, they generate a dazzling brilliance which floods the whole atmosphere; and this fusion of substance and style brings the Enlightenment perfectly to life. The energy of the book seems to flow off in a multitude of directions; but its basic unity is revealed as all roads converge in the end. The structural coherence of *The Persian Letters* makes it uniquely fruitful for studying larger structures of thought and feeling in the Enlightenment as a whole—perhaps even more fruitful than the *Spirit of the Laws,* in whose shadow it has always stood. To show this will require long and intricate explication of a kind that *The Persian Letters* has always deserved but has never received. I want to focus on *The Persian Letters* as a kind of spectrum, on which many of the central ideas of the

5

Enlightenment are projected, so as to bring their inner relationship, the unities and conflicts among them, to light. By locating the idea of authenticity on such a spectrum, we can begin to grasp its full meaning and value.

The letters of which the book consists are circulated among Usbek, a Persian sultan, who has left home to travel in the West and who settles for a long period in Paris; Rica, his friend and traveling companion; Usbek's wives, whom he has left behind; and a cadre of eunuchs who guard and govern the wives in the sultan's name. The book moves on two levels simultaneously: one is Usbek's experience of Paris during the Regency of Philippe, Duc d'Orléans; the other is the interplay between Usbek and his wives and *fonctionnaires* at home. Mainly, however, the Parisian themes have pre-empted the commentators' attention. The reputation of *The Persian Letters* has primarily rested on its satirical picture of a beautiful but decadent and corrupt *ancien régime* on the verge of disintegration; secondly, on the trenchant indictments of Christian fanaticism and intolerance—perhaps even (though it is not agreed) of Christianity itself—which Montesquieu puts into the Islamic Persians' mouths; and, finally, on the cultural relativism which points the way toward the *Esprit des lois* and modern social science. The character of the sultan has been almost universally dismissed as a mere literary device: the use of an outsider's point of view to throw the religious, political and social absurdities within Parisian society into bolder relief. Indeed, the whole Persian aspect of the book has been written off as exoticism or pornography, an unfortunate lapse on Montesquieu's part, though not a fatal one.[2] In fact, however, the

2 The only critics I know who understand the seriousness of the Persian aspect are the late Franz Neumann and his former student David Kettler: Neumann's introduction to the Thomas Nugent translation of the *Spirit of the Laws* (New York: Hafner, 1949), especially xiii–xix;

story of Usbek and his wives forms both the beginning and
the end of *The Persian Letters;* both dramatically and intellectually it is the framework that gives the book its coherence. It is in Usbek's story, moreover, that much of the philosophical originality and radicalism of the book are found.
And it is here that the problem of authenticity first appears.

The story of Usbek and his wives establishes clearly the
genre of *The Persian Letters*—which, because this story has
always been ignored, has never been understood. Montesquieu's work is in fact one of the first *Bildungsromane,* a
novel of education and self-discovery. At the same time, it is
the first distinctively *political* novel written in the West. Its
personal and political themes are thoroughly intertwined:
Usbek's seraglio is at once a household, a society and a state;
the passions that bind men and women within it are simultaneously those which link masters and slaves, upper and
lower classes, sovereigns and subjects, to one another. Montesquieu carries on the tradition of acute psychological
analysis—analysis of the nuances and complexities of what
Burke called "private society"—that is characteristic of
French *moralistes;* Montesquieu is original, however, in exposing and exploring the intimate relation between personal passion and political action. The model of the seraglio he creates typifies the unity of private and public life.
Thus the freedom or repression, equality or inequality in a
state is a function, not of its merely political organization,
but of the structure of its personal and social life as a
whole.[3]

Kettler's piece, "Montesquieu on Love: Notes on The Persian Letters,"
in the *American Political Science Review,* 58 (1964), 658–61. Cf. also
Jean Starobinski's notes to *Montesquieu par lui-même* (Paris: Editions
du Seuil, 1953), 60–9; and Starobinski, *The Invention of Liberty, 1700–
1789* translated by Bernard Swift (Geneva: Skira Editions, 1964), 55–6,
[3] On the derivation of public institutions from private ones—an Aris-

Usbek, the Oriental despot, has come to the West—so he reveals in the first letter of the book—in search of a liberal education. (*PL*, 1) What he eventually gets—the very last letter drives the point home—is an education in liberalism. But the cost of tuition is catastrophically high: the more enlightened he becomes abroad, the more his authority, personal, social and political, disintegrates at home; even as he is discovering and expounding the glories of freedom and equality in theory, his subjects—his subjected wives—are learning to assert these values in practice. At the climax of his education, and of the book, inevitably, yet with a jarring abruptness, the subjects revolt. Their revolt is abortive and self-destructive, but pregnant with its future: it marks a point of departure in European thought, and prefigures an age of revolutionary action to come. "My language, no doubt, seems new to you"—so writes Roxane, formerly Usbek's most loving and beloved wife, now the leader of the uprising. (161) And, indeed, it *is* a new language: *The Persian Letters* announces the emergence of a radically new form of individualism in European civilization. If we examine the language of this new individualism carefully, we will see how and why the ideal of individual *authenticity* emerges.

At first glance, the individualism of *The Persian Letters* does not seem particularly new at all: it seems to fit quite comfortably within the framework of conventional seventeenth-century natural-law theory, as it had been developed by Grotius and Pufendorf, Althusius and Locke.[4] It is char-

---

totelian principle—cf. *PL*, 94 and *Esprit*, 1.2. On each society as a totality encompassing all spheres of life, cf. *Esprit*, XIX.5ff.; it is perhaps the basic idea in the book. (Numbers cited in *The Persian Letters* designate the Letter, not the page; those in the *Esprit des lois* designate the Book and Section. English translations from *PL* are by J. Robert Loy (New York: Meridian, 1959); those from *Esprit* are by Thomas Nugent.)

[4] For a general statement of this theory, see A. P. d'Entreves, *Natural*

acteristic of this theory to posit, as Usbek does, "that men were born to be virtuous and that justice is a quality as proper to man as existence." (10) Similarly, the link between this abstract, formal conception of justice and a theory of social and governmental contract—in the myth of the Troglodytes which Usbek expounds (11–14)—was standard procedure in Montesquieu's day. Later on, Usbek brings together the whole family of modern natural-law ideas: "Justice is a true relationship of appropriateness which exists between two things and this relationship is always the same, no matter by who considered, whether it be God, or an angel, or finally, a man." Moreover, he adds, using Grotius' radical formulation: "even were there to be no God, we should always love justice. . . . Free though we might be of the yoke of religion, we should never be free from that of equity." [5] Thus "justice is eternal and not dependent on the conventions of men." Indeed, "if it should so depend, this would be a horrible truth that we should have to hide from ourselves." (83) It is precisely Usbek's ideas of natural law that are most explicitly turned against him in the end, and turned into the battle cry of the oppressed: "I have rewritten your laws," Roxane writes defiantly in her (and the book's) last letter, "after the laws of nature." (161) It seems only just that a society which denies the natural rights of man should be destroyed.

These passages are often cited as characteristic of Montes-

Law: an Introduction to Legal Philosophy (London: Hutchinson's University Library, 1951), 48–63; George H. Sabine, *A History of Political Thought* (3rd Edition, London: Harrap and Co., 1951), 354–68, 461; also Alfred Cobban, *In Search of Humanity: The Role of the Enlightenment in Modern History* (New York: George Braziller, 1960), 94–7, 161–2.

[5] Montesquieu anticipates here the Kantian conception of God as an ideal that is regulative of our conduct but not constitutive of anything: even if there were no God, Montesquieu says, we should still "do our best to resemble that being of whom we have such a beautiful idea, who, if he were to exist, would be, of necessity, just."

9

quieu's thought. And yet, by themselves, they run counter to one of the basic insights of the book, of Montesquieu's work and of the Enlightenment as a whole: the perception of empirical diversity and cultural relativity. Generally, scholars have acknowledged that the *Spirit of the Laws* raises cultural relativism to a level of sophistication unequalled in the eighteenth century (unless, perhaps, by Herder). But *The Persian Letters,* written a quarter of a century earlier, already contains some of its most striking formulations. Quite early in his stay in the West, Usbek discovers that personal goodness and a viable social life are possible without rigid adherence to Islamic dietary laws— indeed, possible for people who have never even heard of these laws or of the faith itself. He is shocked into a realization whose scope extends far beyond the dietetic: that "objects in themselves are neither pure nor impure." He "cannot think of any quality inherent in the [object] that makes them so." (17) Later on, Rica amplifies this insight: "we never judge of matters except by a secret reflex we make on ourselves"—in other words, by projecting our own image onto the world. Thus "I am not surprised that Negroes should paint the devil in blinding white, and their own gods black as coal. . . ." He is led to the wryly skeptical observation that "if all triangles were to create a god, they would give him three sides." (59)[6] The diversity of cultural and social norms, and the necessity of a relativistic view, are themes that pervade the whole book and underlie all its dramatic action, on both its Persian and Parisian sides. For Montesquieu, as for many other European thinkers, the ab-

[6] Scholarship has recently shown that this dictum is actually Spinoza's (see translator's note to the passage); but Montesquieu's contemporaries took it for his own, and it has always been one of the phrases most often quoted from *The Persian Letters.*

stractions of seventeenth-century natural law collapse in the eighteenth century's encounter with empirical reality.[7]

Before we can assess the full impact of this encounter on Montesquieu's individualism, we must explore its philosophical background. It would be seriously misleading to explain the spread and development of empiricism in the eighteenth century as merely the product of experience. Rather, the empiricists' openness to the world antedated and underlay their worldly experience, and gave that experience its critical force and dynamism. Eighteenth-century empiricists took for granted, and built their world upon, the most impressive achievement of the seventeenth-century rationalists: the Newtonian cosmology, a comprehensive picture of the universe as a whole and man's place in it.

> My dear Usbek [writes Rica], when I see men crawling about on an atom, I mean the earth, which is only a speck of the universe, and proposing themselves as models of divine providence, I don't know how to reconcile such extravagance with such pettiness. [59]

Here Montesquieu depicts the universe as an infinite aggregate of particles of matter in motion. Man and his world comprise a few of these particles—a very few. Even within a given world, different particles move in different orbits. By what right, then, he wants to know, do a very few among these very few particles presume to impose their own peculiar atmosphere on all the rest of nature? This mechanistic argument was to become one of the most trenchant weapons in the arsenal of the *philosophes*. It cut boldly

---

[7] The gradual transition among the *philosophes* and their allies from rationalism and natural law to empiricist and utilitarian modes of thought is discussed by Peter Gay, *The Party of Humanity: Essays in the French Enlightenment* (New York: Alfred A. Knopf, 1964), 198–201. Cf. also Cobban. *In Search of Humanity*, 172–9.

through the arcane intricacies of the hierarchical scholastic image of the world and projected sharply and clearly a vision of Nature devoid of all normative content. From now on, Nature meant, simply, all that was. Although it depicted Nature as morally neutral, this vision itself was far from morally irrelevant. *All* that was: the vision opened the way to a heightened sympathy with many forms of human life and action which up to then had been condemned categorically as "contrary to nature": for *nothing* could be contrary to Nature now. Thus Montesquieu uses the Newtonian cosmology as the basis for a daring and skillful defense of suicide: "am I disturbing the order of providence," Usbek asks, "when I change the modifications of matter? . . ."

> When my soul is separated from my body, will there be any less order and less arrangement in the universe? Do you believe that this new combination will be any the less perfect and less dependent on general laws? Do you think the world has lost something thereby? Or that the works of God will be less great . . . ? Do you believe that my body, having turned into an ear of grain, or a worm, or a piece of turf, will have turned into a work of nature less worthy of her?

Our need to dignify our moral values by attaching the name of Nature to them has "no other source than our pride. (76) We do not feel our insignificance, and come what may, we want to be of value in the universe, to figure in it, to be an important object in it." However it may hurt their vanity, men must face the truth that "all mankind together, [even] a hundred million earths like our own, are but a thin and tenuous atom that God perceives only because of the vastness of his knowledge." (76)[8] If this mechanistic perspective

8 This naturalistic argument was strikingly original and modern. The

seemed to lessen man's stature in the universe, yet in another sense it pointed the way toward a new humanism. In debunking the presumption that would impose a set of rigid forms on the living plurality of nature, it vastly expanded the range of legitimate human experience, it opened infinitely the horizon of what was possible for man in the world. Only against this new, open, empirical horizon could human energy freely express and unfold itself. The right of the individual to self-annihilation was only one aspect (though a crucial one) of his general self-liberation.

But although empiricism had many liberating effects, its consequences for individualism proved to be profoundly ambiguous. For if, on the one hand, it overthrew authoritarian claims to legitimacy through Divine Law, on the other it undercut liberal criticisms of existing authority in the name of Natural Right. The rising success and prestige of empiricism posed crucial questions for political thinkers. After Revelation had been discredited by critical analysis, and Nature emptied of moral content, what standards of value remained? By what criteria could existing institutions be evaluated and judged? Finally, what claims—if, indeed, any claims at all—was the individual subject entitled to make on the political order, and how could these claims be justified?

In the course of the eighteenth century, this last question took on a special urgency. For, as empiricist modes of thought gradually spread, utilitarianism in social and political thought became more and more widely accepted; and

---

defense of suicide before Montesquieu, even in writers as modern as Montaigne and Bayle, had been based on classical concepts of honor. Montesquieu's argument was seminal for the whole eighteenth century; it was adopted by the *philosophes* and developed most cogently by Hume. Cf. Lester Crocker, "The Discussion of Suicide in the Eighteenth Century," *Journal of the History of Ideas*, XIII (1952), 47–72.

utilitarianism threw the whole idea of *individual rights* into serious trouble. It was true that all utilitarians affirmed every man's right to be happy—as happy as was compatible with the happiness of other men. But the practical force of this right was compromised by both the radical and conservative poles into which eighteenth-century utilitarianism was split. On the Left, Helvétius proposed to make men happy by making them to order, perfectly suited to whatever environment the legislator might create for them. The question of individual rights would simply never arise because individuals would be constructed with no loose ends, no capacity for feeling needs or making demands which their environment did not already satisfy. On the Right, the theories of Hume and Burke made it virtually impossible for an individual to express discontent with any existing institution. The mere fact that an institution *was* existing, that it had lasted over time, was enough to establish *prima facie* that it actually did satisfy the people within its reach: for if it did not satisfy them, so the argument went, they would not put up with it.[9] Neither form of utilitarianism could offer any principled objections to despotism: repression, for the eighteenth-century utilitarian, was evil only insofar as it made people unhappy. Men could be totally manipulated, divested of every trace of freedom, treated as marionettes—so long as they were content with the strings. Indeed, this combination of systematic unfreedom and apparent contentment prevailed in all existing states for most of the eighteenth century. With a few exceptions, utilitarians were satisfied with it; when they became critical, it was manifest unhappiness rather than latent unfreedom that they sought to cor-

[9] A plausible enough argument in settled times, somewhat less plausible in the midst of upheaval and revolution. Ironically, it was precisely in the midst of an epoch of revolution that it was developed most vigorously and subtly.

14

rect. As long as empiricist attitudes and arguments could contribute to the defense of such a *status quo,* the liberating force of empiricism was neutralized. The possibilities of human experience might indeed be indefinite, but a repressed humanity—even if happily repressed—was clearly in no position to exploit them. The more the *philosophes* explored and illuminated the world, the more they heightened the contrast between what man could achieve in an ideal world and what men did achieve in the empirical one. In practice men were kept from taking possession of a world which in theory had been declared their own.

Montesquieu perceived the inadequacies of both the rationalistic and the empiricist views of the world, of both natural law and utiliarianism as modes of political thought. He wanted to extend the individual liberty which natural-right theories had promoted, while avoiding the dogmatism of the natural lawyers. He wanted to match the concreteness and realism of natural science, without giving up a critical and normative view of the concrete political reality he observed around him. This tension in his thought generated a search for a new synthesis, for some clear principle on which individualism could rest. It was at this point, in the uncharted country beyond both natural law and utilitarianism, that the politics of authenticity hesitantly, obliquely began.

Happiness, Freedom and the Right of Authenticity

The seraglio which Montesquieu portrays in *The Persian Letters* is an ideal type, a kind of experiment in thought: it is the model of a happy despotism,[10] a repressive society

[10] Strictly speaking, Usbek's kingdom is not a despotism, since, ac-

which apparently satisfies all its members. Natural-law theory might vent moral indignation against Usbek for violating the rights of man; but he could dismiss such criticism as mere dogmatism, based on moral values imposed arbitrarily on his system from "outside." Montesquieu's own critique of a repressive society is much more complex. A repressive system, he argues, fails to fulfill its own immanent standard: it is incapable of satisfying any of its members, even the most privileged; precisely when it appears most stable, it is actually decomposing from within.[11] Starting from utilitarian premises, Montesquieu reaches conclusions which formerly only natural-law arguments were used to defend. In the course of his journey, however, he enlarges the idea of individual rights significantly beyond the frontiers to which natural-law theory had brought it. No social system, Montesquieu tries to show, can provide human happiness, unless it posits, and its government guarantees, a basic human right: the right of every man *to be himself*. We must trace the intricate course of conceptual and psychological analysis by which Montesquieu arrives at this revolutionary concept.

The sultan Usbek, as we first see him, is a man who apparently has everything and is determined to enjoy it. His self-assured, complacent voluptuousness suggests the typical pleasure-loving aristocrat of Montesquieu's age, making a

---

cording to Montesquieu's categories, the spring of human action in a despotic state is fear alone (*Esprit,* III. 3), whereas Usbek's wives are also bound to him by love—although a love which itself contains a large ingredient of fear.

[11] The conceptual model for my description of this system and its decomposition is suggested by Hegel's "Dialectic of Master and Slave," in the *Phenomenology of the Spirit,* translated by J. B. Baille (2nd edition, London: George Allen and Unwin, 1931), chapters 4–6. It should be mentioned, however, that Hegel was a devoted reader of Montesquieu, and may well have been influenced by *The Persian Letters* in working out his dialectical model.

comeback in the wild days of the Regency after the austere absolutism of Louis XIV:[12] The leisured *homme de goût* who felt entitled to all the gratification he could afford, who patronized Boucher and the Rococo, and who devoured *The Persian Letters* and numerous other tales of the seraglio in search of pornographic thrills. In short, the protagonist of the book typifies its audience, and his fate prefigures their own.[13] "You are the faithful guardian of the most beautiful women in Persia," Usbek addresses his chief eunuch in Ispahan. This job will require ceaseless vigilance because these women are "what is most precious to me of all my worldly possessions." He warns the guardian to "preserve your humility among those who share my love; but make them feel at the same time their utter dependence." (*PL,* 2) Usbek loves his wives, then; but he loves them as beautiful *things,* as objects he can use or mold—or break, as he points out (20-1)—according to his will. The women, for their part, far from resenting this status, seem to cherish it.

[12] At one point, Montesquieu seems explicitly to equate Usbek with Louis XIV himself. Thus, "People have often heard him say that, of all the governments in the world, that of the Turks or that of our august šultan would please him best—so much significance does he attach to Oriental politics." (*The Persian Letters,* 37). It is important to remember that, as a lifelong partisan of the French nobility against the claims and aims of the kings, Montesquieu was particularly sensitive to abuses of *royal* power. Cf. Neumann's Introduction, xix–xxix; Franklin Ford, *Robe & Sword: The Regrouping of the French Aristocracy after Louis XIV* (Cambridge, Mass.: Harvard University Press, 1953), especially 238–245. But if we see the Persian theme as nothing more than an allegorical indictment of Louis's court (or his state), we miss much of its richness and depth. For one thing, the sexual and intellectual libertinism of the Persians, and their unashamed pursuit of happiness, clashes very sharply with his severity. Moreover, Ubsek's rank in Persian society is aristocratic, similar to Montesquieu's own stature in France: he addresses other aristocrats as his peers; he has neither the pretensions nor the power of a king.

[13] On his audience and ambience, cf. Arnold Hauser, *The Social History of Art* (4 volumes, New York: Vintage Books, 1958), III, 33–36; also Starobinski, *Invention of Liberty,* 10–14, 54–56.

They lament his absence, and cry plaintively with longing
for him. Although they have never been allowed to see any
man but Usbek, they are certain that they would love him
alone even if granted complete freedom of choice, for "in all
the world, there can be only you worthy of being loved." (7)
Their love does not blind them to their lowliness in his
eyes; indeed, it is precisely his contempt for them that
makes him so "worthy" of the love they have to give. In
probably his most pornographic passage, Montesquieu con-
veys vividly the source of Usbek's appeal. Zachi, one of the
wives, is remembering with nostalgic joy a past instance of
Usbek's wisdom in resolving a famous quarrel among his
women. Each wife, it seems, had hoped to win Usbek's heart
over the others through richness of ornament and finery.
The symbolism of clothes is central here, as it will be
throughout the great tradition of radicalism which *The Persian Letters* begins. The women aimed to charm their master through the beauty with which they covered themselves.
Usbek had "admired how far the zeal of pleasing you could
carry us," but he declared the means misdirected: for it was
not ornaments, but human beings, that gave him pleasure.
Hence he ordered all the women to strip naked and "present themselves to your view in all the simplicity of nature."
At this point, Zachi's mouth virtually waters as she describes
his judicial procedure:

> Happy Usbek, what charms were displayed before your
> eyes. We saw you wander long from one delight to the
> next; your wavering soul remained for a long time in a
> state of indecision; each new grace extorted its tribute
> from you; we were all, in the twinkling of an eye, cov-
> ered with your kisses; you extended your curious regard
> to the most secret spots; in a trice, you made us assume

a thousand different positions—ever a new command
and ever a new submission. [3]

And once she found herself in this position, she says, "a passion much more keen than ambition made me want to
please you" (3); the energy of this passion inflamed her,
brought her to his notice, and she won.

We will see how, as *The Persian Letters* progresses and
eighteenth-century thought develops, nakedness becomes
the archetypal form, the primary symbol of authenticity. At
this point, however, nakedness appears as the epitome of *in-*
authenticity. First of all, nakedness here is enforced, compul-
sory. Second, and more important, it is one-sided, not
mutual: Usbek's clothes remain on in this scene—he wants
to expose his wives' most intimate being, while concealing
his own. Moreover, in their sexual play, the women are going through motions which are prescribed for them; the
master strips them down to "the simplicity of nature," only
to deck them out in complex roles. The alienation of the
whole routine is conveyed in Zachi's prose: "What charms
were displayed before your eyes"; "we saw you wander from
one delight to the next"; "each new grace extorted its trib-
ute from you": the women are observing their "charms" and
"delights" with detachment, as objects wholly outside themselves. However, the more shameless he is in manipulating
them as objects for his pleasure—"ever a new command,
and ever a new submission"—the more willing they are to
make themselves simply objects. The relation between the
sultan and his wives seems reciprocal: both parties would
seem to be getting what they want. Montesquieu has created
what looks like the perfect pornographic utopia: a static,
ideally satisfying social order based on the roles of domination and submission, a sadomasochistic Garden of Eden.

But the serpent of self-analysis soon undermines this garden. Usbek should be perfectly happy: he has the women both ways, they are bound to him by both love and power. Yet a curious *malaise* gnaws at him. It leads him to feel obsessively jealous, and to enforce ever-increasing isolation and repression on his wives. But it is not basically the instability of his power that plagues him (as it does the Platonic tyrant in Book Nine of the *Republic*): "even if my slaves were faithful," he says, "I should still find it difficult to feel secure." Indeed, once he begins to analyze the sources of his discontent, he is forced to admit that "It's not so much that I love them. In this respect, *I find myself in a state devoid of feeling [insensibilité] leaving me with no desires at all."* And it is from this emptiness, "from my very coldness, [that] there grows a secret jealousy that devours me." (6) Usbek has everything, but it is no good to him, for he feels nothing. His situation is paradoxical: fullness brings only emptiness. His power over his wives, which at first seemed total, now turns out to be hollow. He is terrified of losing their devotion; but even when it is forthcoming, he can get no satisfaction from it. "Ah, my dear Usbek," Zachi mourns, "if only you knew how to be happy!" (3) He is the master, but turns out to be even more dependent and unhappy than the slaves he keeps.

As the Persians pursue the source of their *malaise,* they come to realize that it is structural, integral to the status by which they define themselves. Thus Rica observes that for all the strictness with which Persian women are preserved for their husbands alone, "their much-boasted fidelity doesn't obviate the disgust [which their husbands feel] that always follows on the satisfaction of the passions." It occurs to Rica that their women may be so unsatisfying to them because they "belong too strictly to us, [and] such calm possession leaves us nothing to desire or fear." (38) Usbek perceives this same trouble. Before long he sees the society of his seraglio in a new light as

> a uniform existence, without enjoyment. Everything smells of obedience and duty. Even the pleasures are sober, and the joys severe, and they are practically never relished except as manifestations of authority and subservience. [34]

Precisely this fullness of power which he claims over others generates the emptiness of being which he feels within himself. Apparently a system of domination and submission presses all natural feelings into a rigid form and ultimately suffocates their life. Compulsion is unnatural and finally destroys the capacity for joy—the capacity both to receive and to give.

Out of this antithesis of nature and compulsion the idea of authenticity develops. Rica, writing to Usbek from Paris, comments casually that he has really known women only since arriving in the West; that he has learned more about them in a month in Paris, he says, than he could possibly learn after thirty years in a seraglio. He explains:

> With us, their characters are all the same because they are forced into a mold. *We don't see people as they are, but as they are forced to be.* In that servitude of heart and mind there is talk only of fear, which has but one language, and no talk of nature, which expresses itself in such varied ways and appears under so many forms. [63]

In this passage, Montesquieu is posing an ingenious and imaginative solution to one of the profoundest problems of the Enlightenment. He shows that the idea of nature can still be used fruitfully as a norm, while doing justice to the empirical diversity of nature as the Enlightenment experienced it; he enshrines diversity itself as the essence of nature. From his mechanistic and atomistic vision of nature he derives the norm of individuality as a universal moral standard for man. Nature, which expresses itself through an infinite diversity of forms, endows every man with a personality uniquely his own, which he should express and cultivate. And yet, Montesquieu, empiricist that he is, must acknowledge that the human individuality and diversity that seem so "natural" to him find precious little expression in the empirical world. In order to make this predicament intelligible, he is forced to work out a new conceptual scheme: and it is here that the theory of authenticity acquires a life of its own. Human institutions, Montesquieu thinks, belong (like everything else that exists) to nature, yet they turn radically *against* nature: they mold men to fit prescribed social roles, destroy their natural individuality, *force them to be what they are not.* This idea opens up a whole new theoretical perspective. We can now see how the "natural" self of man is threatened by his "social" self; how the spontaneity of "people as they really are" is repressed by the social roles they are forced to play; how the human variety which nature produces is subverted by the uniformity of character which society demands. At this point, Montesquieu introduces a new standard of value into European social and political thought. The basic question, now, is how much freedom do the members of any state or society have *to be the individuals they are*—how far, in other words, is human authenticity allowed to unfold?

Only when men retain their natural individuality—their authenticity—can they participate in nature as a whole, and enjoy the forms of happiness that nature has made available to man in the world. A man can be happy only if he can be—*himself*. But a society which deprives every man of the primary source of his happiness cannot hope to satisfy its members; hence it must inevitably disintegrate from within.

Usbek's personal unhappiness reflects this social and political impasse. Sexuality, which nature has provided as a medium of human happiness, is only a cul-de-sac for him. His wives' lack of spontaneity deprives him of satisfaction and eventually even drains him of desire. Yet if they were to manifest spontaneity, he would be unable to recognize it. Fatima captures his dilemma: "You men are very cruel. You treat us as if we were without feelings, yet you would be very displeased if this were so." (7) Both Usbek's system of political authority and his structure of personal identity force him into this position. He defines himself by his role as a ruler, a master. Hence, if his sexual relations are to be a genuine expression of his personality, they can only be "manifestations of authority and subservience." (34) He must force his natural sexuality into the rigid framework of his social role: sex must confirm his own identity as a master, and his wives' identity as slaves. Thus he is forced to treat his sexual partners as mere objects, devoid of feeling and will of their own. Before long he grasps the futility of this game: to possess mere objects only leaves him empty in the end. In order to find satisfaction in his wives, he comes to see, he would have to recognize them as fellow human beings, endowed with a spontaneity equal to his own. To recognize his wives' personal spontaneity, moreover, would necessarily mean granting them social and political freedom to express it. Usbek's ultimate enlightenment is manifest in a letter in which he criticizes Christian and Western family life, and argues for the right of divorce—not only for men, as in Islam, but for women as well:

> Into such a free action [as marriage], where the heart should play so important a role, restraint, necessity and the very fatality of destiny were introduced [by the Christians]. . . . They tried to stabilize the heart—which is to say, the thing in human nature that is most variable and inconstant. People, burdened with one another . . . were tied together irretrievably and without hope. They acted after the manner of those despots who had live men tied to dead bodies.
>
> Thus not only was the sweetness taken away from marriage, but its very end as an institution was threatened. By wanting to tighten its bonds, they loosened them, and instead of bringing hearts closer together, as they claimed, they only separated them forever. [116]

Usbek now realizes that a woman can satisfy a man only when she gives herself to him freely—and hence revocably. Because all persons are free and their wills are alterable, the happiness one person can give another is necessarily contingent. Certain and irrevocable possession thus defeats its own ends: the ingredient of freedom is essential to any pleasure that possession can give. Usbek, however, is not free to take the practical consequences of the principles he has arrived at. To concede his wives (and subjects) any capacity for feeling and will of their own, to admit the relevance of their consent, would be to renounce his dominant status, the rock on which both his country's social structure and his own personality are founded. Usbek's situation is paradoxical: his only real identity is unmasked as an *un*real identity, built on a lie, thriving on inauthenticity, emptying him of

24

his natural life, ultimately deceiving and defeating only it-self. And yet, because his whole life has been enclosed in a system of falsehood, the false identity it has conferred on him is all he has. Even as the political ground of this iden-tity gives way beneath him, he clings desperately to the rock of his bad faith, and crumbles with it in the end. Usbek's fate shows that in a system of mastery and slavery, no man can be master; the more like a master he looks, the more total a slave of the system he is. The freedom and happiness which mastery promises are delusory: they are available only to men and women who remain the individuals that nature made them. It is only by giving up his social status as a master of men that one can regain his natural identity as a man, can become his authentic self.

Usbek's dilemma reveals the inherent weakness of repres-sive society: it ultimately fails to satisfy even those at the top. But equally important, such a society cannot satisfy those at the bottom. Perhaps this is even more important, because it is from the bottom that revolutions come. In his treatment of Usbek's wives, Montesquieu shows how the love of submission which supports a repressive system can develop into a love of freedom that destroys it. The theme of authenticity is central to their development: in rebelling, they assert and prove that they are not the persons—or rather, the non-persons—that their master thinks they are, and that they themselves once thought they were.

Although the women begin, as we have seen, by abasing themselves, they find the role of slavery entirely appropri-ate, accept without question the status of sexual objects which this role imposes, and complain only of being left alone at night. Here, as elsewhere, it is their masters who first develop the ideas that will eventually set them free. Thus Montesquieu puts into Rica's mouth one of the first modern arguments for the full equality of women. Rica asks whether natural law subjects women to men, and recounts the feminist case, as he has learned it in Paris:

> Nature never dictated such a law. The dominion we hold over them is a veritable tyranny. They have allowed us to keep it only because they are more gentle than we are. . . . These advantages over us, which ought no doubt to have secured superiority for them if we had been reasonable, have made them lose it because we are not.

Thus, it is not innate inferiority that keeps them in their place; if anything, it is a moral superiority, a refusal to lower themselves to the ethical level of their masters. Rica goes on: "Why, then, should we have any advantage? Is it because we are stronger?" Here, he is confronting a traditional conservative argument: men are endowed by nature with superior powers and talents; it is their natural function to command and protect women, who are endowed with less. (This is, in fact, the view of Rica's own Islamic faith.) As evidence, conservatives point to the paucity of feminine achievement. Rica acknowledges this, but contends that it proves the exact opposite of what it is supposed to:

> Their powers [*forces*] would be equal if their education were also equal. Let us put them to the test in the manner of talents [when they are] not enfeebled by their present education and then we shall see if we are so strong. [38]

Lack of achievement stems, not from natural debility, but from inferior education; equality of education will generate equality of achievement. Proof of how much education can do for women is manifest in Paris, where women virtually

26

control the destiny of France, and constitute a powerful "state within a state." (107) Rica's argument for equality in education has become classic, and is one of the staples of Western liberalism. Whenever oppressed groups have sought freedom and equality, it has played a significant part —most recently, perhaps, in the movements for Black and Women's Liberation. It plays a significant part in *The Persian Letters,* too, but only as the oppressed Persian women learn gradually to educate themselves.

By being left alone the women learn that they can live without their master and that they have feelings and ideas of their own.[14] Their first source of power is *self-awareness.* They learn to use their inner lives against their master— inner lives which are inexorably beyond his control.

> And yet, Usbek [writes Zelis], you must not imagine that your lot is happier than mine. I have enjoyed here a thousand pleasures unknown to you. My imagination has worked untiringly to make me appreciate them properly. I have lived, and you have only languished.
>
> Even in this prison here where you hold me, I am freer than you. You could not possibly redouble your concern for guarding me without my drawing pleasure from your worry. Your suspicions, your jealousy and your heartaches are only so many proofs of your dependency. [62]

The women are coming to know themselves as human beings. They see themselves as "living" in that they can stand

---

[14] The women could not free themselves unless Usbek were absent from the scene. His departure, however, is not a mere contrivance for the sake of the plot; it is inherent in the structure of their relationship. He is impelled to leave because his relations with them are boring, unsatisfying; he is bored with them because they are unfree; they are unfree because he requires their submission in order to prove himself.

apart from their roles and find them wanting; Usbek, on the other hand, merely "languishes" because he is trapped in a role assigned by himself. So long as he persists in treating them as objects, a whole dimension of their being is hidden from him: the dimension of depth. So long as he refuses to acknowledge their capacity for an inner life, he will never be able to get through to what is going on inside them; yet they have forced him to face the fact that *something* is going on. Now he can no longer rest securely in the masturbatory world he created for himself. His wives are forcing him to recognize that he is playing his autoerotic games with real people, and that he is putting pressure on a mass of live amunition which might explode at any moment and blow him to bits. Usbek's sense of self depends on his wives' sense of selflessness. As soon as the slaves assert themselves authentically, the master's inauthentic self is doomed.

The women's self-awareness evolves gradually from thought into action.[15] As they come to know themselves, they discover a vital, natural resource in their struggle for recognition: their *sexuality*. At first, they saw their sexual desires only as chains that linked them inexorably to their lord and master; they could conceive no means of satisfaction other than the man who had enslaved them. (7) But their heightened awareness is evident in Zelis' ironic remark to Usbek: "We must *practice our role of subordinate* so that it may hold us firm through the critical period when *the passions begin to appear and encourage us toward independence.*" (62) This passage crystallizes the philosophical importance of the eroticism that pervades *The Persian Letters:* Montes-

[15] Montesquieu is perhaps the first writer to illuminate this process by which men move from acceptance of servitude to revolution. For the conceptual and intellectual dynamics, Hegel's account in the *Phenomenology*, Chapters 4–6, is still unsurpassed; for the social and psychological dynamics, see especially Erving Goffman, "The Underlife of a Public Institution," in *Asylums: Essays on the Situation of Mental Patients and Other Inmates* (New York: Anchor Books, 1961), 171–320.

quieu is proposing here nothing less than a transvaluation of sexuality. The two main cultural attitudes toward sex in the early eighteenth century were a traditional Christian moralism which condemned categorically the sins of the flesh, and a neo-pagan libertinism which took amoral delight in sex as in everything "natural." Although he clearly sympathizes more with the pagan attitude than with the Christian one, Montesquieu stands apart from them both. His approach to sex is deeply moralistic; but because his morality is the morality of *authenticity,* he comes to the radical conclusion that sexuality has positive moral value. Sexuality is the most vivid expression of Nature—and hence of individuality—in man. As such, it is integral to the formation of personal identity: sex is a medium through which every individual can not only *enjoy* himself, but actually *define* himself. When Usbek's wives finally revolt against him, they do so by taking lovers: now they can be authentically naked, by choice, in mutuality. Roxane, in her manifesto and suicide note—the letter with which the book abruptly ends—sums up all the women have learned about themselves and their world:

> Yes, I have deceived you. I seduced your eunuchs, I took advantage of your jealousy, and out of your horrible harem I managed to make a place of pleasure and delight.
>
> I am going to die; poison will soon course through my veins. For what have I to do here since the only man who has held me to life [her lover, who has been killed] is no more? I am dying, but my shade shall not fly off unaccompanied. I have just sent ahead of me those sacrilegious guardians who have spilled the loveliest blood in the world.
>
> You should be thankful . . . that I lowered myself

to the point of seeming faithful to you, and because I kept in my cowardly heart all that I should have proclaimed to the whole earth.

You were surprised not to find in me the transports of love. If you had known me well, you would have found there all the violence of hate. . . .

How could you have thought that I was naïve enough to imagine that I was put in the world only to adore your whims? That while you pampered yourself with everything, you should have the right to mortify all my desires? No! I might have lived in servitude, but I have always been free. I have rewritten your laws after the laws of nature, and my spirit has ever sustained itself in independence. [161]

The Stoics, too, could have invoked the laws of nature, but they wouldn't have acted so radically as to rewrite political laws in their image. This is because the Stoics' conception of nature was spiritual, ethereal, transcendental. For Montesquieu, and for the whole eighteenth century, nature is corporeal, material, immanent. When Montesquieu represents sex as the outward and visible form of nature, he underscores the ideal that nature must *express itself* concretely in the world and in the flesh. Expression of one's natural sexual desires must necessarily mean rejection of repressive social roles which deny the right to be oneself; the wives' assertion of sexual choice and preference is *ipso facto* a declaration of political independence. The act that defines them as women establishes them as *Menschen,* members of the human community; it is an achievement which destroys the myth of their inferiority which was used to keep them down. Sexuality is perhaps the central symbol of *The Persian Letters.* On one hand, it stands for itself, and expresses a demand for greater freedom in sexual life: thus Montesquieu defends adultery and promiscuity (38, 55), divorce (116) and even incest (67). On the other hand, it embodies the authenticity of the individual, and expresses a demand for profound changes in the structure of social status and political authority which will permit the full authenticity of the self to unfold.

There is still another sense in which the wives' uprising fulfills the laws of nature. Implicit in the whole structure of *The Persian Letters,* though never explicitly stated, is a pre-Freudian theory of repression and compensation. Such a theory is logically necessary in order for the idea of nature to function both descriptively and normatively at once. It must be explained how nature, if she is "violated" by men, will "reassert herself"; otherwise the word "nature" will no longer describe the reality of the empirical world, but instead will be just another ideal arbitrarily imposed on the world. In *The Persian Letters,* we are told that nature makes every man an individual. But the authoritarian society we see in Persia fits men into Procrustean roles, and acts as if human individuality simply were not there. What is to become of nature now? At this point the idea of *revolution* takes on a crucial importance in political thought.[16] A repressive society creates a radical gap between people's *social* identities—the roles they are forced to play—and their *real* identities. Montesquieu is one of the very first thinkers to see personal identity as a *problem.* In a repressive society it cannot be taken for granted, but must be *achieved:* men cannot *be* themselves *within* such a system, but must strive to *become* themselves, *against* the system. So long as individ-

---

[16] Jean Starobinski is the only critic I know who grasps the significance of this revolutionary theme. See *Montesquieu par lui-même,* 65–9. But he fails to see how tightly it is woven into the fabric of the work.

31

uals are "de-natured" by roles of servitude, they can assert themselves as individuals only by overthrowing that servitude. Revolt is the only mode of authenticity a repressive society allows; and when nature is repressed, revolt is inevitable. The act of revolution restores the balance of nature: thus, it is not an historical accident, but a biological necessity. This fusion of personal authenticity with revolutionary class-consciousness opened up vast human possibilities which have been fulfilled abundantly in the two centuries between Montesquieu's time and our own.

Usbek has inadvertently taught his wives the language of authenticity so well that they finally use it against him. A despot can only learn the hard way: his moment of self-discovery is simultaneously the moment of his ruin. And yet, the revolutionaries are doing him the biggest favor of his life. In destroying themselves as slaves, they are simultaneously destroying his false, hollow, self-defeating identity as master; and he, unlike them, survives the purgation. It is not clear whether a chastened, educated Usbek, stripped of his most precious possessions, would be capable of starting anew and creating an authentic life for himself. But it is clear that, for Montesquieu, both repressive societies and the repressed personalities that fill and sustain them— masters and slaves alike—must go: for it is only from their ruins that authenticity can arise. Thus the theory of revolution grows out of, and develops alongside, the ideal of authenticity. Both these ideas in themselves, and the relationship between them, constitute vital parts of the legacy Montesquieu passed on.

The Rise of Radical Individualism

The ideal of authenticity, as it first appeared, generated a form of individualism that can only be called radical, for its aims clashed sharply with all forms of authority that existed at the time. *The Persian Letters* was the first manifesto of this new individualism, and it appears quite early in the book. Usbek, having lost his belief in the universal and absolute validity of Islamic dietary laws, has come to believe that "objects in themselves are neither pure nor impure"; he "cannot think of any quality inherent in the [object] that would make them so." This perception is in itself nothing new; in the thought of Montaigne and Pascal, for instance, it constitutes a basis for cultural relativism. But Montesquieu draws very different conclusions from it: he arrives at a personal relativism which addresses rigorous categorical demands to all cultures alike. Usbek reasons that "our senses should be the sole judge of the purity or impurity of things." But every man's sensations, he realizes, are unique. Therefore, he concludes:

> Since objects do not affect men in the same way, since what gives an agreeable sensation to some produces a disagreeable sensation in others, it follows that the data of the senses cannot serve as a rule, *unless* one states that *each man according to his fancy, can decide this point for himself,* and *distinguish for his own purposes the things that are pure from those that are not.* [17]

Each individual, in other words, must create good and evil for himself. This proposition is only a conceptual expansion of the ideal of authenticity: it translates the demand that each man should live his own life into the language of moral philosophy, and states it in the form of a categorical imperative. This ethical individualism logically entails the individual's right to judge the *society* he lives in: whether or not it is "agreeable" to him, to what extent it helps him to fulfill "his own purposes."

33

The right of authenticity forms the nucleus of Montesquieu's defense of suicide. If he were to kill himself, Usbek says, he would "only [be] using a right given to me." He asks:

> Why should they want me to go on working for a society of which I am no longer willing to be a part? Why should they insist, despite my feelings, that I hold to a convention that has been made without my consent? Society is founded on mutual benefit. But when it becomes a burden to me, who can keep me from renouncing it? [75]

Montesquieu's argument here is strikingly original. For the Stoics, and for Montaigne, the right to suicide was derived from a concept of *honor* that was supposedly accepted by the whole of society: a man should do away with himself rather than allow himself to be placed in a dishonorable situation. Montesquieu, however, bases this right on a claim which *every individual* holds *against* his society. Every man is entitled to withdraw his consent from a society which he feels is denying him his proper share of "mutual benefit"; suicide is merely the ultimate form of withdrawal. This defense of suicide shows how closely the ideal of authenticity and the principle of *consent* are intertwined.

But although suicide is the most extreme mode of withdrawal, it is not the only mode. The individualism which in some circumstances justifies suicide will in other circumstances legitimize revolution. Thus Usbek defends the English Revolution of 1688, in a manner which would surely have startled most of its revolutionaries:

> . . . the impatient temperament of the English scarcely allows their kings any time to consolidate their author-

34

ity. Submission and obedience are two virtues that they make least of. On this score, they say extraordinary things. According to them, there is only one bond that can produce attachment in men: gratitude. A husband, a wife, a father and a son are bound mutually only by the love they have one for the other, or by the benefits they make possible one for the other. These various motives of gratitude are the origin of all kingdoms and all societies.

But if a prince, rather than seeking to have his subjects live happily, tries to oppress and destroy them, the principle of obedience ceases to operate; nothing binds them, nothing attaches them to him, and they return to their natural freedom. [104]

It is crucial that this standard should apply to *"all* kingdoms and *all* societies," to the roles of husband and wife, father and son, as well as sovereign and subject. Individuals must remain free to reject any system of roles which fails to fulfill their purposes, and return to an anarchic freedom. We can understand fully Montesquieu's argument here only if we grasp its connection with his defense of divorce (116), which symbolic function should now be clear. The value of all human relationships—private and public, personal and political alike—depends on how much they allow the individuality of every man to express itself. In order to maximize individuality, all relationships must be governed by the consent of the individuals themselves.

The radical individualism of *The Persian Letters* leads to a radical egalitarianism. If all individuals are to fulfill their personal purposes, no one man's purposes may count for more than those of any other. Thus Usbek bestows extravagant praise on modern republics such as Holland and Switzerland, in which both freedom and equality are most fully realized, with beneficent results.

> Nothing will attract foreigners more than freedom and the abundance that always follows from it. The first is sought after for itself, and we are led by our needs to seek out the country where the other is found. . . . The very equality of citizens, which ordinarily produces equality of fortune, brings abundance and life into every organ of the body politic and extends such benefits generally.
>
> The same cannot be said of countries subjected to arbitrary power: the prince, the courtiers, and a few individuals possess all the wealth, while the others groan in extreme poverty. [122]

The equality Montesquieu idealizes here is not merely "formal"—like the purely legal equality promulgated in the *Esprit des lois* (VIII.3)—but clearly "substantive," an equality of *fortune* as well as status. Moreover, it is perhaps the first distinctly *modern* conception of substantive equality. It departs completely from the traditional, primitivistic dream of equality which has recurred throughout the history of Western culture, especially among peasant and proletarian sects, and which had reappeared as recently as the English Civil War: the equality of a simple, static, face-to-face, agrarian economy based on scarcity and frugality.[17] Instead, Montesquieu envisions equality within a modern,

[17] On the persistence of this ideal throughout Christian history, despite repeated (and draconic) repression by Church and State, cf. Ernst Troeltsch *The Social Teachings of the Christian Churches,* translated by Olive Wyon (2 volumes, New York: Harper Torchbooks, 1960), especially pages 39–88, 328–82, 694–728. For its influence on modern secular radical movements, cf. E. J. Hobsbawm, *Primitive Rebels: Studies in Archaic Forms of Social Movement in the 19th and 20th Centuries* (New York: Norton, 1965).

urban, dynamic economy, based on growth and abundance. Although he does not develop it, and indeed soon abandons it, this model of equality—like so much else in *The Persian Letters*—is seminal for two centuries of social thought.

The radical individualism in Montesquieu's thought runs counter to an attitude which pervades all his work and which has always formed the center of his reputation: his *legalism*. In the *Spirit of the Laws* Montesquieu offers what has since become the classical liberal definition of freedom: "Liberty is the right to do what the laws permit. . . ." If a citizen could do what the laws forbid, "he would no longer be possessed of liberty, because all his fellow-citizens would have the same power." (XI.3) This definition is elaborated a little later: political liberty is essentially *security*, the ability to calculate the consequences of one's actions. (XII.2) By legalistic criteria, men can enjoy freedom within virtually any political system, so long as certain procedural standards are observed. (XII.4ff.) Only despotism precludes freedom, because despotism is regulated by the "momentary will of the prince," (IV.16) and has no "fixed constitution" or "settled laws." (III.8) This conception of liberty grows out of Montesquieu's empiricism: he wants an idea of freedom flexible enough to encompass the great diversity of political systems he knows.[18] So long as a system works smoothly and holds together securely, he wants to say, the men in it are free. The *content* of its laws does not matter; they will guarantee freedom so long as they are "enacted as general ab-

---

18 At the same time, and in the same place, we find a baldly dogmatic natural-law definition of freedom: it is "the power of doing what we ought to do, and not being forced to do what we ought not to do." (XI.3) This outright contradiction is never resolved, or even acknowledged in the *Spirit of the Laws; The Persian Letters*, I have tried to suggest, is more critical and toughminded.

37

stract rules and administered by independent courts," governed by some set of established *forms*.[19] Thus Montesquieu's idea of freedom here poses no threat to his beloved *parlements* or to the aristocratic privileges they conserved and consolidated. This legalistic idea and its political implications are already visible in *The Persian Letters;* but Montesquieu's earlier work contains a trenchant critique of legalism which his later work omits.

If freedom were simply the power to do what the laws allow, the women of the seraglio would have little to complain about. "You are the scourge of evil and the pillar of fidelity," Usbek advises his chief eunuch, "you make them carry out the laws of the harem." *(PL, 2)* Again, when he is enraged at his wives, he berates them for violating the "laws of duty" which he has conferred on them. (21) These references to law are not entirely ironic. Usbek's system does in fact operate according to more or less predictable rules; he does not change his will from moment to moment, and his wives know what to expect of him; although they are engaged in constant intrigue to obtain preferment over one another, he treats them with a certain disinterestedness (a function, perhaps, of his uninterest), and demands a uniform decorum and submissiveness of them all. Within the framework of a repressive system, the women are certainly secure—far more secure, as Usbek points out, than they would be in the world outside. (26)

Later on, Usbek universalizes the legalistic standard. The

---

[19] Cf. Franz Neumann's Introduction, lxi–lxii. Neumann emphasizes Montesquieu's contribution to the theory of the nineteenth-century *Rechtstaat,* and to the collapse of liberalism that attended it in Germany: the German bourgeoisie learned to put up with anything, so long as forms were observed, and canonized Montesquieu as one of their teachers. Whether Montesquieu would have approved of his putative pupils is very much an open question.

true way for man to please God, he says, after the manner of the eighteenth-century Deist, is "to observe the rules of society and the duties of humanity." This can be done by "practising all the duties of charity and human kindness in [men's] behalf and never violating the laws under which they live." (46) He recognizes no possible tension between particular laws and universal duties, between the society in which one happens to live and humanity as a whole. At the very end of his travels, however, Usbek abruptly discovers the profound contradiction which the façade of legality conceals. He writes from Paris in 1720, at the height of the economic catastrophe set off by the financial speculations of John Law: "I have seen a nation, noble by nature, perverted in the flashing of an eye, from the lowliest of subjects right up to the greatest. . . . I have seen a whole nation in which magnanimity, candor and good faith have from all time been regarded as inborn virtues, become the basest of nations. And I have watched the disease spread, even to its healthiest members." Usbek raves on, traumatically shocked. What shocks him most deeply, however, is the extent to which "They called forth odious laws as guarantee of the most cowardly action and gave to injustice and perfidy the name of *necessity*." (Montesquieu's emphasis.) When a law is odious, its very certainty and stability only reinforce the evil it does. Usbek tells a melodramatic tale of the bankruptcy of an honest man. "I have left a whole family in tears," the villain boasts, "wiped out the dowry of two fine girls, and deprived a little boy of his education. The father will die of grief and the mother is perishing from sadness. Still," he says as he retires serenely at night, "I did no more than is permitted under the law." (146) Usbek now perceives that when the content of a law is unjust, formal legality only formalizes its victims' ruin—a dubious form of

39

freedom. The importance of this perception is underlined by its place in the dramatic structure of the book. Usbek's critique of legalism comes on the verge of the climax, and marks his very last moment of innocence: the next letter reveals the incipient upheaval that will destroy his power and glory. The knowledge he expounds at this moment describes and prefigures the fate he is about to undergo; he does not know it, but it is his own reflection he sees. His own laws are about to be "rewritten . . . after the laws of nature" (161): it is only natural that any repressive system of laws, however formally legitimate, should meet such a fate. Radical individualism, as it emerges here, is not opposed to law in itself. But it resists the legalistic tendency to sanctify procedure while obscuring substance, to reduce the plasticity of human freedom to the rigidity of legal forms. It insists on critical scrutiny of the *content* of laws, of what they do to men.

The ideal of authenticity, when its implications are worked out, calls into question still another of the basic concepts in Western political thought: the concept of *virtue*. The traditional, classical definition of virtue is formulated most succinctly by Montesquieu himself in the beginning of the *Esprit des lois*: the politically virtuous man is one "who loves the laws of his country and who is actuated by the love of those laws." (Montesquieu's Explanatory Note.) The *Esprit*'s notion of virtue, like its notion of freedom, is peculiarly legalistic and conservative: it is capable of supporting virtually any existing political system. The only condition it imposes is that a system be *repressive*: for Montesquieu describes virtue as "a *self-renunciation* which is ever arduous and painful." (IV.5) It is a renunciation which men will not undertake of themselves; if it is to be enforced, it must be forced. Thus censorship is necessary in a virtuous republic, to keep men from expressing ideas which might prove subversive. (V.19) Sexual liberties, too, must be punished draconically, and women must be kept in subjection, lest feminine charm and vivacity sap the virtue of the solid citizenry. (VII.8 ff.) Indeed, all outlets for passion apart from patriotism must be closed: "The less we are able to satisfy our private passions, the more we abandon ourselves to those of a general nature." (V.1) For Montesquieu, here, the epitome of a virtuous society is an order of monks. Why is it, he asks, that monks seem to be attached to such a repressive style of life? It is because

> their rule debars them from all the things by which the ordinary passions are fed; there remains only the passion for the very rule that torments them. The more austere it is, the more force it gives to the only passion left them. [V.2]

This notion of virtue draws a sharp line between the self and society: the self is virtuous only when it surrenders its freedom and submits to the laws which society imposes on it. Once again, however, the conservative authoritarianism of the *Spirit of the Laws* finds its most astute critique in the radical individualism of *The Persian Letters*.

The discussion of virtue in *The Persian Letters*, like the discussion of law and liberty, begins with Usbek's instructions to the chief eunuch on how to govern his wives. "Your tireless attentions," he says, must "uphold virtue when it vacillates. If the women you are guarding tried to abandon their duty, you would make them give up such hope." (2) Here, just as in the *Esprit*, Montesquieu identifies virtue with submission. Since virtue is a negation of the self, it seems perfectly reasonable to protect the women from any experience that might generate a will to self-expression: hence they must be denied all "worldly education" and kept locked up in "a joyful state of happy inability to transgress." (26) But Usbek himself, flaring up in a moment of anger, inadvertently lights the spark that will explode his kind of virtue. Outraged at Zachi for an assignation she has had with a eunuch, he writes:

> You will perhaps tell me that you have always been faithful. Come now! How could you have been anything else? . . . How could you have broken the bolts and the doors that held you? *You vaunt much a virtue that is not free.* . . . [20]

Devotion, he sees, is devoid of meaning and value when it is compelled; virtue can be ascribed to it only if it is freely given. A conversation Usbek has with a Frenchman extends and deepens this idea. Virtue, the man tells him, is composed of "feelings" which "stem from nature"; in our terms, it is inherent in the authentic personality of every man. The Frenchman then expresses dismay that Persians "were forced to live with" a mass of slaves,

> whose hearts and minds always reflect the baseness of their social position. These cowardly people weaken in you feelings of virtue which stem from nature, and they have been destroying such feelings in you since the very childhood they tyrannize. [34]

The Frenchman is being elaborately ironic here, though his irony is lost on Usbek. He seems to be blaming the slaves for the master's lack of natural virtue; but if his words are examined carefully, the responsibility turns out to devolve on the whole repressive system that enslaves them. Nothing, after all, is "forcing" the Persians to live with slaves—except their own desire to be masters. If the masters find themselves corrupted, drained of their natural virtue, they have only the social system which made them masters to blame. The brute fact of human enslavement is a living refutation of the premise of human freedom on which virtue must rest.

Montesquieu has worked himself into a paradoxical position. He began by identifying virtue with submission to the social and political system under which one lives. Meanwhile, however, he has demonstrated brilliantly that a *repressive* system—one which denies the right to authenticity, and which withholds the freedom and equality necessary to exercise this right—systematically destroys the possibility of virtue. How can virtue express itself in a system whose whole structure works to repress it? Montesquieu does not state an explicit answer, but *The Persian Letters* contains a few striking intimations. Consider the wives' conduct at a moment when they are on the verge of open revolt:

> Meanwhile, your wives no longer show any reserve. Since the death of the great eunuch, *everything seems permissible to them.* . . . Each day sees further corruption of morals. No longer is there to be found on the countenance of your wives *that strict, vigorous virtue which was in times past enthroned there.* A *new sense of joy,* spread throughout these halls, is, to my mind, infallible proof of some new satisfaction. In the most minute things, I notice *liberties unknown up to now.* Even among your slaves there reigns a certain indolence toward duty and observation of rules which surprises me; they no longer possess that ardent zeal to serve you which once seemed to quicken the whole seraglio. [151]

Montesquieu's exact words are important here. The report does not exactly say that the women are *entirely* lacking in virtue. What he says is that they have lost a *particular kind*

of virtue—*"cette vertu mâle et sévère qui regnoit autrefois"*
—a virtue that reigned over them autocratically and kept
them in subjection. Perhaps, however, they are actuated by
a different kind of virtue? A virtue appropriate to a person
for whom "everything seems permissible," a virtue based on
newly won "liberties" and on the "joy" the individual finds
in himself. We get one glimpse of what this new virtue
might look like in action: Roxane invokes it in her final
manifesto. She has just asserted her natural individuality:
"I have rewritten your laws after the laws of nature, and my
spirit has ever sustained itself in independence." She must
now reject a form of virtue that is based on a denial of the
authentic identity she has just created. "I have dared to pro-
fane the name of virtue by allowing submission to your
caprice to be called by that name." (161) True virtue, presumably, is embodied in what she is doing now. But if Roxane's actions are virtuous, the idea of virtue has taken on a
new life. Traditional virtue, best explicated in the *Spirit of
the Laws,* entails painful self-repression; *The Persian Letters* opens up the possibility of a virtue that is based on pleasure and self-*ex*pression. Traditional virtue consists of love
for one's country and its laws; here, however, in a system of
repression, virtue must turn *against* the country and its
laws. Traditional virtue is conservative, a pillar of the *status
quo;* we are faced now with a virtue that is profoundly revolutionary, whose deepest impulse is to overthrow a repressive *status quo.*[20]

[20] Montesquieu did not develop this new idea of virtue, and indeed
eventually abandoned it; but he never gave up the radical individualism
on which it had been based. The traditional notion of virtue that appears in the *Spirit of the Laws* is draconically repressive; but Montesquieu himself does not advocate the repression it entails. It is
essential to understand that the idea of virtue serves two basically different purposes in the two works. Throughout the *Letters* virtue is projected as *the* ideal, as the thing which men were born for. (10) In the

44

Montesquieu's Image of Authenticity: The Metropolis[21]

The Persian Letters is usually read as a satirical and critical commentary on Parisian life during the Regency of the Duc d'Orléans. This emphasis is unfortunate. It obscures the fact that Montesquieu is one of the very first writers to bring to life the whole new world of possibilities opened up

---

Esprit it lacks this normative value: it merely describes *one* ideal among many, one of the several possible alternatives to despotism, and not at all the one Montesquieu most prefers. This is not simply because as sociological commentators tend to think, he is trying to be "scientific" and valuefree. (Cf. Emile Durkheim, *Montesquieu and Rousseau: Forerunners of Sociology,* translated by Ralph Manheim [Ann Arbor: University of Michigan Press, 1960], 15 ff.) The *Esprit des lois,* a work of consummate maturity, is in fact a deeply pessimistic book; it is devoid of any trace of the radical ideals and hopes that pervade the youthful *Persian Letters.* The *Letters* argued that fidelity, devotion, virtue— human commitments in general—logically entailed human freedom; the *Esprit* sees the two as empirically, psychologically incompatible. Montesquieu does not derive this conclusion from any philosophical argument; he takes it for granted as simply a sad fact about human nature. In opting for constitutional monarchy as the best of all possible models, Montesquieu feels that he is opting for freedom: for a relatively unregulated state in which wise government can arrange things so that (in the familiar eighteenth-century liberal manner) "each individual advances the public good, while he thinks only of promoting his own interest," (III.7) and so that its citizens can become "good *subjects*" without having to be what they will never choose to be, "good *men.*" (III.6) Within the monarchy, as Montesquieu pictures it, human passion can express itself freely, with no restraints other than the rules of honor which individuals prescribe for themselves; (V.19; VII.8–12) but any hope that virtue might grow out of this interplay of passions and personalities has long since been given up. Montesquieu has replaced his youthful radicalism with a liberalism more appropriate to a pessimistic view of the world. It was too much to hope for a society in which men would choose to be virtuous; it is enough, now, to settle for one in which they are at least free to be themselves.

21 The theoretical basis of this chapter is Georg Simmel's essay, "The Metropolis and Mental Life," reprinted in *The Sociology of Georg Simmel,* translated and edited by Kurt Wolff (Glencoe, Illinois: The Free Press, 1950), 409–24.

by the *metropolis* which Paris had become.[22] His vision of the metropolis marks unmistakably the modernity of his sensibility. *The Persian Letters* is filled with detailed description and evocation of metropolitan life which point the way toward the great works of modern realism. But Montesquieu is not content to merely describe the metropolis, he endows it with philosophical meaning and value: it is the ideal medium for authentic life. His Persian visitors discover the metropolitan virtues in the course of discovering themselves.

Usbek and his friends grow to appreciate the Parisian life as they perceive the *ennui* and emptiness of their own. Parisians, they see at once, are so much happier. "Persian women," Usbek observes, "are more beautiful than those of France, but the Frenchwomen are prettier. Impossible not to love the former, and equally impossible not to be happy with the latter." Montesquieu's choice of words here brings out a crucial antithesis. *"To love"*: his relation to Persian women is purely transitive; the flow of feeling is all one way, from a subject to an object. *"To be happy with"*: this is a wholly different sort of relationship, a relationship of "withness," of mutuality. The capacity for mutuality presupposes a certain temperament: a woman must be "gay and sprightly," as the *parisiennes* are, not "gentle and modest" like the residents of the seraglio. It takes a specific social and political climate to make people gay: "You simply cannot find there [in Persia] the *freedom of mind* . . . that I see here *in every rank and profession.*" (34) Usbek is learning

---

22 Carl E. Schorske discusses the city as a recurrent image of liberation and cultivation in Enlightenment thought: see his essay, "The Idea of the City in European Thought"; in Oscar Handlin and John Borchard, editors, *The Historian and the City* (Cambridge, Mass.: M.I.T. Press, 1963), 95–114. Curiously, Schorske discusses neither Montesquieu nor Rousseau.

that libertinism must become liberalism in order to fulfill itself. This is the lesson of the metropolis: for it is only here, where the liberty of every man in every rank is respected, that the happiness and self-fulfillment which Usbek (and every other man) seeks can be found.

The Persian Letters evokes with a vivid immediacy and power the best of metropolitan life and the pervasive freedom that flows through it. We see Rica almost bowled over by the city's speed: "We have been in Paris for a month and have continually been in motion. . . . Perhaps you will not believe this, but for the month I have been here, I have seen nobody walking. There are no people in the world who get so much out of their carcasses as the French: they run; they fly." (24) This breathless pace bespeaks a great concentration of energy and intensity of life. Their sheer frequency of interaction is amazing: "if man is a social animal, the Frenchman is more of a man than any other. He is man personified, for he seems to be made only for society." (87) But this sociability is not a function of leisured decadence: it does not divert men from serious work. Usbek points out the flourishing state of art and science, craftsmanship and business in Paris. It is true, he acknowledges, that the most important motive behind all this activity is self-interest; and it is true that self-interest, when it is carried to excess, can corrupt a people. (11–12, 146) But it is far from destructive here and now. Instead, it generates an "ardor for work" which "passes along from social class to social class, from the artisans right up to the nobles. . . . [This] spirit is caught by the nation. Work and industry are everywhere. Where, then, is this effeminate people you talk so much of?" The Parisians work not merely for "necessities," but for "superfluities" as well. Hence they are never content; their satisfactions only generate new needs, their desire is open-ended

47

and insatiable. Montesquieu, who has studied the English economists, sees this incessant striving not as a sign of decay, but of social health. "If the inhabitants [of Paris] were courageous enough to give up so many of the things they need, that people would grow weaker every day, and the state would become so enfeebled that no power would be too small to conquer it." (106) The metropolis differs from all traditional societies not only in the quantity but in the quality of its work: The Parisians' sources of income, Rica comments, "consist only in their wit and ingenuity. Each man has his own, and he exploits it as best he can." This continuous activity of mind and release of energy make Paris "the mother of invention." (58) In its infinite dynamism and productivity, Montesquieu's metropolis is a microcosm and a symbol of nature. Like nature, the metropolis is mechanical and individualistic, not organic and collective, in its sources of life. Hence its life expresses itself through the infinite diversity of its atoms. "Foreigner that I am," says Usbek, "I found nothing better to do than to study the crowd of people who come here endlessly and who always have something new to offer me." (48) Usbek, whose whole identity has always been based on the repression of human nature and diversity, is enthralled by the spectacle of natural life in all its authenticity, which he is beholding for the first time.

Montesquieu's picture of the metropolis, like his vision of the nature it expresses and symbolizes, suggests radical ideas. Paradoxically, the social instability of the metropolis is a potential source of political stability for the state which the metropolis supports. "To keep a prince powerful," Usbek writes, "his subjects must live in pleasure. He must work to secure all manner of superfluity for them, devoting to this as much attention as to the necessities of life." (106)

An economy of superfluity can develop, however, only if all men are engaged in incessant activity which is open-ended and imposes no inherent limits on them. But the social condition for the abundance which every modern state requires clashes radically with the social structure on which every existing state is based. This tension between state and society is evident in France. In the corrupt and chaotic French state, political power is a function of social caste; it derives its authority from an uneasy combination of magic, traditional reverence and force. Amidst the energy and health of metropolitan society, on the other hand: "Liberty and equality reign in Paris. Birth, reputation, even military glory, however brilliant, will not save a man from the crowd in which he is lost." (88) Montesquieu perceives very clearly the leveling and liberating force of the city street and its crowd. The perpetual motion of metropolitan life breaks down and sweeps away all the fixed social roles which would impose a deadening rigidity on its flow. Paris can be no respecter of *personae* because the only laws it recognizes are laws of motion; it tends toward a state of permanent revolution. In 1721 Paris is still governed by Versailles. But it will be only a matter of time before social history overflows into political history, and the modern city rings down the curtain on the traditional state.[23]

The citizens of the metropolis are exposed to a continuous bombardment of stimuli, a dazzling flux of constantly changing forms of life. In order to withstand its pressures, they have learned to see through the pretensions to absolute

[23] The event which moved Burke to lament that the decent drapery of life had been torn away was the march of the Parisian crowd to Versailles on October 5, 1789, when several thousand people, led by women, surrounded the royal palace and brought the king and queen back to the city, to reign among the people. Cf. George Rudé, *The Crowd in the French Revolution* (New York: Oxford University Press, 1959), 61–79.

validity and sanctity with which every form of life surrounds itself. Only one thing is sacred for them: the individuality of every human being. Their "freedom of mind"
from all absolutes (34) releases each individual to be himself. In such a climate, Rica soon perceives his exotic, aristocratic Persian costume as a mask, a stereotype that conceals
him both from the Parisians and from himself. "All this," he
says,

> made me decide to put off the Persian costume and
> change over to one in European style, just to see if
> there would remain anything admirable in my face.
> The test made me understand *what I was really worth.*
> Free of all foreign embellishment, I found that I was
> more soberly judged. . . . I immediately fell into a
> void. [30]

Although Rica is momentarily upset by the verdict of the
metropolitan crowd, he recognizes them as qualified to
judge: they know how, he feels, to see men as they are.
Usbek learns to understand this in his own way. At first, he
is scandalized by the looseness of manners and morals in
Paris. "Women here have lost all reserve," he writes Roxane: "They appear before men with faces uncovered. . . ."
These women without veils are symbolic of Parisian—and
metropolitan—life as a whole. What seems to shock Usbek
most profoundly about this life is the *openness* with which
it is carried on. Thus he tells Roxane to be grateful for the
seclusion with which her own life is enveloped:

> Yes, my Roxane, if you were here, you would feel out-
> raged by the frightful shamelessness into which your
> sex has slipped. You would flee these abominable
> places; you would sigh with regret for that sweet retreat
> where you meet with innocence, where you are sure of

yourself, where no danger causes you to tremble, where, finally, you can love me without fear of ever losing the love you owe me. [26]

At this point, Usbek still takes the seraglio for a place of maximum security, where a woman can be "sure of herself" —fastened to her place by her sense of shame and her lack of self-esteem—and her dominant husband sure of himself, and both of them sure of one another, sure of the roles in which they are fixed. In time, however, he comes to see that the seraglio is actually a place of maximum deception and *in*security; that all the fixed identities within it are chimerical, the very opposite of what they seem; and that the veils he has thrown over his wives only screen out his source of knowledge of who they really are. Once this becomes clear, the openness of the metropolis appears as a blessing, its shamelessness as a welcome honesty, a breath of fresh air. At the same time, in observing the energy and diversity of the Parisian crowd (48), Usbek has learned to participate in it, and to seize for a fleeting moment an individuality that eludes him in his life as a whole. When Rica states the idea of authenticity, Usbek is ready to receive it, and to perceive its social implications:

> Dissimulation, that art so practiced and so necessary among us, is unknown here. Everything speaks out; everything is visible; everything is audible. The heart shows itself as clearly as the face. In their customs, in their virtue, even in vice, something akin to naiveté is always visible. [63]

In the transparency of the metropolitan atmosphere, appearance and reality can unite. Here men's real thoughts and feelings—both virtuous and vicious—can emerge. Only where the veils are torn away do trust and security in

51

human relations become possible; it is only in the metropolis that men can truly speak to men.

A central theme of *The Persian Letters* is that a person can get satisfaction only *with* other people, not *from* them; that to enjoy them, one must respect their authenticity. The freedom and equality of the metropolis, which the book evokes so well, provide the ideal medium in which the authenticity of everyone can subsist. But this medium, in enlarging the possibilities for human happiness, alters radically the forms in which men can experience happiness. Usbek fails to perceive these new forms when he is preoccupied with his own life. For himself, he conceives of happiness as something purely *static,* immobile, eternal. He fears any assertion of autonomy by his wives because it would necessarily change their relationship to him; and he feels any change whatever as a threat to his happiness. In observing the metropolis, however, he discovers a basically new way of being happy; a *dynamic* happiness. Parisians, he notes, find an abiding joy in the total liberty—that is, total license—of their sexual relations. Transience and inconstance present no problem to them and even provide a source of enjoyment. "Their peace of mind is not based on the confidence they have in their wives; on the contrary, it stems from the bad opinion they have of them." The Parisians regard a husband who loves his wife and insists on keeping her to himself as "a man lacking the attraction to make himself loved by another woman": such a man, it is said, "takes improper advantage of the law to make up for the charm he lacks. . . ." (55) This *charm* is the Parisians' secret. Living in an open society where the freedom of every person in every rank is respected, and where personal diversity and individuality are constantly out in the open, they have developed a sense of *self-esteem.* They feel their own personalities as their most valuable assets; hence they do not need to possess each other exclusively and eternally in order to secure for themselves the means of happiness. "After all," they say, "were we to be unhappy in our status as husbands, we should always find some way of making up for it in our status as lovers." (38) They have a basic confidence in themselves; hence they can afford to play a plurality of roles without having to stake their whole identity on the success of any particular one. If social freedom has conferred a sense of personal dignity on them, this dignity has in turn enhanced the value of their freedom. These Parisians are in fact a new type of personality, brought into being by modern times and by the metropolis, introduced by *The Persian Letters* into European thought. On one hand, they are remarkably flexible, sensitized to a life of perpetual change and mobility; on the other hand, for all the metamorphoses they go through, their underlying sense of self remains intact. They embody a new principle of personal identity: an individuality that exists apart from social status, and maintains itself independently of any roles the individual might play.

The impact of *The Persian Letters* has always been oblique and ambiguous. Its radical individualism has never fit comfortably into any of the standard political formulae; indeed, it has come to be a stumbling block in the way of all parties that would claim authority over the lives of men. Nevertheless, in its perception of the repressive character of all established states, in its demand for an authentic existence that would transcend the established repressions, and in its understanding of the liberating forces which modern times had engendered, *The Persian Letters* pointed a fruitful direction for the political thought of its age.

53

INTERLUDE

Diversion and Discovery: The Self in Enlightenment Thought

> Every healthy effort . . . is directed from the inner to the outer world.
>
> GOETHE TO ECKERMANN
>
> How can one be glad of the world, unless one is flying to it for refuge?
>
> KAFKA

Pascal: The World as Obstacle to the Self

WE HAVE SEEN how the ideal of authenticity arose out of men's experience of the first great wave of modernization in the West. It suddenly seemed possible *to be oneself in the world:* to fulfill the self's potentialities not by getting out of this world, but by getting into it. By penetrating the life of the world more deeply than ever, man could discover hidden sources of power and glory that lay in the depths of the self; only if these buried treasures were brought out into the open could their true, ultimate value be revealed. The Paris celebrated in *The Persian Letters* symbolized the infinite new possibilities which the modern world had opened up for men; Montesquieu's Persia—

and his Versailles—represented the old, traditional, repressive social and political forces that were holding men back.

And yet, there was much that was wrong with this picture, alluring as it seemed. Was it really so easy to be oneself in Paris? Pascal, one of the most toughminded of modern men, argued that it was impossible. If one took a hard look at the world, it appeared that not only was *Deus absconditis*,[1] but man himself was missing. The activities men engaged in did not constitute an expression of the self, but rather a displacement and a disguise; not a fulfillment, but an endless emptiness. Pascal picked up the echoes of this emptiness in the second section of his *Pensées*, which he entitled "The Misery of Men without God." [2]

The problem of self-alienation first arose for Pascal out of his observation of the pervasive vice of *insincerity*. "Human life," he commented bitterly, "is only a perpetual illusion. No one speaks of us in our presence as he does in our absence. Human society is founded on mutual deceit." This evil "is no doubt greater and more common among the upper classes; but the lower are not exempt from it. . . ." Although Pascal's indictment encompassed the whole structure of society, he saw nothing specifically social about the

---

[1] *Deus absconditis*, or "The Hidden God": a doctrine, professed by the most radical of Jansenists in seventeenth-century France, according to which the world, both natural and human is totally devoid of divinity. This heresy maintains that there is nothing in the world from which anyone could legitimately infer the existence of God, and hence that belief can spring only from a wholly groundless faith. Lucien Goldmann sees this doctrine as the key to Pascal's thought, and as one of the milestones in the development of modern radicalism: *Le dieu caché: Etude sur la vision tragique dans les Pensées de Pascal et dans le théâtre de Racine* (Paris: Librairie Gallimard, 1955). Cf. also Erich Auerbach, "On the Political Theory of Pascal," in *Scenes from the Drama of European Literature*, translated from the German by Ralph Manheim (New York: Meridian Books), 101–32.

[2] I have generally followed the translation of W. F. Trotter (New York: Modern Library, 1941), who uses the numbering established by Leon Brunschvicg.

vice he condemned. "Man, then, is only disguise, falsehood, and hypocrisy, both in himself and with regard to others. He doesn't wish anyone to tell him the truth, he avoids telling it to others; and all these inclinations, so far removed from justice and reason, have a natural root in his heart." (*Pensées*, 100) The mutual deceit on which society was founded was simply the sum of all individual deceptions.

Why should men go to such lengths to conceal themselves? Pascal, arguing from traditional Christian premises, held that men were insincere to hide their innate viciousness, a viciousness of which they were only too well aware. If others saw us as we are, they would only hate and despise us, for we are all basically hateful and despicable. "This embarrassment in which [man] finds himself produces in him the most unjust and criminal passion imaginable: he conceives a mortal hatred against that truth which reproves him and convinces him of his faults. He would annihilate it; but unable to destroy it in itself, he devotes all his attention to hiding his faults, both from others and from himself. . . ." The ultimate source of this embarrassment, and of the deceit that sprang from it, was what Pascal called *amour-propre*, "self-love": "The nature of self-love and of the human self [*le moi humain*] is to love nothing but itself and to think of nothing but itself." (100) But Pascal's argument here, although theologically exemplary, was not psychologically plausible. For if men could really love themselves in spite of full knowledge of their faults, why should they hate their fellow men for being the sort of beings they knew themselves to be? A self-love based on self-knowledge would be far more likely to give these faulty men an empathy with their faulty neighbors, and to generate a climate of mutual acceptance. In any case, self-love did not help to explain an ambience of pervasive insincerity and self-disguise.

Pascal must have sensed the inadequacy of this analysis, for he developed a far more complex and radical view of the roots of self-alienation. In a long series of fragments, he explored the idea that all human activity was an endless search for *divertissement,* "diversion." What men sought most of all in the world, he argued, was a way out of themselves. They escaped into it, leaving everything behind, not only their vices but their virtues as well. For his most striking piece of evidence Pascal chose that figure whom the world most exalted, the man who seemed to him to "have everything": the absolute monarch.

> Yet, when we imagine a king attended with every pleasure he can feel, if he be left without diversion, and be left to consider and reflect on what he is, this feeble happiness will not sustain him; he will necessarily fall into forebodings of dangers, of revolutions which may occur, and finally, of inevitable disease and death; so that if he be without what is called diversion, he is unhappy, and more unhappy than the least of his subjects who plays and diverts himself.

And this was why "kings are surrounded with persons who are wonderfully attentive in taking care that the king be not alone and in a state to think of himself, knowing that he will be miserable, king though he be, if he should meditate on himself." (139, 142) Pascal's vision here focused not on human *insincerity* but on a far more profound form of self-alienation which I will call *inauthenticity:* the determination of men to hide themselves not merely from others, but from themselves. Insincerity, whether rooted in self-love or self-hatred, requires that a self be "there" to state the deception; inauthenticity is a situation from which the self has altogether disappeared. Pascal's discussion of *divertissement* revealed a world marked not by excess but by an absence of self.

The archetype of diversion was *le jeu,* the game. "Men occupy themselves following a ball or a hare; it is the pleasure even of kings." (141) The compulsive, self-defeating behavior of the gambler offered a perfect symbol of man's insatiable need for diversion. (139) But the structure of the game underlay not only man's leisure-time pursuits, but his more serious and weightiest works; there was no essential difference between them. Thus:

> The [proper] order of thought is to begin with one's self, with its author and its end. But what does the world think of? Never of this, but of dancing, playing the lute, singing, making verses, trying to grab brass rings, etc., fighting, making oneself king, but without ever thinking what it is to be king, or to be a man. [146]

For the Pascalian king, kingship itself was a diversion. The life of the great aristocratic functionary was equally alien to the man who lived it.

> What is it to be chief intendant, chancellor, first president, but to be in a condition where from early morning a large number of people come from all quarters to see them, so as not to leave them an hour in the day in which they can think for themselves? And when they are in disgrace and sent back to their country houses, where they lack neither wealth nor servants to help them when the need arises, they never fail to be wretched and desolate, because there is no one to keep them from thinking of themselves. [139]

All the roles in society were spiritually bankrupt, empty of meaning for man. The more important they seemed, the

61

more vacuous and absurd they actually were. Yet men pursued them, so as not to have to confront and contemplate themselves.

Why were men so afraid to contemplate themselves? Pascal was sure he knew: for his own contemplation had revealed to him "the natural poverty of our feeble and mortal condition, so miserable that nothing can comfort us when we think of it closely." (139) The human condition he lamented here was not the innate viciousness so familiar to Christian rhetoricians and their audience, but a *malaise* far more profound: the cosmic futility of man, the absurdity of his vices and his virtues alike. This theme was developed in one of Pascal's profoundest and most beautiful meditations, concerning "man's disproportion." (72)

> For in fact what is man in nature? A nothing in comparison with the infinite, an all in comparison with nothing, a mean between nothing and everything. Since he is infinitely removed from comprehending the extremes, the end of things and their beginning are hopelessly hidden from him. . . .
>
> This is our true state; this is what makes us incapable of certain knowledge and absolute ignorance. We sail within a vast sphere, ever drifting in uncertainty, driven from end to end. When we think to attach ourselves, to fasten ourselves to any point, it wavers and leaves us; and if we follow it, it eludes our grasp, slips past us, and vanishes forever. Nothing stays for us. This is our natural condition, and yet most contrary to our inclinations. We burn with desire to find a solid ground, and an ultimate, sure foundation on which to build a tower that will reach to the infinite; but the groundwork crumbles beneath us, and the earth opens to abysses.

Locked in his room alone, meditating on the ultimate structure of the universe, Pascal was led to view the human condition as an impasse. This terrified and paralyzed him; it led him to the view, moreover, that resigned inertia was the only rational mode of conduct for man.

> If this be well understood, I think we shall remain at rest, each in the state in which nature has placed him. Since the sphere which has fallen to us as our lot is always distant from either extreme, what does it matter that man should know a little more about how things work? . . . In comparison with these infinities all finites are equal, and I see no reason for fixing our imagination more on one than on another.

The great error of men who searched for diversion was to ascribe meaning and value to things, to people, to relationships with the world. So long as they persisted in their error, and continued to expend their spirit on worldly things, men would never be themselves. The world, and all its opportunities for action, were fundamentally alien to man.

Pascal's analysis of inauthenticity was powerful and persuasive, yet fundamentally unsatisfactory. The basic difficulty stemmed from his definition of the self.

> Nothing is so insufferable to man as to be completely at rest, without passions, without business, without diversion, without study. He then feels his nothingness, his forlornness, his insufficiency, his dependence, his weakness, his emptiness. There will immediately arise from the depths of his heart weariness, gloom, sadness, fretfulness, vexation, despair. [131]

Pascal was trying to show that all worldly activity was an attempt to escape from the self. But he had actually settled the argument in advance, by defining the self as something *a priori* distinct from the world. He conceived the self as inexorably severed from all worldly relationships. Thus passion, business, study, sensual satisfaction, intellectual engagement, were all alien modes of being. Only when completely inert, cut off from everyone and everything, devoid of passions or cares, locked in contemplation, was man truly himself. Pascal then cited man's persistent need for action in the world as proof of his self-alienation. But the data he had observed in fact proved nothing of the kind. He was able to reach his conclusion only by begging the essential question: what was man's authentic relation to the world? "I have discovered," he said, "that all the unhappiness of men arises from a single fact, that they are unable to stay quietly in one room." (139) But this inability might be the source of all man's happiness as well! Indeed, if the natural fruits of solitary reflection were what Pascal said they were, it is hard to see how an active man could fail to gain in happiness. The emptiness man felt in the void might reveal not the emptiness of his nature, but the unnaturalness of the void. Pascal asserted without argument that the world was a stumbling block for the self. But the most striking thing he observed—man's inability to feel at home in solitude and at rest—could have been explained even more plausibly by a radically opposite view: that the world was man's native element, and activity in the world the only medium for his authentic self-expression.

The inadequacy of Pascal's analysis came across most vividly in his discussion of the king. He inferred the inauthenticity of kingship from the fact that the "royal dignity" was not "sufficiently great to make its possessor happy by the mere contemplation of what he is." (142) Pascal, normally so toughminded, was taken in here by the fictions of kingship: that it was a *dignitas non moritur,* existing in itself, independent of the men who inherit it, bear it and pass it on, holding the state together.[3] But these fictions had never been so dramatically exposed as in Pascal's own time, with the French monarchy seriously threatened and the English one actually dissolved by civil war. The political history of the seventeenth century should have made it clear to him that "royal dignity" could not be passively contemplated in itself: its reality had to be proved in action. If the kings of France had rested alone in their rooms, as Pascal prescribed, their royal dignity would have been instantly overthrown—and Pascal's own class and religious faction would have helped in the overthrowing. It would not have satisfied King Louis XIV to merely reign; he could never have enjoyed his royal dignity, or felt himself "every inch a king," except by actively ruling his country. In this respect kings were no different from other men. To take any man away from things, from other men, and from the possibility of action, would be to take away his sole means of being himself. Pascal was shrewd in his intuition that even the men of his age who were most deeply engaged in worldly activities were somehow not fulfilling themselves; but he was mistaken in thinking that they were deprived of self-satisfaction by their engagement and worldliness *per se*.

Thus, although Pascal diagnosed brilliantly man's alienation from other men and from himself, he failed to explain it. His observation of how forlorn men felt apart from the world was especially pertinent at the end of the seventeenth century. But it showed only that men were coming to feel more and more at home in the world; that, after centuries of Christian culture, human nature was becoming worldly once again.

[3] The ideology of kingship in the West is best explicated by Ernst Kantorowicz, particularly in *The King's Two Bodies: A Study in Medieval Political Theology* (Princeton, N. J.: Princeton University Press, 1956).

Voltaire: The World as Vehicle for the Self

This new worldliness was perhaps the central theme in French thought throughout the eighteenth century. We can see it expressed vividly and eloquently in the Enlightenment's most sustained critique of Pascal, Voltaire's discussion of the *Pensées* in Number 25 of his *Lettres philosophiques.*[4] Voltaire sought "to take the part of humanity against this sublime misanthrope, to show that we are neither so wicked nor so unhappy as he says. . . ." (Introduction) He was quick to detect Pascal's unwarranted assumptions about human nature, and to draw opposite conclusions from the evidence Pascal had introduced. Thus Pascal had said: "Man is so wretched that he would grow weary [*s'ennuieroit*] even without any external cause, merely from his peculiar condition. . . ." (*Pensées*, 139) Voltaire replied: "On the contrary, man is fortunate in precisely this; and we should be grateful to the author of nature, that he attaches *ennui* to inaction, in order to force us to be useful to others and to ourselves." (xxvi) Pascal was scandalized that a man who had just lost his only son could completely forget his sorrows by immersing himself in the hunt for a wild boar. "This man does well," Voltaire answered, "dissipation is as sure a cure for sorrow as quinine for fever. So don't revile nature, which is always so ready to come to our aid." (xxvii) Indeed, if we only remembered that nature was rational, we would understand man's need for occupation and action not as a *divertissement* from himself, but as his authentic self-fulfillment. For "Isn't it absurd

---

4 These letters, composed in England between 1728 and 1730, first appeared in 1733. All my citations are from Letter 25; numbers designate Voltaire's paragraphs. I have used the critical edition, edited by Gustave Lanson (Paris: Hachette, 1930), in which Letter 25 appears in Volume II, 184–244. Translations are my own.

to think that man's senses, so perfectly suited for action, are really meant only for contemplation?" (xxiv) Instead, we should infer from the human capacity for activity in the world that "Man is born for action. . . . For man, not to be *occupé* is not to exist." (xxiii)

But it was not enough merely to justify man's need to occupy himself; Voltaire went on to defend the structure and distribution of occupations as it was in his society. Thus, for a lifelong partisan of the *thèse royale,* it was disturbing that Pascal should insist on the inexorable unhappiness of the king. Perhaps, as Plato had suggested in Book Nine of the *Republic,* the despot, the *bad* king, was bound to be unhappy; but surely not *every* king, not kings *as such!* "A wise king can certainly be happy at home with himself" [*chez lui*]; individual cases of the sort Pascal dwelt on applied only to the particular men he cited, and "prove nothing about the rest of mankind," or about the role of kingship itself. (xxv) Voltaire was equally upset by the idea that there might be something structurally amiss at the bottom of the social order. Pascal had commented that "The most important thing in life is the choice of a calling; yet this is decided by chance [*par hasard*]. Custom makes men into masons, soldiers, slaters." (97) The basis on which social roles were assigned to men—or at least, to men of the lower classes—was basically contingent, fortuitous, absurd. Voltaire did not contest the description, but he saw no need to worry about it. "Who else [but chance and custom] should fix soldiers, artisans and mechanical workers in their places? There is no special art or genius required for these jobs; and for things that all the world can do, it's perfectly natural that custom should apportion them." (xxi) Voltaire was perfectly correct when he pointed out that in the European society of his day most occupations were so empty of meaning that it basically did not matter what men did. But in leaving it at that, he was intimating that it *should* not matter. Even though man defined himself, and proved his very existence, by being *occupé* in the world, the nullity of most men's occupations seemed to be no cause for concern.

Voltaire was not indifferent to the sufferings of the mass of men. But he was firmly convinced that the world in which he was so comfortably at home had to be fundamentally beneficent. His belief in a cosmic world-order[5] precluded any systematic critique of the ordering of society. Thus Voltaire insisted that the world was far from being the desert island Pascal said it was:

> As for me, if I look at Paris or London, I see no reason for the despair M. Pascal speaks of. The city I see is not at all like a desert island, but populated, opulent, civilized [*policée*]; the men in it are as happy as human nature allows them to be. . . . To see all men as criminals is the idea of a fanatic; to see the world as nothing but pleasure and delight is the view of a Sybarite. But to think that the earth, men and animals are all that they should be in the order of providence is the idea of a wise man. [vi]

If Pascal had categorically rejected the world, Voltaire just as categorically embraced it. His false consciousness here was typical of the *philosophes* as Peter Gay describes them:

> The philosophes cultivated their connections with power, and their fraternizing with the enemy cost them heavily. It distorted their tactics, long circumscribed their freedom of action, sometimes seduced them into

---

5 It is precisely this optimistic faith which Voltaire later attacked so bitterly and trenchantly in *Candide*. But he never really assimilated the moral insight and imagination that made *Candide* a modern classic.

intellectual dishonesty, and blurred their radicalism, not only for others but for themselves as well. . . .

The intellectual revolution over which the Enlightenment presided pointed to the abolition of hierarchy as much as to the abolition of God. But most of the philosophes found much to cherish in the existing order.

Seeking to distinguish themselves, the philosophes had little desire to level all distinctions; seeking to be respected, they had no desire to destroy respectability. Their gingerly treatment of the masses, which became less patronizing as the century went on, reveals their attachment to the old order and their fear of too drastic an upheaval. [*The Enlightenment* I, 24–7] [6]

The *philosophes* were the first group of thinkers to see clearly the vast range of possibilities for human self-expression in the world. Elated by the beauty and grandeur of their vision, however, they lost sight of the great gap between what they saw and where they stood, between what was possible for man and what was real for men, between the human world as it might be and European society as it was. For a long while the Pascalian insight into the spiritual bankruptcy of social norms and roles was obscured. The mainstream of Enlightenment thought submerged the clear boundaries Pascal had drawn between being *a king*—or a common laborer, or any of the roles which European society assigned to men—and being *oneself*.

Self, State and Society in the Enlightenment

So far we have seen several approaches to the problem of authenticity. The Stoics, and Pascal in their tradition, made

[6] *The Enlightenment: An Interpretation,* Volume 1, *The Rise of Modern Paganism* (New York: Alfred A. Knopf, 1966).

total indictments of the societies they lived in: all existing social roles, they felt, prevented men from being themselves. But they did not understand the social basis of alienation. What kept men from being themselves, they thought, was worldly activity as such, not any particular kinds of activity, not any particular arrangement of the world. Hence they did not look closely into exactly *how* men became alienated from themselves in society. Radical though it was, the Stoical critique remained too abstract to have any political impact. In the eighteenth century, however, thinkers were coming increasingly to think of human nature and its potentialities as belonging essentially to this world. For some of the *philosophes*—Voltaire, for instance, in his early critique of Pascal—authenticity was no problem at all: men were fulfilling themselves perfectly well in the world as it was. For others, however, authenticity could be understood for the first time as a political issue. Thus Montesquieu argued in *The Persian Letters* that men could be themselves only where they were free and equal; a state which denied human freedom and equality had no claim on the obedience or loyalty of men. Unfortunately, he never related his theoretical insight directly to the social and political conditions around him. Still, we can extract one concrete political theme from *The Persian Letters*: a dualistic view of State and Society which condemned the traditional, authoritarian French state and celebrated the modern, liberal Parisian society. The young Montesquieu felt perfectly at home in the individualistic, dynamic, cosmopolitan metropolis which was just beginning to emerge. He was confident that this distinctively modern society contained the means for liberating all men to be themselves—if only the state would let it alone. Thus the theory of authenticity in *The Persian Letters,* though revolutionary, was profoundly optimistic.

In this it prefigured the ideology of the revolutionary bourgeoisie in 1789, who in general were quite happy with the structure of French society, and sought only a redistribution of political power to reinforce and legitimize the social power they already held.

Rousseau fought this optimism all his life. The state and society, he believed, were a unity: the repressive states of his time were not imposed arbitrarily on European society, but grew organically out of it. It was the social system as a whole that alienated men, not only from one another, but from themselves:

> It has often been noticed that in the course of their lives *the majority of men are quite unlike themselves (sont dissemblables à eux-mêmes)*, and often seem to *transform themselves totally into different men.* But it wasn't to establish so well-known a fact that I planned to write my book; I had a more original and more important end in mind. I wanted to trace the causes of these changes, and to concentrate on those which depended on us, in order to show how *we might ourselves control them, so as to make us at once better and more certain of ourselves.* [*Confessions* IX, 408][7]

Here Rousseau returned to the most radical aspects of the theory of self-alienation: the problem, as he defined it above, was not simply that men *appear* "unlike themselves,"

---

[7] The book Rousseau refers to, a project conceived in 1756, was to be entitled *The Morals of Sensibility* or *The Wise Man's Materialism.* He abandoned it, however, before it had got far. All citations of Rousseau's writings are, unless otherwise noted, from the Pléiade *Oeuvres Complètes* (Paris: Gallimard, 1959). This monumental edition, edited under the direction of Bernard Gangebin and Marcel Raymond, will not be complete for many years; I have used it for all the works it covers. Translations are my own. All Rousseau's autobiographical writings appear in *Oeuvres Complètes,* Volume I. Where the *Confessions* are cited, Roman numbers designate the book, Arabic numbers the page.

but that they actually *"are* unlike themselves." Moreover, he saw the emerging modern society which the *philosophes* loved so well not as a triumph over alienation, but as its grotesque culmination. At the same time, he had absorbed the insight and outlook of the Enlightenment, and this made the problem far more complex for him than it had been for his precursors. He had to explain how it was possible for men to have "transformed themselves totally into different men," expelled themselves completely from a world to which they completely belonged. And he had to show how, given the full measure of man's self-alienation, it was nevertheless possible for men to become themselves in such a world.

II

Who Am I?
Rousseau and the Self
as a Problem

Rousseau's Originality

IN *The Persian Letters,* Montesquieu suggested, with great dramatic brilliance, what explosive political force the demand for authenticity might contain. But the schematic abstractness and the complex symbolism of the *Letters* muffled its impact: it was read by everyone, relished by many, appreciated by a few, but understood by no one at all. (Stendhal, a full century later, may have been the first.) It was only in the second generation of the Enlightenment, through Rousseau, that the search for authenticity came into its own. Rousseau gave it a personal immediacy and urgency that his age could not ignore; he forced his contemporaries to acknowledge that the self was a *problem* as pressing for them as it was for him. In forcing this problem to the surface of consciousness, moreover, he showed how repressive, how profoundly alien to the self the modern world really was. Throughout his life and works he explored the tensions between the self and the world with a depth, an intensity, an imaginative vision that no one has ever matched. Indeed, he carried the search for authenticity as far as it could go in a pre-revolutionary age. Many of the frontiers he discovered were soon surpassed, and some of his signposts proved deceptive; but he was the first one there. He claimed the ground for mankind, and drew the maps we still must use to get as far as he.

From the Essays to the Confessions

The personal force of Rousseau's search for authenticity comes across most vividly on the first page of his *Confessions*. He boldly announces:

> I am forming an enterprise which has no precedent, and whose execution will have no imitator. I want to show my fellow-men [*mes semblables*] a man in all the truth of nature; and that man is myself.
>
> Myself alone [*moi seul*]. I know my heart and I understand men. I am not made like anyone who exists. I may not be better, but at least I am different. Whether nature did well or ill in breaking the mold in which she cast me, you can tell only after you have read me.
>
> Let the last trump sound when it will, I will come with this book in hand to present myself before the Sovereign Judge. I will proclaim aloud: Here is what I did, what I thought, what I was. I have told the good and the bad with the same freedom [*franchise*]. . . . I have shown myself as I was: contemptible and vile when I was; good, generous, sublime when I was. I have unveiled my inner being [*dévoilé mon intérieur*] as You yourself have seen it. Eternal Being, gather around

me the numberless crowd of my fellow-men: let them listen to my confessions, groan at my indignities, blush at my depravities. Let each of them in turn reveal his own heart at the foot of your throne with the same sincerity. And then let any one of them who dares, say: "I was a better man than he." [1, 7]

Readers have often questioned the authenticity of Rousseau's very first words. Is his enterprise really unprecedented? In many ways his project of self-revelation seems merely an echo of Montaigne's. Consider, for instance, Montaigne's address to the reader of his *Essays:*

I want to be seen here in my simple, natural, ordinary fashion, without pose or artifice; for it is myself that I portray. . . . Thus, reader, I myself am the subject matter of my book. . . . [*Essays*, 2]¹

Or again, at greater length, the beginning of his essay on Repentance:

Others form man; I describe him, and portray a particular one, very ill-formed, whom I should really make very different from what he is if I had to fashion him over again. But now it is done.

Now the lines of my painting do not go astray, though they change and vary. The world is but a perennial movement. All things in it are in constant motion—the Earth, the rocks of the Caucasus, the pyramids of Egypt—both with the common motion and with their own. Stability itself is nothing but a more languid motion.

¹ Page numbers for Montaigne are from the *Complete Essays*, edited and translated by Donald Frame (Stanford: Stanford University Press, 1965).

I cannot keep my subject still. It goes along befuddled and staggering, with a natural drunkenness. I take it in this condition just as it is at the moment I give my attention to it. I do not portray being: I portray passing . . . from day to day, from minute to minute. My history needs to be adapted to the moment. I may presently change, not only by chance, but also by intention. This is a record of various and changeable occurrences, and of irresolute and (when it so befalls) contradictory ideas: whether I am different myself, or whether I take hold of my subjects in different circumstances and aspects. So, all in all, I may contradict myself now and then; but truth, as Demades said, I do not contradict. If my mind could gain a firm footing, I would not make essays, I would make decisions; but it is always in apprenticeship and on trial.

I set forth a humble and inglorious life; that does not matter. You can tie up all moral philosophy with a common and private life just as well as with a life of richer stuff. Each man bears the entire form of man's estate.

Authors communicate with the people by some extrinsic mark; I am the first to do so by my entire being, as Michel de Montaigne, not as a grammarian or a poet or a jurist. If the world complains that I speak too much of myself, I complain that it does not even think of itself. [610–1]

Rousseau was fully aware of Montaigne's attempt to understand and describe the uniqueness and totality of his being, and to develop a new literary form appropriate to self-revelation; his works are full of acknowledgments of his debt.[2] Nevertheless, in asserting the originality of his proj-

2 Cf., for instance, *CC*, I. 1001, 1036, 1150, 1176, 1791–3, 1834, 1855, 1862.

ect, Rousseau was basically right. Despite the similarity of their rhetoric, the meaning of autobiography—and of authenticity—had changed profoundly in the two centuries between them.[3]

In trying to understand this change, we might begin by noting Montaigne's apparent effortlessness: self-revelation seems to come naturally to him. "Others form man; I describe him. . . ." It is unnecessary to add anything new; the self does not have to be created: it need only be noticed and described. Thus the gift most important to Montaigne is sensitivity, the capacity for richness and depth of perception. He perceives himself not as sharply distinct from the world, but rather as continuous with it through space and time: he changes "from day to day, from minute to minute," impelled from outside "by chance" or "by intention" from within. The self cannot be grasped, but only evoked. Personal identity is a continuous flow; Montaigne's art, as he conceives it, is a spontaneous overflow. Virtues and vices, greatness and pettiness, will pour out, separate, interpenetrate; it does not matter, moral categories can never encompass the plenitude of personality. There is nothing problematical about the self: it is simply, pervasively, *there*.

This genial self-certainty, perhaps Montaigne's most engaging quality, is strikingly absent in Rousseau. Autobiography appears to him not as a spontaneous effusion, but as a conscious decision, a project, an "enterprise" that must be painstakingly "formed," an undertaking so arduous that it will never be imitated. Montaigne's self was separated only very loosely from the world around it, capable of expanding or contracting in any direction, open-ended in both space and time; although he was perpetually "on trial," a defini-

[3] My account of Montaigne is indebted to Erich Auerbach's discussion in *Mimesis: The Representation of Reality in Western Literature*, translated from the German by Willard Trask (New York: Anchor Books, 1957), 249–73.

tive verdict could never be reached. Rousseau's self, on the other hand, appears as a closed book; his readers are to judge him as if they were at the eschatological End of Time —and as if they themselves had to be judged by the rules they set.[4] Moreover, his image of the mold and his insistence on depicting "myself alone" [*moi seul*] make it clear that he wants the self to be sharply demarcated in space—inner as well as outer space. Finally, Rousseau sees the self as profoundly divided within itself: its inner life is hidden from the outward view of men, seen by God alone. This division must be overcome: the human *intérieur* must be *dévoilé*, so that the subject can share himself with his *semblables* with a community of his fellow-men. Up to now we have seen ourselves and each other as through a glass darkly, but now we must see face to face. This revelation is to occur, however, not *donc*, at the Last Judgment, as Christian theology would say (I *Corinthians*, 12.13), but *nunc*, now, as the book is read and felt and understood; and not in Heaven, face to face with God alone, but here in the world, in a community of men. While Montaigne was content to expand or contract the boundaries of the self haphazardly wherever the stream of consciousness might flow, Rousseau demands an intricate process of definition and selection, rejecting some aspects of experience and placing special emphasis on others, to separate what properly belongs to the self from what does not. If Montaigne is like a friend leading us on a leisurely tour of his house, Rousseau confronts us like a weird messenger, an Ancient Mariner, who seizes us and takes us by force on a trip into a psychic underworld.

4 Rousseau, we might say, tries to draw the reader into the box with him as a fellow-defendant: he sees the task he is imposing on himself as obligatory for all men, although probably unattainable by most. Montaigne, who does not feel himself under this sort of pressure, puts no such pressure on us.

Such a confrontation is essential in a world where "the majority of men are quite unlike themselves, and often seem to transform themselves into different men": it is only by cutting through the structure of this world that we can get in touch with the buried life of the self. The project of bringing the self to the surface is necessarily subversive to a society that has driven the self underground. At the same time, ironically, it is only from the ground of this society that the self can authentically live and grow.

An Age of Ambiguity

Rousseau, then, perceived new dimensions of complexity and ambiguity in the relationship between the self and the world. The originality and richness of his perception are evident from the very start of his career as a thinker. Consider the beginning of his work of social criticism, the *Discourse on the Arts and Sciences.*

> It is a great and beautiful spectacle to see man raising himself from nothingness by his own efforts; dissipating, with the light of his reason, the shadows in which nature enveloped him; *lifting himself above himself;* soaring in spirit up to the celestial regions; like the sun, traveling with giant steps through the vast extent of the universe; and, what is still greater and more difficult, *returning into himself,* to study man and get to know his nature, his duties and his end. (*OC,* III. 6) [5]

This is one of Rousseau's most important sentences: its structure prefigures the inner structure of the Enlightenment as a whole, and marks very precisely Rousseau's place

---

[5] Page numbers for the *Discourses* and for all political writings, are from Volume III of *OC.* Translations are my own, though I am indebted to those of G.D.H. Cole (London: Everyman, 1950).

in it. The movement of this sentence is vividly cinematic: starting from a fixed point, its perspective gradually widens and heightens to encompass a vast expanse; suddenly its focus constricts drastically, and zooms in on the starting point itself. That point is man. In the first clause, man's own will raises him from nothingness to being. In the second clause, the light of his reason enables him to penetrate the darkness with which nature surrounded him, and to raise himself *"au-dessus de soi-même."* In the third clause, his spirit lifts him still further, into celestial regions. Through human will, reason and spirit, we have advanced from nothingness to being to self-transcendence. In the fourth clause, man, having reached the heavens, appears as the sun, sweeping his rational, spiritual light over all the universe. But at this point a tension appears: how can enlightened man expect to master the whole world while living beyond himself? Is he not part of the universe too? If the empire of light and reason is to be genuinely universal, man must turn his light on the source of light: on himself. He must turn inward, and examine "his nature, his duties and his end." It is significant, however, that when Rousseau makes his demand that human intelligence and energy turn inward, he introduces it not by means of a new sentence, but through a fifth clause, whose structure is parallel to the other four. Moreover, the adjectives he uses to describe the change he seeks are quantitative—*"plus grand et plus difficile"*—indicating a difference in degree rather than in kind. The movement of this sentence is not a polar antithesis—a form of which Rousseau is generally so fond—but rather a continuous flow. In other words, Rousseau announces his program of a "return into himself" not as a sharp break with the spirit of his age, but as an integral part of an ongoing historical process. This continuity is emphasized in the very next sentence: "We have seen all these marvelous things renewed within the last few generations." "*All* these marvelous things"—*both* exploration of the universe *and* scrutiny of the self—are aspects of Enlightenment; through both, man makes himself more and more thoroughly at home in the world.

But if Rousseau's search for authenticity was a natural outgrowth of the Enlightenment, it was at the same time a radical indictment of that society out of which that Enlightenment had grown. We can see the basis for this indictment if we ask ourselves why Rousseau insisted that man had to *"return into himself"* in order to achieve self-knowledge. This was a very different method from the methods used so successfully by physical scientists in exploring the rest of the universe. Man did not need to "get inside" the multitude of phenomena in order to understand them; why, then, should he have to explore himself from within? If man were part of the totality of the world, why wouldn't it suffice to observe empirically the ways in which men manifest and present themselves in the world? Rousseau's separation of the methods appropriate in physical science from those essential to the study of man discloses one of his fundamental themes. A new method was needed for man, he believed, because human behavior in the world was profoundly *alien* behavior; it revealed less about what men *were* than about what they were *not*. This paradoxical idea pervades his work. "How happy it would be to live among us," he said longingly, "if only our outward faces were mirrors of our hearts. . . ." In fact, however, "A man doesn't dare appear as he is; he is under a perpetual restraint." Rousseau's society seemed to confront men as a medium not for revealing, but for concealing themselves. The primary symbol of this society, again and again in Rousseau's writings, is the *veil:* "that

83

uniform and deceptive veil of politeness . . . which we owe to the light of our century." (*Arts and Sciences,* 7–8) Or alternately, as suggested by Saint-Preux, hero of *La Nouvelle Héloïse,* the *mask:* "Up to now," he wrote Julie after his first encounter with Paris, "I have seen many masks; when am I going to see the faces of men?" (*Julie,* II.14, 236)[6] "The good man [*homme de bien*]," he said in his First *Discourse,* "is an athlete who loves to wrestle stark naked; he despises those vile ornaments which cramp the use of his powers, and which were probably invented only to hide some deformity." (8) Years later, recollecting his Second *Discourse,* he said: "I demolished the petty lies of men; I dared to strip their nature naked. . . ." (*Confessions,* VIII. 388) In order "to know man's nature, his duties and his end," it was necessary to tear men's veils and costumes and masks away, to discover the faces and bodies and souls beneath them.[7]

---

[6] Rousseau's *Discourse on the Progress of the Arts and Sciences* is in *OC,* III. Citations from *Julie, ou la Nouvelle Héloïse* designate the Part, then the Letter, then the page; page numbers are from *OC,* Volume II. Translations are mine. For a discussion of Rousseau's veil-imagery, cf. Jean Starobinski, *Jean-Jacques Rousseau: la transparence et l'obstacle,* pp. 23–26.

[7] The distinction which Rousseau was trying to make between empirical qualities and "natural" (or "essential" or "ideal") ones was difficult to formulate in the language of his time. According to Erich Auerbach's essay "La Cour et la Ville," the seventeenth-century French idiom *se connaître,* literally "to know or recognize oneself," was ordinarily used to signify "to know one's position in society." This mode of self-knowledge, required for any *honnête homme,* "implied a recognition and observance of distances"; this sort of recognition meant not only tacit consent, but active approval. Thus, imperceptibly, the self *as social custom defined it* merged in men's minds with the self *as it essentially is.* Accordingly, when a seventeenth-century manual of deportment said that "all things should remain within the limits appointed to them by nature," it meant not only that "a ruby, however perfect and beautiful it may be, can never hope to become a diamond," but that men were like stones: "so anyone who hopes to raise himself higher, or more precisely, to change his nature, to make himself something other than he was, is wasting his time and trouble." Again, in contemporary dis-

At this point, the contrast with which our chapter began is all the more striking. Montaigne, expressing the deepest aspirations of the Renaissance, wanted the stream of consciousness and self-consciousness to flow over all the world; nothing within the range of possible human experience was alien to him. Rousseau, two centuries later, was convinced that, in the course of its own spontaneous flow, the stream had become polluted by alien elements which had clogged and finally reversed its natural flow. Paradoxically, however, the primary source of this alienation was men themselves: *they "transform themselves* into totally different men." (*Confessions,* IX. 408) The alienation Rousseau perceived in his world was *self*-alienation.

It is only by locating Rousseau's project of self-examination and self-revelation within the context of self-alienation that we can grasp its full meaning and power. Rousseau did not conceive of confession as St. Augustine

---

cussion of Molière's *Le Bourgeois gentilhomme,* it was commonly said that Monsieur Jourdain, in his passion to raise himself to nobility, "forgets his limits, *il se méconnait." (Scenes from the Drama of European Literature,* 165, 174f., 245.) The aspirations of the bourgeois to raise himself were simply an absurd confusion, an elementary mistake: thus French classicism avoided—or, rather, postponed—discussion of the rights of man and citizen.

The corruption of language that dulls men's critical faculties, and blurs the disparity between things as they are and things as they should be (and could be), is a leitmotif in contemporary radical thought. It is discussed incisively in Orwell's seminal *1984;* in Ernest Gellner, *Words and Things* (Boston: Beacon Press, 1959); in C. Wright Mills, *The Sociological Imagination* (New York: Oxford University Press, 1959); in Herbert Marcuse, *One-Dimensional Man* (Boston: Beacon Press, 1964). All these writers err, it seems to me, in portraying this sleight-of-mind as a peculiarly contemporary problem. As Auerbach's material suggests, it is rather an old story. Indeed, it is only in modern times, through Rousseau and his contemporaries, that the difference between *is* and *ought* has been clearly articulated in moral philosophy, and that a psychological vocabulary has emerged in which the potentialities of the self and the conditions for its fulfillment (or "actualization") could be talked about.

had, as the disclosure of a *fait accompli,* the revelation of a pre-existent unity of self. Rather, he saw the value of his end-product as inseparable from the process of its creation. The process of confessing, for Rousseau, was a process of unmasking, of differentiating, of integrating, of *bringing his authentic self into being.* Philosophers up to now had exhorted man to *know* himself; the point now, far profounder and more difficult—which perhaps should have been the point all along—was for man to *be* himself.[8]

---

[8] Jean Starobinski arrives at this paradox only very late in his remarkable book, *Jean-Jacques Rousseau: la transparence et l'obstacle* (Paris: Plon, 1957). His conceptual apparatus limits him to an issue that seems to me far less rich and interesting: "the antithesis of appearance and reality." He portrays Rousseau, first of all, as a suffering, guilt-ridden human being, obsessed with proving the purity of his true motives and the ultimate goodness of his actions, and so vindicating himself in the eyes of a hostile world which he felt had manipulated and rigged appearances against him; beyond this, as a radical thinker who could transcend his personal obsessions, as a trenchant critic of social conditions which forced men to be insincere and hypocritical with one another, and kept them from revealing their thoughts, their feelings, themselves "as they really are." Thus Starobinski focuses on Rousseau's concern with "the impossibility of communication among men," and his attempts to restore a lost paradise which would permit "*la transparence réciproque des consciences, la communication totale et confiante.*" (1–10) In these formulations, only the appearances of the self, its outward forms, are problematical; its underlying inner reality is taken for granted. Man's happiness would be complete, it is supposed, if men could only strip away the masks and show the true selves that are really *there.* This definition of the problem diverts Starobinski from Rousseau's much more radical idea that *the inner reality was itself a problem,* that the self was only a potentiality, something yet to be attained. Eventually, in discussing the problems of confession and autobiography, Starobinski works his way around to the idea that Rousseau eventually gave up (or, perhaps, would be logically compelled to give up) his pursuit of "a pre-existent self which he sought to express completely"; "no longer *pursuing* his true self *in* a fixed past, he *became* his true self *in the act of writing about* his past." Thus Rousseau ascended to "the free creation of the self. It's no longer necessary for the self to go back into the past to search for its source: its source is here and now, in the present moment, in the flow of its emotions. The present is just as pure as the past if the past is relived through present feelings. Thus the important thing is not to *scrutinize* oneself, or to *judge* oneself, but to *be* oneself." Indeed, Rousseau's "need to keep writing and justifying himself only proves that he hasn't yet begun

The society of eighteenth-century France, in which Rousseau found himself, was a strange conglomeration of tradition and modernity. In the Parisian metropolis, all the newest and most daring ideas and modes of behavior sprang to life, developed and grew; at the same time, alongside it, the French countryside went on existing as it always had, immured in the depths of the middle ages. The ambiguities of this social structure, and the difficulties it presented for Rousseau, prefigured a predicament which radical social critics all over the world have encountered since his time. Marx formulated it vividly in his own conceptual language, in the preface to the first edition of *Capital:*

> we . . . suffer not only from the development of capitalist production, but also from the incompleteness of that development. Alongside modern evils, a whole series of inherited evils oppress us, arising from the passive survival of antiquated modes of production, with their inevitable train of social and political anachronisms. We suffer, not only from the living, but from the dead. *Le mort saisit le vif. [Capital,* I. 13][9]

---

to be himself, that he hasn't attained indivisible unity of self, that *the task is always ahead of us."* (247–9) Unfortunately, this idea remains tangential to the book. Starobinski makes no attempt to integrate it into the structure of his argument. Moreover, he seems to see the issue as a purely aesthetic one: the problem of authenticity is the problem of finding the ideal *language* of authenticity. He mentions it as one of the central problems in "modern *literature,*" but does not appear to see it as any sort of problem in modern *society.* The argument of this book is that the search for authenticity is central to the experience both of modern society and of the modern state; and that Montesquieu and Rousseau were the first to explain how and why this should be so.

[9] *Capital.* Volume I, translated by Samuel Moore and Edward Aveling (Chicago: Charles H. Kerr & Co., 1906). In the twentieth century we have become familiar with this sort of polarization—ultramodern cities surrounded by stagnant, underdeveloped countryside—as a standard feature in pre-revolutionary societies. It can be found in Russia, China, Cuba, Vietnam.

Rousseau was at one with the *philosophes* in their indictment of the Old Regime. Indeed, he grasped its moral
bankruptcy more fully and criticized it more trenchantly
than anyone in the eighteenth century. At the same time, he
perceived the fatal flaws in the alternative which the *philosophes* embraced, the distinctively modern social system that
was just emerging. Throughout his work, Rousseau showed
how *all* the existing modes of personal identity—both traditional *and* modern—were actually modes of depersonalization, stumbling blocks which kept the individual self from
coming into its own.

Self-Alienation
in Traditional Society

The domination of the land as an alien power over men is already inherent in feudal landed property. The serf is an adjunct of the land. In the same way the lord of an entailed estate, the firstborn son, belongs to the land. It inherits him.[10]

KARL MARX

IN THE TRADITIONAL social structure which had dominated Europe for over a thousand years, men derived their feelings of personal identity from social roles which were, in Ralph Linton's formula, *ascribed*. "Ascribed statuses," Linton writes, "are those which are assigned to individuals without reference to their innate differences or abilities. They can be predicted and trained from the moment of birth." (*The Study of Man*, 115)[11] Ascribed roles

[10] This formulation occurs in Marx's early manuscript on "Rent of the Land." In *Economic and Philosophic Manuscripts of 1844*, translated by Martin Milligan (Moscow: Foreign Languages Publishing House, 1956), 61.

[11] *The Study of Man* (New York: D. Appleton-Century, 1936). Linton's work has become classic for contemporary role theory. Cf. especially his chapter on "Status and Role," 113–131.

are particularly conducive to social stability; on the other hand, they inevitably stifle the energy and initiative of the individuals who must fill them. Similarly, on an individual level, the man whose whole future life is laid out for him at birth, who came into the world only to fill a pre-existing niche, "is much less likely to be disappointed than a man living under our own system, . . . where the limits for ambition are not socially defined." This is because, although "membership in a rigidly organized society may deprive the individual of opportunities to exercise his particular gifts, . . . it gives him an emotional security which is almost unknown among ourselves." (131) Rousseau lived at a moment when the ascribed identities which had developed out of feudalism were placing an unbearable strain on an increasingly large number of men. Rousseau understood very vividly the psychic costs of ascriptive identification. Throughout his writings he criticized the traditional series of roles in European society, and urged their dissolution.

The Nobility and the Peasantry:
Personal Feelings versus Social Forms

At the pinnacle of traditional society, Rousseau saw an aristocracy which cultivated *sensibilité* and the expression of feeling in literature, but whose whole economic and social life cut them off from their own deepest senses and their most personal feelings. In the first part of the *Confessions,* Rousseau reflected on this:

Among the people, where great passions express themselves only on occasion, natural feeling makes itself heard more often. In the highest ranks, it is absolutely

90

stifled, and beneath a mask of feeling, it is always self-interest or vanity that speaks. [IV. 147]

These aristocrats did not denounce or denigrate emotion, as their seventeenth-century predecessors had; indeed, they officially encouraged its fullest expression. Rousseau argued, however, that the social forms which they used to convey personal feeling served only to conceal and constrict it. All his life he denounced the aristocratic standard of *politesse*. The style of manners which radiated from the French court imposed "a vile and deceptive uniformity" on men, so that "all souls seem to have been cast in the same mold. Politeness demands this, decorum decrees that; one always follows custom, never one's own nature [*son propre génie*]." (*Arts and Sciences,* 8) Individual *génie* was systematically repressed by the intricate social code of *galanterie*. Gallantry, Rousseau said, had been instigated by women; yet, "It would not be hard to show," he argued in the *Letter to d'Alembert,* "that instead of gaining by these practices, women lose. They are flattered without being loved, served without being honored. They are surrounded by agreeable people, but they no longer have lovers; and the worst of it is that the former, without having the feelings of the latter, usurp all their rights." [12] Men were constantly professing their passion, their devotion, their love. But these feelings could manifest themselves only through a prescribed structure of courtly conventions. The conventionalization of love, however, destroyed precisely what was most beautiful about love: its *individuality*. "Is there a question

[12] Page numbers for the *Lettre à d'Alembert sur les spectacles* are from the English edition, edited and translated by Allan Bloom as *Politics and the Arts* (Glencoe, Ill. The Free Press, 1960). Where my translations differ from Bloom's, I have consulted the Classiques Garnier edition of *Du Contrat social* and other writings, (Paris, 1962).

of love in all this tedious jargon? Don't those who use it use it equally for all women? And wouldn't they be upset if one believed them to be lovers of one woman alone?" Gallantry forced the intercourse between men and women into rigid molds; it was impossible for a man and a woman to encounter one another as individuals. At the same time, all the richness of emotion that love might evoke—"this terrible passion, its frenzies, its palpitations, its transports, its burning expressions, its even more energetic silences, its inexpressible looks . . ."—was congealed into a few stereotyped forms. It was no wonder that the men and women in high society were so often unfaithful to one another; a system that suppressed the individuality of people could never generate bonds of fidelity between one individual and another. The "general spirit of gallantry stifles both genius (*génie*) and love." (104) Aristocratic *moeurs* separated people from each other because it separated them from themselves.

If the aristocrats of Rousseau's day were incapable of loving one another, they were sealed off even more tightly from any intimacy that cut across class lines. Rousseau experienced very vividly the contradiction between ascribed status and personal feeling. He owed much of his fame, and at times even his survival, to some of the most eminent noblemen—and noblewomen—in Europe. He was particularly indebted to the Maréchal and the Maréchale de Luxembourg. The Luxembourgs gave Rousseau a house on their estate at Montmorency, arranged for the publication of *Emile,* made every effort to protect him from repressive authorities, and helped smuggle him out of France in 1762 after every effort failed. Throughout their long, deep, troubled friendship, both husband and wife showed great affection, respect and solicitude for Rousseau; the Maréchal's letters in particular radiate an exquisite grace. Rousseau loved them deeply; even in the second part of the *Confessions*, when he was sure that everyone had turned against him, he acknowledged how much their friendship had meant to him. Nevertheless, he was constantly troubled by the relationship, in which he saw something problematical at the core.

In his very first letter to the Maréchal,[13] Rousseau accepted the offer of a lodging, but insisted on elaborate "conditions" for their whole relationship, conditions based on two very different rationales. On one hand, he said: "I know that my respect for your person doesn't release me from the respect due your rank; but I know even more certainly that . . . poverty too has its dignity, which any lover of virtue must take into account." He continued: "Reciprocal esteem brings all classes together; no matter how elevated you might be, no matter how obscure I might be, the glory of each must be recognized by the other." This was no protest against the existing class system; indeed, Rousseau was reinforcing that system, by insisting on its inherent equity and fairness for all. On the other hand, in the same letter, Rousseau declared that among friends *"I know only one language, that of friendship and intimacy."* (April 30, 1759; *CG*, IV. 230–2) This meant that true friendship was a relation which ignored all class distinctions—and hence, which denied their claims to existential validity. But if this were so, then friendship across class lines would be possible only insofar as men's class identities—identities implanted in them since birth by the whole social system—could be obliterated.

After their friendship had developed, Rousseau was often

---

13 References to Rousseau's letters are cited from the *Correspondance Générale*, edited by Théophile Dufour, in 20 volumes (Paris: Librairie Armand Colin, 1924–30).

sanguine about it. "You don't know how sweet it is," he wrote the Maréchal, "to see that inequality isn't incompatible with friendship, and that a man can have someone greater than himself for a friend." (End of August 1759; *CG*, IV. 300) "It was in one of these transports of affection that I said to the Maréchal, as I embraced him: 'Ah, Marshal, before I knew you I used to hate the great [*les grands*], and now I hate them all the more, since you have shown me how easy it would be for them to make themselves lovable.'" (*Confessions*, X. 527) Even at such moments, however, Rousseau saw how precarious the whole relation was. In order to sustain it, he said, "You must remain what you are, and I must remain what I am." To remain *what they were*, for Rousseau, meant to reject the conventional social roles appropriate to a wealthy noble and a poor commoner: "Don't try to be my patron; I promise you, in turn, not to be your panegyrist. . . . If, however, you insist on patronizing me, giving me gifts, obtaining favors for me, drawing me out of my estate, and if I accept your benefits, you'll have gained nothing more than a hack in me, and you'll be nothing more than just another aristocrat [*grand*] in my eyes." (*Ibid.*) Thus Rousseau did all he could to avoid any action or gesture that might be subsumed under the roles of traditional hierarchy. He refused to accept money from the Maréchale—even in return for work he had actually done, in making her a copy of *Julie*. (October 29, 1759; *Ibid.*, 321–3) Again, at a time when he was afraid that he had offended and alienated her: "if you were less of a great lady, . . . I would throw myself at your feet, I would spare neither obeisance nor pleas to placate your dissatisfaction, whether it was well-founded or not. But in the rank you are, don't expect me to do what my heart demands." (November 15, 1759; *CG*, IV. 334) Here, ironically, the gesture of submission would have been emotionally appropriate; but because the Maréchale was a noblewoman, to whom all commoners owed obeisance, the ritual and social significance of the act would have absorbed its personal, emotional meaning. Again, although Rousseau warned his noble friends against "drawing me out of my estate," he did his best to draw them out of theirs. He refused to see the Luxembourgs in their native element, "in the midst [*milieu*] of that crowd, inseparable from your rank, with which you are constantly surrounded." (May 27, 1759; *Ibid.*, 257) He would visit them only when they were alone; in other words, only when he could relate to them independently of the roles which their rank imposed.

The conflict between class and personality kept Rousseau and the Luxembourgs from ever becoming completely intimate. A brief sequence from Book Ten of the *Confessions* reveals some of the tensions that pulled them apart. Rousseau tells first of having offered his portrait, painted by Latour several years before, to the Maréchal and his wife. They soon reciprocated and gave him theirs. In the eighteenth century, such a gesture had great symbolic weight: it meant nothing less than the giving of oneself. (X. 531) But these feelings of mutuality could not last; and Rousseau next describes the social forces that undermined them. He had always supported ardently the repeated efforts of the French bureaucracy to impose financial reforms. Accordingly, when Etienne de Silhouette was dismissed from his office as Controller General in 1759, through pressures from the great financial interests, Rousseau wrote him a letter of condolence. (The letter is datd December 2, 1759; *CG*, IV. 343) Madame de Luxembourg asked for a copy, which Rousseau gladly supplied. But he did not know then the fact which he later came to see as the key to the whole situation: that she "was herself one of the money-grabbers who had interests in the farming of taxes, and who'd got rid of Silhouette." In view of her position, he saw in retrospect, his views were bound to "excite the hatred of a friendly and powerful woman, to whom I was growing more attached day by day, and whose displeasure I was far from wanting to incur. . . ." (X. 532) The discovery of his economic ideals may have been disturbing to her; the discovery of her economic reality was shattering to him. It meant that the wealth and power with which the Luxembourgs had helped and protected him sprang from the very system that had persecuted him and forced him to flee all over Europe. Their generosity, of which he had drunk so deeply, flowed from a polluted source. He had come to love these good people by abstracting their human essence from their roles in an evil social system; he had not realized how deeply embedded in the system they were.

In retrospect he came to see their relationship in a new light. If their whole lives were so deeply rooted in the social life of the *noblesse,* perhaps the real source of their benevolence toward him was not so much friendship as *noblesse oblige.* At this point in the *Confessions,* Rousseau inserted a letter which, although chronologically earlier, expressed what seemed to him the next logical step. "How I hate all your titles," he had written the Maréchale, "and pity you for bearing them! You seem so well-fitted to enjoy the charms of private life. If you only lived at Clarens! I would go there to find my life's happiness. But the Chateau de Montmorency, the Hotel de Luxembourg! Is this where Jean-Jacques should be seen?" Rousseau was not saying that their good feelings toward him were a sham; what he was saying was that *all* their personal feelings were stifled by the social forms and functions that they fulfilled. Their desire and capacity for "the charms of private life" were thwarted by the public roles which they had inherited and were forced to play; the titles they bore down on their own impulses and emotions hardest of all. The heart's affections could express themselves only in a context of *equality,* in which equivalent feelings were exchanged and shared. (X. 533. The letter is dated August 13, 1759; *CG,* IV. 298) Their social position repressed their *sensibilité,* and kept them from experiencing Rousseau as an individual person; he appeared to them rather as a personification of an abstract category. Essentially a member of a lower class, he was a candidate for largesse, but never for mutuality. Rousseau pronounced a definitive verdict on their friendship in the *Confessions:*

> In my relationships I have never been capable of moderation, or of simply fulfilling the duties of society. With me it has always been all or nothing. Soon it was all; and seeing myself made much of by people of their importance, I overstepped the limits and conceived a friendship with them of a kind permissible only between equals. I expressed it by complete intimacy [*familiarité*] in my manners, while they never deviated from the politeness [*politesse*] to which they had always accustomed me. [X. 522]

These noble lives were governed and circumscribed by a class code of privileges and obligations. The code mediated all their personal relationships, forced their feelings into the fixed forms of "the duties of society," and prevented them from experiencing the equality and mutuality which "the language of friendship and intimacy" required.

Rousseau's indictment of the nobility focused on their *politesse,* on the genteel *moeurs* which had radiated from

97

the French court since the time of Louis XIV. But the intellectual force of his critique extended far beyond the courtly world, and touched the basic idea on which all traditional systems of power must rest; the idea that a man's dignity could be inherited, that it had a meaning and a value which antedated, survived and transcended the particular man who bore it. Rousseau's critique of traditional, ascribed stratification, is stated most concisely by Milord Edouard, the benevolent and free-minded English peer, in a letter to Julie. He exhorts her to resist her father's pressure to marry Wolmar, a noble of her own rank, and to remain with Saint-Preux, the commoner whom she loves. Edouard warns:

> You will be sacrificed to the chimera of rank [*la chimère des conditions*]. You will have to contract an engagement that is repudiated by your heart. You may get public approval [*l'approbation publique*], but it will be contradicted by the unceasing cry of your conscience; you will be honored but contemptible. It is better to be forgotten but virtuous. [*Julie*, II. 3; 200] 14

The chimera of rank, enforced through a conformist public opinion, set itself against both the heart and the conscience of individuals. Erecting social barriers between man and

14 Rousseau underscores this indictment with an ironic footnote: "The chimera of rank! This is an English peer talking! Mustn't all this [*tout ceci*] be a fiction? Reader, what do you think?" This note plays on the eighteenth-century literary convention that a novel is merely a record of factual events. It is certainly implausible that an English lord should disdain "the chimera of rank"; but if this provocative phrase was not spoken by an actual person, if it was indeed a "fiction," then it could only be ascribed to the creator of fictions, to the author himself. Thus Rousseau disengages his indictment from the dramatic context in which it occurs, forces the reader to confront it directly, and implicity affirms it as his own. Moreover, the identity of the fictional "*tout ceci*" remains suggestively ambiguous: might it not designate the whole chimerical system of rank that has made Edouard a peer in the first place?

man, it kept people from expressing their most powerful impulses and fulfilling their deepest needs. The depersonalization of personal relations was no mere by-product of aristocratic rule, but its categorical imperative. If personal, individual qualities—the heart, the conscience—were posited as the basis of human value, the whole rationale for ascribed class dignity would collapse.

If "the chimera of rank" cramped the self-expression of the men at the top of traditional society, it was even more enervating to those at the bottom. Although Rousseau often celebrated the life of the peasantry, which seemed to him particularly rich in possibilities for protective self-seclusion and retreat (we shall consider this theme at length later on), he understood its drawbacks very well. If peasants in their rural isolation were free from the conformist social pressures [*l'approbation publique*] that choked the courts and salons, they were at least as thoroughly enslaved to the dead hand of the past. They conformed as mindlessly as did the nobility, not to the expectations of peers who surrounded them, but to the traditions of ancestors who had preceded them. In the Second Book of the *Emile,* Rousseau showed how far the mass of peasants actually were from being themselves. "There are two sorts of men," he said, "who are constantly engaged in physical activity, and who pay very little attention to cultivating their minds: peasants and savages. The former are rough, crude and clumsy; the latter are known, not only for their keen senses, but for their subtlety of mind [*esprit*]. In general no one is duller than a peasant, or sharper than a savage." It would have been totally contrary to Rousseau's epistemology, and to the whole purpose of *Emile,* to say that these peasants were *born* dull; he argued, rather, that their environment *made* them dull. They were made dull, first of all, by the static inertia of the social system in which they lived; and second, by the particularly passive, submissive role which that system imposed on them. The peasant "always does what he's been told, what his father did before him, what he himself did in his youth. He exists entirely according to routine. He spends his life almost like an automaton, constantly occupied with the same tasks; with him habit and obedience have taken the place of reason." (II. 82–3) [15] Thus the closed, stagnant hierarchy of rural life socialized the men in its lowest ranks—that is, the vast majority of men—into automatons, programmed to live and act mechanically according to traditional routines. Individual thought or feeling, insight or initiative, could only be destructive to these traditions and routines. Hence it was essential for traditional society to keep individuality from developing, at the bottom as well as at the top.

At every level, then, traditional society interposed *social distance* between man and man; across this gulf, no genuinely *personal* relationships could grow. "We never sympathize with other people's woes," Rousseau wrote, "unless we know we may suffer the same ourselves." But social distance stifled their sympathy. "Why is it that kings have no pity on their subjects? Because they never expect to be men themselves." The man who held the very highest rank in a traditional society elevated himself not only above other men, but above humanity itself; he merged himself with the *dignitas non moritur* of his crown, and mocked the mere mortality of man's estate. Again, at a slightly lower level, "Why are the rich so hard on the poor? Because they have no fear of becoming poor. Why do the nobles have so much contempt for the people? Because the aristocrat knows he

[15] *Emile*, translated by Barbara Foxley (London: Everyman, 1955). Roman numbers designate the Book, Arabic numbers the page. Where my translations differ from Foxley's, I have consulted the Classiques Garnier edition (Paris, n.d.).

will never be a commoner." (*Emile,* IV. 185) The whole realm of human feeling and experience which the lowliest man shared with the most elevated was systematically denied. Every man was reduced to a function of the rank which he acquired at birth—or, perhaps more accurately, to paraphrase Marx, the rank which acquired him.

Thus self-alienation was built into the life situation of the traditional ruling classes. But this particular mode of self-alienation was rich in social and psychological benefits: it brought them power, deference, security. If they could not be personally touched, neither could they be personally threatened; the social barriers which cut them off from other people and from their own feelings also gave them a sense of identity that was impregnable. It was easy to see why the upper classes were willing to make the sacrifice of self which their social roles demanded.

But the passive submissiveness of the peasantry, and of the lower classes in general, presented a much more difficult problem. "Servitude is so unnatural to man," Saint-Preux wrote, "that it could not exist without some discontent." (*Julie,* IV. 10, 460) In fact, however, both the extent and the intensity of servitude in European society were on the rise: men were increasingly polarized into rich and poor, strong and weak, masters and slaves. (*Discourse on the Origin of Inequality,* 187) And the oppressed classes, far from revolting, had learned to "love their own slavery." (*Arts and Sciences,* 7) Rousseau was continually troubled by this fact. Why, he wondered, should the vast majority of men embrace the roles of servitude which traditional society sought to impose on them—roles which deprived them of their freedom and denied their individuality? How could men who were born free be induced to help forge their own chains?

Submission and Recognition

Rousseau's own experience of servitude provided clues. In 1728, newly converted to Catholicism, penniless and homeless in Turin, he was taken on as a valet by a Countess de Vercellis. At first, he recounts in the *Confessions,* Mme. de Vercellis was interested in his life story, and encouraged him to confide his deepest feelings; beneath the servant's livery, presumably, she discerned a man of *sensibilité.* But although she wanted him to open his heart to her, she kept hers closed to him. Her interest in him was abstract, formal, mediated by social distance; "she never said a word to me that betrayed any affection, sympathy or kindness." She imagined that "by concealing [her own] feelings [she] would be more successful in penetrating another's." What she did not understand was that her coldness and distance would "only deprive [him] of the courage to show" his feelings. Rousseau could express himself only in a context of mutual openness and trust. Where mutuality was lacking, the springs of his feeling dried up. Hence "My replies were so timid that she must've found them banal and boring. Eventually she stopped questioning me, and spoke to me only to give me orders." Because the Countess saw nothing of Rousseau's inner life she assumed he had none, and treated him accordingly, as an automaton that existed only to receive and execute commands. "She judged me less by *what I was* than by *what she had made me;* and since she saw in me nothing but a lackey, she prevented me from appearing to her in any other light." (*Confessions,* II. 81–2) But he himself had collaborated in the falsification, by acting as if her image were true. On one hand his outward servility functioned as a mechanism of defense against an oppressive situation, while his inner life continued to go on underground.

On the other hand, ironically, it helped to reinforce the oppression: by acting as if he had no feelings, he made it legitimate to treat him like an automaton without feelings.
What forced Rousseau into this impasse was his need for
recognition. Hegel formulated this human need in his
Phenomenology.[16] This meant that Rousseau could be himself only insofar as his self-identity was confirmed by others;
what they would not recognize, he could not assert. Thus
Mme. de Vercellis was able to turn off the flow of his
feeling by refusing to take it seriously and recognize it for
what it was worth. This suggested ominous possibilities: the
power to mold men into whatever shape one willed. In a
traditional hierarchy, this power belonged to the hereditary
ruling classes; the men at the bottom were forced to define
themselves according to terms dictated from above. Even
when the men at the bottom of a traditional society tried to
overthrow their servile roles, their need for recognition held
them down. Rousseau learned this from his first childhood
attempt at rebellion. While working as an engraver's ap-
prentice, he relates in the *Confessions,* he began to make
petty thefts. He depicts these thefts as perhaps the one possible form of protest against a brutally repressive system
which he had no power to change:

> My master's tyranny finally made his trade, which I
> should ordinarily have liked, unbearable to me, and
> drove me to vices which I should otherwise have de-
> spised, such as falsehood, idleness and theft. . . .
>
> I was used to living on terms of perfect equality with
> my elders; to knowing of no pleasures which were not
> within my grasp; to seeing no dish of which I did not

16 The dynamics of recognition are discussed brilliantly in Hegel's
elaboration of the "dialectic of master and slave."

have a share; to having no desire which I did not express; to letting every thought in my heart rise to my lips. Imagine my fate in a house where I dared not open my mouth, where I had to leave the table before dessert was served, and the room as soon as I had no more duties to perform there. Confined continuously to my work, I saw enjoyments everywhere for other people, and privations for myself alone. The thought of the liberty in which the master and the journeyman lived multiplied the weight of my subjection. When there were arguments about the subjects I knew best, I dared not open my mouth. Finally I came to covet in my heart everything I saw, only because I was deprived of everything. [I. 31–2]

This passage brings out the polarity of two radically contrasting social systems. In the first, Rousseau enjoyed freedom and equality; his thoughts and feelings were valued in themselves, and he was encouraged to express them; although only a child he was treated as a man, as an end in himself. In the house of M. De Commun, the master engraver, on the other hand, Rousseau was defined purely and simply as a machine, which existed in order to work. Accordingly, when he had no work to do in any given place, he had no right to be there. He was entitled to only so much food as his body required to remain in working order; dessert, which would have brought him pleasure unrelated to his function, was superfluous—it would have been like pouring extra oil into a motor, or it might have suggested that Jean-Jacques was something more than a motor. He "dared not open [his] mouth," because his master would not allow that he might have something of his own to say; to admit him to "arguments about the subjects [he] knew best" would have been a tacit admission that he had some experience, some knowledge, some existence independent of his role. Every item in the traditional household routine was a ritual affirmation of its social structure, and hence of Rousseau's abject position at the bottom of that structure. Against such a background, the act of stealing took on a special meaning: it was Rousseau's only way of asserting himself. The things he stole—e.g., food—were important to him not so much in themselves as for their symbolic value. "I was never *absolutely* undernourished at my master's; the austerity of my diet was painful to me only in *comparison with the luxury he enjoyed.*" (33) Thus his thefts improved his position relative to his master, and allayed a radical inequity in the distribution of wealth. Moreover, on a deeper level, Rousseau was demonstrating that his master's definition of him as a working machine was false, that he was a human being with a will of his own, capable of redefining and changing the structure of events in his own way.[17] But the system whose grip Rousseau was seeking to slip out of was not willing to let him go so easily. It had its own definition for him: a *fripon,* a thief, a scoundrel. Thus, in his master's eyes, his thefts had no reasons, merely causes: he stole, not for any human purpose, but through an animal reflex, or a mechanical reaction; not to redress a social imbalance, or to prove his freedom, but simply because he was a *fripon* and it was part of the degenerate nature of a *fripon* to steal. By the same fatality, it was part of the nature of a *fripon* to be beaten—not to deter him from stealing, for

[17] Perhaps to underscore the innocence and essential legitimacy of his enterprise, Rousseau describes an attempt to steal some apples from the larder. (34) The complex technical aspects of the operation are recapitulated in painstaking detail; a certain suspense is built up over whether the attempt will succeed, and whether the culprit will avoid capture; the overall tone is one of wry good humor. In view of the Biblical symbolism of stolen apples—which Augustine re-echoes early in his *Confessions,* with another story of a childhood theft of fruit— the most striking thing about this passage is what it leaves out: the whole experience of guilt.

that would be a hopeless endeavor, but to give the scoundrel his due. Gradually, imperceptibly, a kind of tacit convention grew up between Rousseau and his master:

> Soon I had received so many beatings that I grew less sensitive to them; finally they seemed to me a sort of compensation for my thefts, which made it right for me [*me mettoit en droit*] to go on stealing. Instead of looking back and thinking of my punishment, I looked forward and contemplated vengeance. I judged that to be beaten like a scoundrel authorized me to be one. I found that thieving and being beaten belonged together, indeed, that they were in a sense a single state; and that if I fulfilled my part of the bargain, I could leave it to my master to do the rest. Assured of this, I began to steal with a much easier conscience than before. I would say to myself: "Well, what will happen? I'll be beaten? Let it happen: that's what I was made for." [34–5]

"*I judged that to be beaten like a scoundrel authorized me to be one.*" Here Rousseau accepted his master's definition of him, and abandoned his own attempt to define himself. He had begun by rebelling against an unjust system; he ended in a position of seeming to buttress a legitimate one. Since the *fripon* was of evil nature, his actions were necessarily wrong; in acknowledging himself as a *fripon,* Rousseau was admitting himself in the wrong. The real purpose of punishing a *fripon* for wrongs he could not help but commit was to reaffirm a rightful structure of authority. In allowing himself to be treated as a *fripon,* and in learning to recognize himself in that role, Rousseau was tacitly conceding the legitimacy of his master's power: for the actions of a *fripon* could be defined categorically as wrongs only when directed against a system of power which was defined as essentially right. In exchange for this concession, the system accorded him a recognition which it had previously withheld: for the first time, it "authorized [him] to be" something. Whereas before Rousseau had hardly been granted the right to exist, now, as *fripon*, he suddenly found himself a virtually indispensable man: without his "deviant behavior," the system could not assert its basic norms; only by binding him up could it maintain its own social bonds intact. Inadvertently, then, Rousseau let himself be encompassed and absorbed; he became a parasite within the system from which he had tried to cut himself loose. It was a mark of strength and elasticity of traditional society that it could circumscribe social protest within the blind alley of crime— and that it could force the protesters themselves, trapped by their need for recognition, to accept the criminal label and act out the compromising role in which their masters cast them.[18]

The Captive Imagination

But Rousseau's inability to break free of the system he rebelled against did not stem from any poverty of imagina-

[18] Sartre, in his brilliant study of Jean Genet, discusses at length a case strikingly similar to Rousseau's. Genet, an orphan in the care of peasant foster parents, was identified at the age of ten as "a thief." His response was not merely to accept the role in which he had been cast, but to play it to the hilt. He went on to make thiefhood a project, a life's work; he "resolved to become what crime made of me." *Saint Genet: Actor and Martyr*, translated by Bernard Frechtman (New York: Mentor Books, 1964), 26–85. Perhaps the living example of an independent, intransigent father who accepted no one's definitions helped Rousseau to escape the imposed identity which the orphan Genet desperately embraced.

E. J. Hobsbawm has shown that principled theft typically appears as the most primitive form of social protest in static, traditional societies. Even thieves whose motives are entirely selfish find it advantageous to depict themselves as "social bandits," Robin Hoods, friends of the people and enemies of their oppressors. But social banditry is a blind alley, because it offers no structural alternative to the structured oppression it fights. *Primitive Rebels*, Chapters 1–3.

tion. Indeed, his very richness of imagination helped, ironically, to keep him in his place. The faculty of imagination is inevitably dangerous to any rigidly stratified society, since it inspires men to conceive alternatives to the order that is imposed on them. But traditional society in Rousseau's time had learned to use this faculty, and so to control not only men's actions, but their fantasies as well. Toward the end of Book One of the *Confessions*, Rousseau describes how his youthful imagination served to hold him down. He begins by explaining why, although his sexual desire was very intense throughout early adolescence, he made no attempt to assert himself with women. "In this strange situation my restless imagination took a hand," he recollects, "which *saved me from myself*. . . ." He then explains how the imagination worked against the self:

> What it [the imagination] did was to nourish itself on situations that had interested me in my reading, recalling them, varying them, combining them, and *making them so completely mine [me les approprier tellement] that I became one of the characters [personnages] I imagined,* and saw myself always in the pleasantest situations of my own choosing. So, in the end, the *fictional situation in which I had put myself made me forget my real situation which had so dissatisfied me.* . . . [My imagination] had modified my passions, and restrained them by *making use of those very passions to curb themselves.* So it is that I have been slow to act through an excess of desire. [I. 41; emphases mine]

Rousseau's imagination had been engendered by his passions; it had sprung from the tension between the intensity of his desires and the obstacles which his environment placed in their way. But at some point imagination had made a leap, and established itself and its creations in a separate realm, independent of the real situation out of which it had grown. In the brave new world of the imagination no shadow fell between what was and what ought to be; desire and fulfillment were one. The imagined world was "so completely mine" in a way the real world could never be; a world in which Rousseau was the leading *personnage* could compensate for, and perhaps even blot out, a world in which he was not even a *personne*. Indeed, he could be not only the leading personnage but the *auteur*, dictating his terms to the world, directing and controlling the play as a whole. Thus his desires could be cultivated, refined, developed in complete safety—with a guarantee that they would never be acted out. Utopian ideals need not clash with obdurate realities; the oppressed subject could comfortably lead a double life:

> It is a very strange thing that my imagination never manifests itself more agreeably than when my situation [*mon état*] is least agreeable, and never less cheerfully than when everything is cheerful around me. My poor head can never submit itself to things as they are. It cannot merely decorate; it must create. . . . If I want to paint the spring, it must be winter; if I want to describe a lovely landscape, I must be enclosed by walls; and, as I've said a hundred times, if ever I were confined in the Bastille, it's there that I would draw the picture of liberty. [IV. 171–2]

Thus the imagination freed the "head" from subjection to "things as they are"—but only by detaching it from the body, which remained confined in its Bastille. It split men in two, and so diverted their discontent from its source in their lives. This split enabled the social system which oppressed them to run on without interruption. The autonomy of the imagination, then, could facilitate the heteronomy of the imaginer—"saving him from himself," by protecting a society which kept the self repressed.

Traditional society circumscribed not only the form of imaginative life, but the very content of the fantasies which men imagined. Rousseau often yearned nostalgically for a secure niche in a traditional order—perhaps "the tranquil, obscure rank of a good artisan, especially in a superior trade like that of an engraver in Geneva"—in an ascriptive order which "would have contained me in my sphere, and offered me no way out." At such moments, longing for repression, he invoked the imagination as a pillar of constraint.

> Since my imagination was rich enough to embellish any state with illusions [*pour orner de ses chimères tous les états*], and powerful enough to transport me, according to my whim, from one state to another, it mattered very little what walk of life I was actually in. Never mind how great the distance between my place and the greatest castle in Spain, I found it easy to establish myself there. [I. 43]

But the imagery which Rousseau uses here to depict his fantasy life suggests that, even in his mind, he was not so free as he thought. In focusing his imagination on "the greatest castle in Spain," he was not really wandering very far from home. This cliché castle was only a mirror-image of his actual surroundings: the identity of the lord of such a castle was just as static, just as rigidly ascriptive, just as unfree as his engraver's role. The structure of his fantasy merely recapitulated the structure of the reality he lived in. His imagination dreamt of a high place in the system instead of a low one; but it failed to transcend the system itself.

And yet, inadvertently, Rousseau's imagination *did* carry him beyond the system. At the close of the First Book of the *Confessions,* he tells the story of his abrupt departure from Geneva at the age of sixteen. He was accustomed, he relates, to play with his friends outside the city gates after dark. Twice he was left outside overnight when the gates were locked, and he was warned of dire punishments to come if it should happen a third time. Rousseau was afraid, and resolved not to go out again after dark. But his resolution did not last, and before long he was locked out once again. When the other boys returned home the next morning, Jean-Jacques remained outside, and resolved to leave Geneva for good. In retrospect he would speak of being locked out as a purely external fate: "I ran up and shouted breathlessly. It was too late. When I was twenty paces away I saw them raise the first bridge. I trembled as I watched its dreadful horns rising in the air, a sinister augury of the inevitable fate which awaited me from that moment on." (I. 41–2) But he himself suggests that his own inclination played an important role in arranging this fate. Although he never cared much for the other boys or for their games, he says, "once I got into things I was more ardent than they and went farther out. Hard to rouse and hard to restrain: this had been a constant trait in my character. When we went walking outside the city I always went ahead, and I never dreamt of returning unless others dreamt of it for me." (41) The medieval city gates are an excellent symbol for traditional society. Although Geneva was a closed society, it was never a *total* society: its bounds were narrow and clearly marked; it locked people out as well as in; it had gaps through which one could slip away. What Rousseau found outside the gates was *space:* space to breathe freely, to move, to stretch his limbs, to let himself be. No doubt the other boys also enjoyed the open space; but they experienced it only as an interlude, a temporary break from their real business in the world. For Rousseau, however, once he had had the chance to *feel himself,* the reality of his place in Genevan society faded away. Had he stayed, he recollected, he would have grown up to be "a good Christian, a good citizen, a good *paterfamilias,* a good friend, a good workman, a good man in every way. I would have loved my situation [*état*]. . . ." (I. 43) But these roles had lost all meaning for him. *"I never dreamt of returning unless others dreamt of it for me."* In deciding not to return, Rousseau was deciding to dream his own dreams—dreams which the realities of Genevan society could not fulfill.

> Although the moment when fear had suggested the project of flight to me was terrible, the moment in which I actually carried the project out was delightful. . . . The only thing I felt was a sense of the independence I believed I had won. Now that I was free and my own master, I believed that I could do anything, that I could achieve anything. I had only to take one leap and I could fly through the air. Confidently I entered the vast spaces of the world. [II. 45]

Abruptly, sharply dramatically, Rousseau had cut himself loose from all the roles and identities with which traditional society had sought to bind him. The situation which Rousseau had created for himself typified perfectly the paradigmatic condition of modern man: free and his own master, dreaming his own dreams, entering the infinite space of the world. Only gradually would he discover—and proclaim—that the modern world, for all its infinite possibilities, stifled and repressed and destroyed the self in its own distinctive ways.

The Hidden Man:
Self-Alienation in
Modern Society

> ". . . his own kin will be the last man in the world to find out anything about Flem Snopes's business."
>
> "No," the first man said. "He wouldn't even be that. . . . Flem Snopes don't even tell himself what he is up to. Not if he was laying in bed with himself in a empty house in the dark of the moon."
>
> WILLIAM FAULKNER
> *The Hamlet*

> In this age of enlightenment, everyone knows how to calculate to the penny the worth of his honor and his life.
>
> *Letter to d'Alembert*

J'*entrois avec sécurité dans la vaste espace du monde. . . ."*

For Rousseau "the world" meant the city, *"la Capitale,"* the metropolis. In the course of his life it came to mean, above all, Paris. Although Paris was located in France, its meaning for Rousseau transcended national boundaries. As Saint-Preux explains, writing home from his first voyage to

Paris, his purpose in going there is "to get to know man [*l'homme*], and my method is to study him in his various relationships . . . that way I might begin to understand the true effects of society." It was essential to "distinguish philosophical observation from national satire. It is not Parisians I'm studying, but inhabitants of great cities." (*Julie*, II. 16, 242–3) Paris was paradoxical at the core; it was unique precisely in its absence of local uniqueness; what made it the city it was, the source of its individuality, was its archetypicality; hence, although it was an empirical place, it could be observed and described philosophically.

The metropolitan society which was crystallizing in eighteenth-century Paris introduced a new category, a new mode of being into the world: *l'homme,* "man" *as such.* Metropolitan man, as Montesquieu had already observed in *The Persian Letters,* enjoyed a new kind of personal identity. He seemed to be totally free, in both body and mind: he was emancipated from all traditional social roles and traditional modes of servitude; he knew how to dream his own dreams, and used his wit and imagination to create a place for himself in the world. He was perpetually active, constantly transcending himself; he could play many different roles, in public and private life, without immobilizing himself in any of them. Where members of traditional, rural societies were constricted by what Linton would call *ascribed* identities, the modern Parisians had developed a system of what he would call *achieved* identity. "Achieved statuses are . . . those requiring special qualities. . . . They are not assigned to individuals from birth, but are left open to be filled through competition and individual effort." (*The Study of Man,* 115) Thus metropolitan society seemed to make it possible, perhaps for the first time in history, for men to *be themselves,* to define and create lives which would be authentically *their own.* Indeed, as Montesquieu had noted, men in this society were uniquely *open:* in Paris no one wore veils any more. "Everything speaks out; everything is visible; everything is audible." *(Persian Letters,* 63) Rousseau recognized this openness; that was why he sent Saint-Preux to the metropolis to "get to know men." And yet, as Saint-Preux soon realized, "under these exteriors, so open and so agreeable, the [Parisians'] hearts are perhaps more hidden, more tightly sealed within themselves, than our own." *(Julie,* II. 17, 255) For instance, Parisian conversation was exciting and educative: "They talk about everything, because everyone has something to say," and yet, "No one says what he thinks, but only what he wants others to think." This was why, despite the city's infinite opportunities for human interaction, and intercourse, "I am never more lonely than when I'm in the crowd." For him who would discover man, the *"vaste espace du monde"* turned out to be empty, a *"vaste désert du monde."* (II. 14, 231–3) "The gravest fault of great cities," Saint-Preux commented sadly, "is that men become different from what they are; society gives them a being different from their own." (II. 21, 273) These modern metropolitan men were just as alienated from themselves as were the aristocrats, peasants and artisans of the traditional, rural, feudal society that Rousseau had left behind. *L'homme* might indeed have come into being in this society, yet he was nowhere to be seen.

Paris Re-examined

The Paris Rousseau criticized was essentially no different from the Paris Montesquieu had celebrated. Rousseau did not call attention to new facts, but rather examined the acknowledged facts of metropolitan life from a radically new perspective. Montesquieu had been captivated by the perpetual motion and energy of the Parisians. For Rousseau, all this activity on the surface only served to mask a profound passivity underneath; these men in a hurry were compulsively driven—driven out of themselves. "You might think that these isolated people living independently would at least have minds of their own. Not at all; they are machines, which don't think for themselves, but are set in motion by springs." Again, "Just as clocks are ordinarily wound up to go only twenty-four hours at a time, so these people have to go into society every night to learn what they're going to think the next day." (*Julie*, II. 14, 234) These mechanical metaphors emphasized that the Parisians' movements were rigidly circumscribed, repetitive, cyclical, ultimately static; they were always on the move, but never really going anywhere; the possibility of progress or self-development never even arose for them. Moreover, as machines, they were impelled from without, not from within; they could be turned on or off, set fast or slow, directed this way or that, by whoever or whatever controlled their motion. These supposedly free men moved with all the repressed rigidity of "a regiment in battle"; they were about as authentic as a company of "puppets nailed to the same board, or pulled by the same string." (II. 17, 250)

As the theatrical model of the puppet show suggests, Rousseau understood that the man-machines of the metropolis were not all programmed in the same way; they played different roles, performed complementary functions in a vast division of labor. "When a man speaks, it's his costume [*habit*], not he, that's expressing a feeling. . . . Each coterie has its own rules, its own standards, its own principles, and will admit no others. . . . There's one mode of reason for the robe, another for finance, another for the sword." (II. 14, 233–4) The metropolis had unveiled a world of infinite variety and diversity, a world that was thoroughly pluralistic. This was the world Montesquieu had celebrated in *The Persian Letters*. But while Paris might appear pluralistic to an outsider (a Persian—or a provincial lord), Rousseau insisted that it was narrowly monolithic from within: the members of each of its many groups adamantly denied the legitimacy of the others, refused to recognize their right to exist. This was most strikingly true of the groups at the top. For the rich and fashionable people who patronized the theater, "the sphere of the world contracts," so that "They themselves are the only inhabitants of the earth; all the rest are nothing in their eyes. The whole world [*tout le monde*] keeps a carriage, a Swiss, and a *maître d'hôtel*. This means that the whole world consists of a very few people. Those who walk on foot—*des Bourgeois, des hommes, du peuple*— are simply not in the world at all. It's necessary to have a coach, not in order to get you from one place to another, but in order to exist." (II. 17, 252) They hoped to entrench themselves in their social roles, and to lock out all the rest of humanity.

There was nothing new about the attempt of a ruling class to freeze itself in its pre-eminent role, to establish social distance between itself and humanity. But while this static mode of identity had served some real function (although perhaps an unjust one) in traditional society, it had no relevance whatever to the facts of metropolitan life. For the crucial fact of life in the metropolis was *change*. Rousseau saw Paris as "a stream" in which "everything changes every moment," and in which no one, not even an observer, could hold still. (II. 17, 245) Anything could happen here: "everything is absurd and nothing is shocking." (II. 14, 235) In such a world it was inevitable that there should be a "perpetual clash of intrigues and cabals, a continual ebb

and flow of prejudices and contrary opinions. . . ." (234)
In traditional societies a man was a master by his rank, a
rank that was ascribed to him from his birth; in modern
society a man became master only through the power he
had, power which he had achieved. But the distribution of
power was in perpetual flux; what had taken a lifetime to
build might be destroyed in a moment. A striking contradiction developed between the permanency of men's pretensions and the transcience of their conditions, between the
solidity of the identities they claimed for themselves and the
fluidity of the roles they actually played. The tenuousness of
these achieved statuses put the men who held them under
severe pressure to prove themselves in their new roles. They
compensated for their greenness and allayed their insecurity through unprecedented cruelty to the men below them.
Thus Saint-Preux could say: "there is probably not a city in
the world where fortunes are so unequal, where the most
sumptuous opulence reigns alongside the most deplorable
poverty." (232)

Rousseau described sensitively in the *Emile* the psychic
process by which the *arriviste* who had moved up from poverty obliterated his past—and obliterated his humanity in
the act. "There are ranks [*états*] which seem to change a
man's nature, to recast [*refondre*] . . . the men who adopt
them." Thus "if I were rich, it would mean that I had done
all that is necessary to become rich. I should therefore be
insolent and base, sensitive only on my own behalf, pitiless
and hard toward all the rest of the world, a scornful specta-
tor of the sufferings of the *canaille*—for that is what I
should call poor men [*indigents*], to make people forget
that I once belonged to their class myself." (*Emile*, IV. 310)
The rich man fits himself into his new role by an act of
redefinition: "*indigents*" were metamorphosed into "*can-

118

aille." Now the essential thing about a poor man was no longer his wretched economic *situation,* but his debased, canine *nature,* of which poverty was simply a natural consequence. Since the poor were animals by nature, subhuman poverty and squalor could be seen as merely their native element. What had made some men rich and others poor, whether the existing distribution of wealth was just, how poverty might be ameliorated—such questions need not be asked. Indeed, they *could* not be asked, for there were no words available in which to formulate them. The new vocabulary stamped contingent, fluctuating events with the seal of eternal, inevitable fate. The *nouveaux riches* came to see themselves as mere vehicles of that fate, capable only of acting out the class roles which their "nature" imposed on them. This belief enabled them to play these roles to the hilt, to exploit the poor without inhibition and without limit —while their power lasted. Ironically, the very equality of metropolitan life had helped generate its most extreme and vicious inequalities. The new freedom, openness and mobility that made it possible for social servitude to be short also made that servitude more solitary, poor, nasty and brutish than ever before.

Political Masks: Liberalism

The social distance which these rich men put between themselves and poor men was ratified and enshrined in the fundamental laws of the modern state. In his analysis of the relation between state and society, Rousseau diverged radically from the *philosophes* and liberal reformers of his time. Like Montesquieu in *The Persian Letters* (though not in the *Spirit of the Laws*), they drew a sharp distinction between political and social life. They saw the partly traditional (and feudal), partly absolutist French state as a drag on the dynamic, metropolitan French society which was just beginning to emerge. They were confident that this distinctively modern "civil society" was capable of liberating all men to be themselves—if the state would only let it alone. The whole trouble with the state was the *arbitrariness* of its incursions into social life, conferring special privileges on some men, imposing special burdens on others. They understood freedom as Voltaire had defined it, as "dependence on nothing but the laws." Hence all men would be free if the state were *constitutional:* that is, if it confined its actions within the limits of a code of general rules, and constituted itself as what Pope had called "a government of laws and not of men," thus allowing the life of society to flow on unimpeded. Rousseau attacked this dualistic view of state and society. The idea of a government of laws—not men—was absurd to him: all laws, after all, were made by men. The state, he insisted, was no mere excrescence parasitically imposed on the life of society; rather, it grew organically out of social life. Thus, if a state was repressive, it was because some power in society had a vested interest in repression, and knew how to use political power to execute its will.

Rousseau demonstrated the social basis of political power by asking two simple questions: first, whom did the power of the state protect? second, whom did it protect them *from?* (Lenin later condensed these two questions into one: *Who —— Whom?*) He used his model of the hypothetical state of nature to bring out, by contrast, the distinctive character of political repression. Already in the state of nature inequality had appeared and some men had begun to exploit others; but because "every man [had been] his own master," these evils had been only transient: our concepts of "domination" and "servitude" would have been unintelligible to natural man. If one natural man felt put upon by

120

another, he could simply move freely to another place. "What if I should happen to meet a man so much stronger than I, so depraved, indolent and fierce that he could force me to work for his subsistence while he remained idle? He would have to take care not to let me out of his sight for even an instant, and to bind me fast before he went to sleep, or else I'd kill him, or simply run away. After all this, let him relax his vigilance for even a moment, let him turn his head at a sudden noise, and I'll be twenty paces off in the forest; my chains will be broken and he'll never see me again." In other words, natural man could be constrained by nothing except physical force; there was no way of holding him in any role he did not wish to fill. "One man might well seize the fruits that another had gathered, the game he had killed, or the cave he had used for shelter; but how could he exact *obedience,* how could there be chains of *dependence* among men who possessed nothing?" (*Inequality,* 161–2) The greatest achievement of the state so far had been precisely to create these chains, to develop non-violent, psychic means for keeping men in their place. Of course, it was not in the interest of *all* men to remain in their places— merely in the interest of those whose places were at the top. It was very clear to Rousseau who gained and who lost from all existing states and laws: "in the state of nature there is an actual and indestructible equality among men. In the civil state there is a vain and chimerical equality of rights." This civil equality, in fact, was only a means by which "the power of the community [was] added to the power of the strong for the oppression of the weak." Against Montesquieu and the liberal constitutionaries of his day, Rousseau argued that "The universal spirit of the laws of every country is always to take the part of the strong against the weak, and the part of him who has against him who has not. . . ."

The rule of law was basically only a false front, a screen for the dominance of the men who made the laws. "From this first contradiction spring all the other contradictions between the real and the apparent which are to be found in the civil order. The many will always be sacrificed to the few, the common weal to private interests; those specious words 'justice' and 'subordination' will always serve as the tools of violence and the weapons of injustice." (*Emile*, IV. 197–8) All states, then, were built on lies, constitutions and laws served only to deceive the oppressed masses into thinking that they were in their rightful place.

Rousseau was more concrete in his indictment of the specifically *modern* state. Here again, in his analysis of the divisions in state and society, Rousseau left the company of the *philosophes*. For them, the main line in French society was drawn between the privileged nobility and clergy on the one side, and everyone else on the other. The main focus of their political energy was a struggle which lasted throughout the eighteenth century, to induce or impel the privileged estates to contribute a fair share to the upkeep of the state. They sought, above all, a constitutional state which would bring about legal equality and a "rule of law." Their project prefigured the ideology of the revolutionary Third Estate in 1789. Although Rousseau endorsed this project in principle, he was unimpressed by its ultimate aims. Legal equality, he felt, would have little effect on the most drastic inequalities of the day; indeed, it might even reinforce them. The range of Rousseau's vision extended far beyond the conditions of 1789. The real unit of power in modern society, he saw, was no longer descent, but money; increasingly the crucial division was one of class, not of status; the decisive social roles were no longer nobles and commoners, but rich and poor. Hence the oppressiveness of the modern

state took a distinctively economic form: it "provides a powerful protection for the immense possessions of the rich, and
hardly leaves the poor man in possession of the cottage he
has built with his own hands. Are not all the advantages of
society for the rich and powerful? Are not all the lucrative
posts in their hands? Are not all privileges reserved for them
alone? Is not the public authority entirely on their side?" It
was not so much that the rich could always afford to buy
preferment; their privileges came to them in advance, *a
priori*, as "the rich man's right." (*Political Economy*,
271–2)[19] The institution of the state "bound new fetters on
the poor, and gave new powers to the rich; destroyed irre-
trievably all natural liberty; fixed forever the law of property and inequality; converted clever usurpation into in-
alienable right; and, for the sake of a few ambitious men,
subjected all mankind to perpetual labor, servitude and
misery." (*Inequality*, 178) The ideas of law, right, justice,
which the state had brought into being, had only served as
screens for the exploitation of the weak by the strong. The
main achievement of the modern state so far had been to
freeze existing inequalities as they were, to consolidate the
fluid, transient roles and identities of modern economic life
into a solid social structure, and to give this system a blessing of "legitimacy." Thus the modern state was a powerful
agency of repression; but the agent that used it and refined
its powers was modern society. It was this society as a whole
that alienated men from themselves.

Cultural Masks: Neoclassicism

Against the political repressiveness of Versailles, the *philosophes* had exalted the liberal Parisian culture. In foster-
ing the growth of culture—the creation and appreciation of

19 Article for *Encyclopédie*, 1755; page numbers from *OC*, III.

art, the development of science—the metropolis was vastly expanding the range of possibilities for human self-expression. Rousseau never denied these possibilities; rather, he called attention to a basic ambiguity inherent in his culture. On the one hand, in its greatest works, this culture generated an unprecedented fullness of self-activity. On the other hand, in its everyday workings, culture served —just as politics did—to reinforce and legitimize a social system whose whole structure did violence to the self. Thus "Necessity raised up thrones; the arts and sciences have made them strong." Art and science

> fling garlands of flowers over the chains that weigh [men] down. They stifle that feeling of individual liberty for which men would seem to have been born; they make men love their own slavery, and so transform them into what we call "civilized people" [*Peuples policés*]. [*Arts and Sciences,* 7]

Along with its potentialities for self-expansion, culture had given rise to new modes of self-alienation.

The most immediate threat to authenticity in art arose from the relationship between the artist and his audience. "Every artist wants to be applauded. The praise of his contemporaries is the most precious part of his recompense. What, then, will he not do to obtain it? . . . He will lower his genius to the level of his age, and will prefer to create mediocre works which will be praised in his lifetime, rather than sublime ones which won't be admired till long after his death." (21) Psychically as well as economically, the artist was dependent on the responses of his audience. This dependence forced him to create works which echoed their values and flattered their vanities. The more culture developed, the more deeply art was entrenched as an established social role, the more the integrity of the artist was compromised.

In his analysis of Molière's *Misanthrope,* in the *Letter to d'Alembert,* Rousseau described the inevitable tension between the artist's personal vision and his social needs. "Since he had to please the public, [Molière] consulted the most general taste of those who constitute it. According to this taste he composed a model, and according to this model he drew a picture of the contrary failings, from which he took his comic characteristics, various of which he distributed in his plays." Molière's ideal when he wrote was "not . . . a good man [*honnête homme*], but a man of the world [*homme du monde*]. Hence he wishes to correct not what was vicious, but what was ridiculous. . . . Thus, wishing to expose to public derision all the faults which were opposed to the qualities of the likeable man—the man of society—after having created so many other ridiculous characters, there remained to him that one whom the world pardons least: the man who is ridiculous because he is virtuous." This is what Moliére had set out to do in the *Misanthrope:* he had meant to vindicate the dominant values of his age by holding its critics up to scorn and ridicule. But the unconscious force of his nature had overcome the calculated skill of his art: "Although Molière wrote reprehensible plays, he was personally a good man [*honnête homme*]; and the brush of a good man has never been able to paint the features of righteousness and probity in odious colors." Hence Alceste actually emerged as a far more sympathetic and engaging character than Molière had planned: the author could not help but put into his character's mouth the truths he knew himself. "Who, then, is the real misanthrope of Molière? A good man [*homme de bien*] who detests the *moeurs* of his age and the wickedness of his contemporaries;

who, precisely because he loves his fellow-men, hates in them the evils they do to one another and the vices which engender these evils. . . . If there were no scoundrels and flatterers, he would love all mankind. There is no good man who is not a misanthrope in this sense. . . ." Thus "the force of virtue triumphs over the *art* of the author and does honor to his *character*." (*Letter to d'Alembert*, 36–43) Ironically, the ultimate success of the work was a function of its artistic failure. Molière had set out to vindicate the life of *la Cour et la Ville;* but his personal vision and insight had broken through the shell of the artist's social identity, in which he had encased himself, and produced a brilliant, trenchant critique of the values he had aimed to affirm.[20]

But if the authenticity of the artist and his art was endangered by his dependence on the *moeurs* and values of his audience, it could be equally threatened by his independence. As culture developed, and the division of labor became more and more specialized, the pursuit of art—and of science as well—separated itself from the common life of men. Aesthetics had not only disengaged itself from ethics, and established its autonomy, but actually pre-empted the place of morality in the hierarchy of cultural values. Thus, "The question is no longer whether a man is honest, but merely whether he has talent." (*Arts and Sciences*, 25) Men

[20] Thus the play succeeded in spite of, and against, its author's intentions. Nevertheless, Rousseau argued, Molière managed to compromise Alceste's character and dilute his ideological force. ". . . Molière has misunderstood the misanthrope. Can it be that he did so unawares? Surely not. This is how the desire to cause laughter at the expense of his character forced him to degrade it contrary to the truth of its nature." Rousseau identified deeply with this misunderstood misanthrope, and suggested in a footnote that "a man of genius could compose a new *Misanthrope,* no less true or less natural than the old one, equal to Molière's, and incomparably more instructive. I see only one difficulty for this new play: it could not succeed. For whatever one might say, in matters of honor no one laughs with good grace at his own expense. And here we are back to my principles." (42)

were losing interest in the *content* of a work—or an action
—and becoming more and more exclusively concerned with
its *form*. Works were examined and judged not for their
total meaning, but for their *style* alone, for their mere pro-
ficiency of *technique*. As culture refined itself, and men's
preoccupations became more formal and technical, the
process of judgment became increasingly specialized: thus
"We have physicians, mathematicians, chemists, astrono-
mers, poets, musicians, painters; but we no longer have citizens. . . ." (26) Valuation had become more of a profes-
sional prerogative, less of a human one. Human activities
were assessed exclusively by the received standards of their
respective *métiers;* there was no one left to ask general questions about their value—or about the value of these *métiers*
themselves—to the community as a whole. People cared
only that a thing should be done well; no one worried about
whether it should be done at all. In aesthetics, men learned
to venerate greatness, majesty, sublimity, in themselves;
hence, in the state, the great tyrants who oppressed and enslaved them appeared as admirable as the great heroes who
fought to set or to keep them free. "Vice or virtue, what does
it matter, so long as it's presented with grandeur?"
Rousseau saw the theater as a microcosm of modern culture:
"everything that is put on in the theater is not brought
nearer to us, but made more distant. . . . The theater has
rules, principles and a morality of its own, just as it has its
own language and style of dress." (*Letter to d'Alembert,*
25-7) Culture thus reproduced—and, in so doing, reinforced—the structure of modern society: it was divided into
monadically insular sub-cultures; men gave their loyalty entirely to their sub-cultural peers. "The good, the bad, the
beautiful, the ugly, truth, virtue, have only a local and circumscribed existence." (*Julie,* II. 14, 234) Anything was

127

permissible if it was judged successful by one's peers; nothing was permissible if it was not.

There was still another, deeper sense in which modern culture could be said to "fling garlands over the chains that weigh men down." Rousseau believed that the art, the science and the dominant *moeurs* of his time were organically linked in their repressiveness.

> There reigns in our moeurs a vile and deceptive uniformity, and all souls seem to have been cast in the same mold. Politeness demands this, decorum decrees that; one always follows custom, never one's own nature [*son propre génie*]. [*Arts and Sciences,* 8]

It is essential to understand that Rousseau was attacking an art which was governed very strictly by classical ideals whose eternal, universal validity was accepted without question, and a science which assumed that all possible phenomena and experiences could be described exhaustively by physical laws. The prestige of neo-Classical art and Newtonian science in early eighteenth-century culture had generated peculiarly rigid models of human perfection: mechanical precision and statuesque immobility became ideal attributes which men strove to attain; it was believed that perfection could be reached (or in any case approached) through the strict observance of a uniform set of *principes.* By the middle of the eighteenth century it had become fairly commonplace to criticize neo-Classical aesthetics for its repressive rigidity, and to exalt the values of spontaneity, diversity and self-expressiveness in art. Similarly, philosophers of science were beginning to recognize the inexhaustibility of experience, the open-endedness of the scientific enterprise, and the role of individual genius and creativity in scientific discovery. These aesthetic and scientific developments were part of a general movement of ideas which is now usually characterized as "pre-Romanticism." [21] But Rousseau was the only writer who understood the political implications of the Pre-romantic cultural critique. For him, the neo-Classical and Newtonian idea of perfection helped (perhaps inadvertently in science, quite intentionally in aesthetics) to buttress a social system which manipulated and exploited men as if they were *objets d'art* mechanically "cast in the same mold," which endowed dominant norms and styles of behavior with all the inexorable force of cosmological laws, which worked to eliminate all human individuality by denying its very existence. This cultural authoritarianism accustomed men to submit to systems of fixed rules, imposed by external authorities, established for all times, closed to all scrutiny or change, taking no account of the inclinations or needs of the individuals whose lives they ruled. By teaching men to order and evaluate their experience according to received conventions, culture was depriving them of their strongest weapon against political oppression and social exploitation: their sense of *self*, "that feeling of individual liberty for which men would seem to have been born."

The consequences of modern culture, then, were pro-

[21] In the philosophy of science, the seminal work was Diderot's *On the Interpretation of Nature,* published in 1753; for a lucid account of the contest and impact of Diderot's scientific thought, see Henri Lefebvre, *Diderot* (Paris: Editions Réunis, 1949). The aesthetic story, with which I am more familiar, has been told well several times: for example, André Monglond, *Histoire Intérieur du préromantisme français* (2 volumes, Grenoble: Editions B. Arthud, 1929); Arthur O. Lovejoy, who has dealt with this theme tirelessly over the past forty years, *The Great Chain of Being* (Cambridge, Mass.: Harvard University Press, 1936), Chapter 10, and *Essays in the History of Ideas* (New York: George Braziller, 1955), throughout; Jacques Barzun, *Classic, Romantic and Modern* (1943; revised edition, New York: Anchor Books, 1961); Walter Jackson Bate, *From Classic to Romantic* (Cambridge, Mass.: Harvard University Press, 1946); M. H. Abrams, *The Mirror and the Lamp* (New York: Oxford University Press, 1953); Martin Price, *To the Palace of Wisdom* (New York: Doubleday, 1964). So far as I know, only Arnold Hauser, in Volume III of his *Social History of Art* and Jean Starobinski, in *The Invention of Liberty,* have attempted seriously to understand the social and political aspects of Preromanticism.

foundly ambiguous. It had encouraged man to use his reason and sensibility to "gain mastery over the world." But even as men gained mastery over the world—understanding it through science, making it beautiful through art—they were losing their grip on their own situation within it. They were becoming objectively enriched, but subjectively impoverished; better informed than ever about the world's rules, but less and less aware of their own needs—and of their society's ways of frustrating their needs. Among *Peuples policés* the pursuit of culture served as a very efficient spiritual—and political—police: it kept men out of trouble by keeping them out of themselves. This police power was so effective largely because it was so secret: the victims never realized what it was that they were missing. Indeed, the victims themselves were enlisted as collaborators: taught to believe in the rational order of the universe, they learned to accept their place in it as a reasonable one; transfixed by the beauty and grandeur radiating from the commanding heights of society, they could transfigure their lives at the bottom in its vicarious glow. Even the torch of Enlightenment, Rousseau understood, could serve as an instrument of obscurantism: the repressive society that had furnished the fuel and lit the flame had directed the light far away from the immediacy of human life, and frozen it into static, abstract forms of thought and feeling, leaving men in the dark about their personal needs and about a social system that repressed them. If these monuments of beauty and rationality made the oppressed masses "love their own slavery" (7), they simultaneously preserved the ruling classes from pangs of bad conscience about their mastery: so long as one kept one's gaze focused on cultural institutions, and avoided confronting the men beneath them, society appeared basically healthy and progressing every day. The highest art and science of modern times was self-deception.

The State of War: Insincerity and Survival

Throughout this chapter I have been explicating Rousseau's description of the new modes of self-alienation which modern society had introduced. But he did more than just describe this condition: he analyzed it in general terms and tried to develop a theory to explain it. In the following sections I want to examine Rousseau's more theoretical discussion of human identity in the modern age. I want particularly to focus on the paradoxical character of modernity as it appeared to Rousseau: as both the nadir of man's self-alienation and, simultaneously, the medium for his full self-liberation.

In his earliest exploration of self-alienation, Rousseau focused mainly on a phenomenon familiar to French moralists: *insincerity*. He was struck by a glaring disparity between the theory and the practice of modern moral and social life. If a hypothetical ideal observer from some distant land tried to infer the moral beliefs of Europeans from their moral pretentions, he would be impressed with "the politeness of our manners, the affability of our conversation, our constant profession of benevolence, and that tumultuous assembly of all men of all ages and all ranks who seem to have nothing to do from morning to night except to oblige one another." (*Arts and Sciences,* 9) "If all this were sincere, and taken at its word, there would be no people less attached to property, and communism would be virtually established. The rich would be incessantly offering what they had, the poor would always accept, men would find themselves naturally on one level, and Sparta itself would be no more egalitarian than Paris." (*Julie,* II. 14, 232) The first important point about this system of values was its very strict universality: "in the same circumstances, all men act exactly alike." Moreover, it was not only uniform in the de-

mands it made on men, but uniformly repressive. These altruistic *moeurs* might reign, but they could never rule.
They succeeded only in driving men's real, immediate impulses and motives underground, to the point where "we
never know whom we are dealing with."

> What a train of vices attend this uncertainty! No
> more sincere friendship; no more real esteem; no more
> perfect confidence between man and man! Jealousy,
> fear, coldness, reserve, suspicion, hatred, betrayal, all
> hide themselves under this uniform and deceptive veil
> of politeness . . . which we owe to the light of our cen-
> tury. [*Arts and Sciences*, 8–9]

If individuality were driven out the front door by a morality of rigid self-denial, it would only come in the back way
again, in the form of insincerity.

It was no surprise, then, that Parisians, when confronted
with a moral code appropriate for Spartans, should be insincere: the "vile and deceptive uniformity" which the code
imposed on them kept these modern, individualistic men
from fulfilling *leurs propres génies,* their own natures. (8)
But the unnatural uniformity of the code was not enough to
account for the extent and depth of their own insincerity.
There was an inverse ratio between the benign appearance
of social life in the metropolis and its malignant reality.
Thus, instead of the equality which the Parisians' professed
benevolence would necessarily bring about, Rousseau found
an inequality more radical than any in the world. The ex-
tremity and brutality of these contrasts was no accident; it
flowed from the very essence of modern society: a society in
which "everyone thinks of his own interest, and no one of
the common good," and in which "the interests of individuals are always opposed to one another. . . ." (*Julie,* II. 14,

234) The need for insincerity arose from a war of each against all, from a social system in which everyone was a threat to everyone else. Beneath a surface of benevolence, frightful aggressions seethed in modern man's mind: "after long prosperity, after having swallowed up treasures and destroyed multitudes of men, our hero ends by cutting every throat, until, at last, he finds himself sole master of the world. Such is, in outline, the moral picture, if not of human life, at least of the secret pretensions in the heart of every civilized man." (*Inequality*, 203) Ironically, these supposed individualists were themselves "cast in the same mold" (*Arts and Sciences*, 8); their egoistic motives were ultimately just as uniform as the Spartan principles they despised.

This Hobbesian condition was not, as Hobbes had thought, integral to the human condition: it was fallacious, in "speaking of human wants, avidity, oppression, desire and pride, [to] transfer to the state of nature ideas which have been acquired from society. . . ." (*Inequality*, 132) These impulses, and the insincerity which sprang from them, all had historical roots, which—primarily in the *Discourse on Inequality*—Rousseau attempted to trace. So long, he said, as men "understood only tasks that one man could do alone, and confined themselves to arts which did not require the joint labor of several hands, they lived free, healthy, honest and happy lives, to the extent that their nature permitted it and they could enjoy the pleasures of mutual and independent intercourse. But from the moment one man began to stand in need of the help of another, from the moment it appeared useful to even one single man to have provisions enough for two, equality disappeared, property was introduced, work became necessary, vast forests were transformed into smiling fields, which man had to water with the sweat of his brow, and where slavery and

133

misery were soon seen to germinate and grow up with the crops." (*Inequality,* 171) The crucial point in man's history, then, had been the moment in which the human needs began to expand, for this was the beginning of man's self-development. From the very beginning, however, the self-development of *each* man had been opposed to the self-development of *all.* That first proprietor, the man who had enclosed a piece of ground and said "This is mine" (164), had created a sphere of activity for himself in which he could freely fulfill his enlarged needs; on the other hand, he had simultaneously closed off an area of freedom and self-expression to everyone else. The institution of *property* had added the dimension of *competition* to human life. What it gave to one man it *ipso facto* took away from all others; everything any man enjoyed for himself, from then on, was acquired at other men's expense. Moreover, once *any* man *chose* to seek property, all men were *forced* to seek property. "According to this principle, anyone who wanted to consider himself as an isolated individual, self-sufficing and utterly independent of others, could only be utterly wretched. He could not even continue to exist, for, finding the whole earth appropriated by others while he had only himself, how could he ever get the means of subsistence?" (*Emile,* III. 156) If any man did not acquire some sphere from which he could exclude others, there was perpetual danger that others might exclude him.[22]

22 In describing the process through which a few men, by behaving acquisitively and competitively, could sweep all other men along in their wake, Rousseau is heavily indebted to Hobbes. Cf. *Elements of Law,* Part I, Chapter 14, Section 3; *De Cive,* Chapter I, Section 4; and the discussion in C. B. MacPherson, *The Political Theory of Possessive Individualism* (New York: Oxford University Press, 1962), 44. What Rousseau rejected in Hobbes was the idea that human nature, rather than history, was responsible.

Rousseau saw a similar dynamic at work in the genesis of states. Thus, "Once the first society was formed, the others followed necessarily. Men were forced either to become part of the first society, or to unite so as

The further men developed themselves, the harder they were pressed to mobilize themselves as competitors. Every quality, every virtue a man might possess would inevitably appear as a threat to everyone else; it would provoke emulation and retaliation on their part, expose him to greater risks than ever, and escalate an already murderous state of war; yet no man could afford to relax, to stop developing and perfecting himself, for fear that his opponents would surpass and overcome him at once. Now more than ever men were moved by "a devouring ambition [which] inspired them with a vile propensity to hurt one another. . . ." But this aggressive zeal was no overflow of self-activity: it arose "less out of genuine need than from the desire to put oneself above others." As acquisitive, competitive behavior became more and more pervasive, the traditional altruistic ideals of classical *virtu* and Christian *agapé* became less and less relevant to modern reality. At length, the demands of reality had pre-empted men's concern. But rather than supplant the old ideals, modern men had learned to use them for their new purposes. Thus, instead of declaring explicitly their aggressive intentions, they cultivated "a secret jealousy, all the more dangerous in that, to strike its blow with greater security, it puts on the mask of good will." Men could pursue power far more relentlessly, with far less inhibition, if they disguised their might as right. In this climate insincerity was not only understandable; it was inevitable, the self's sole means of survival:

> It is clearly in one's interest to appear different from
> what one actually is. Being and seeming become two

---

to resist it. They had to imitate it in order not to be swallowed up by it. Thus the whole face of the earth was changed, and everywhere nature disappeared. . . ." Eventually these *"grands corps"* covered every inch of space on the earth. *The State of War,* an unfinished essay, in *OC,* III. 603.

entirely different things; and from this distinction springs pompous artifice, lying trickery, and all the numerous vices that go in their train. [174–5]

Market Society and the Dissolution of the Self [23]

Rousseau's first attempts at social criticism focused on the vice of personal insincerity. As he explored the workings of modern society in greater depth, however, Rousseau came to feel that its basic human problem was not insincerity at all, but a far graver *malaise*. To say that men behaved insincerely, that they put on false appearances, implied that their "real" selves stood behind the scenes, pulling the strings of behavior, organizing the whole structure of appearances. This meant that insincerity could grow only in a substratum of autonomy; in order to deceive and manipulate one another, men had to be in full possession of themselves. Rousseau soon concluded that his contemporaries were not free enough to be capable of insincerity.

This lack of autonomy was manifest in the life of nations. Rousseau examined the process by which authoritarian regimes could win the hearts and minds of enslaved peoples. Common sense might expect quiescent, benign peoples to submit most readily, while belligerent and aggressive ones would resist. Quite the contrary, Rousseau argued. "It is no easy matter to reduce to obedience a man who has no ambition to command; nor could the most adroit politician enslave a people whose only desire was to be free. But inequality makes its way easily among ambitious and cowardly men, who are always ready to run the risks of fortune, and

23 I have borrowed the expression "market society" from MacPherson, *The Political Theory of Possessive Individualism,* cf. especially 46–70, but I am using it in a somewhat different sense.

are almost indifferent as to whether they command or obey.
. . ." This explained why peoples who were abjectly submissive at home so often threw themselves feverishly into
wars of conquest and imperialist adventures abroad. The
need to submit and the will to dominate were mirror-images
of one another: "citizens allow themselves to be oppressed
only insofar as they are led on by blind ambition, so that,
looking below rather than above, they come to love domination more than independence, and consent to put themselves in chains in order to put others in chains in their
turn." (*Inequality*, 188) Both these impulses aimed at *inequality*—that is, at an identity which defined the self in
terms wholly relative to others; both rejected *independence*
—that is, an identity which defined the self on terms that
were its own. The polarities of political life, the roles of
master and slave, offered men a means of escape from themselves.[24]

24 This escape was particularly seductive—and particularly destructive—in the realm of international politics. Rousseau was far more
pessimistic about prospects for international peace than about prospects
for domestic reforms within individual states. He believed that the state
of war which prevailed between states was less tractable than the similar
war between man and man because the needs of individual men, no
matter how great modern society might make them, were inherently
finite, ultimately limited, "fixed by nature." On the other hand, "the
state, being a purely artificial body, has no determinate extent, no
appropriate size. No matter how big it gets, it can get even bigger;
no matter how strong it becomes, it still feels weak. Its security, its
preservation, demand that it make itself stronger than its neighbors."
Indeed, the size and stature of the state were "purely relative; it must
compare itself incessantly in order to know itself. . . ." It "depends
entirely on the states that surround it; . . . it becomes small or large,
weak or strong, only insofar as its neighbors expand or contract, grow
stronger or weaker." Moreover, security within a state only places it in
danger from without, because the healthier a state becomes, the more
desirable a target for conquest it appears. Finally, while "nature has
set bounds to the inequality among men, the inequality among [states]
can grow incessantly until one absorbs all the rest." *State of War*, 601–5;
cf. *Inequality*, 178–80. In the essay on the state of war, however, Rousseau restricts the possibility of war to political bodies, and seems to

Rousseau found the same tendencies in economic life. He analyzed the experience of the rich men of his day: why did they pursue wealth with such avidity? According to traditional Western views, both classical and Biblical, the rich man was the epitome of selfishness. The desire for wealth arose out of unusually great appetites: Rousseau saw them very differently: "if we have a few rich and powerful men at the pinnacle of grandeur and fortune," he said, "while the masses grovel in obscurity and misery, it is because the rich and powerful value the things they enjoy *only insofar as other men are deprived of them;* without any change in their condition, they would cease to be happy if the people ceased to be wretched." (189) Riches were valuable only insofar as other men were poor. Thus men pursued wealth not to satisfy internal needs, but to distinguish themselves externally from other men. Far from being excessively selfish, the rich seemed to have no distinct sense of themselves at all. Economic identities, like political ones, seemed entirely mediated, conferred on the self by others.

This peculiar absence of self could also be found in cultural life. Rousseau expended much spirit in criticism of his contemporaries' pursuits of art and culture. Sometimes, however, when he looked very closely, he saw that it was not art or culture that most of them were really after. "They are even valued directly according to their uselessness. . . . The rich think so much of these things, not because they are useful, but because they are beyond the reach of the poor." (*Emile*, III. 148–9) Here Rousseau was describing what Veblen later called "conspicuous consumption." These patrons looked through the works of art they patronized; they

---

disallow the Hobbesian war between man and man which the *Discourse on Inequality* describes so well. Cf. Stanley Hoffmann's discussion, "Rousseau on War and Peace": *A.P.S.R.* LVII, 2 (June, 1963), 317–33.

cared only how these works would appear to the eyes of others. They saw culture as merely a competitive asset, among other assets—"servants in livery, equipages, rich furniture, fine clothes, spacious courts and gardens, public entertainments, useless professions such as dancers, singers, players, and all that multitude of objects of luxury, amusement and idleness which strike the eyes of all. . . ." If the rich were left alone with these objects, to contemplate or use them in solitude, they would not know what to do with them: for *"their whole purpose is to be seen, without which they would be useless."* (*Political Economy*, 276) Puritanical as he was, Rousseau preferred sheer voluptuousness to this calculation. Hence, he said, "if I were rich . . . I should be unlike them [the rich men of his day] in one way: I should be *sensual and voluptuous rather than proud and vain."* (*Emile*, IV. 310) Sensuality, by contrast, was a direct, immediate, personal response; and it was precisely the human capacity for personal response that modern society was destroying.

Indeed, personal response and involvement seemed to be absent from even that most personal of spheres, sexual relations. Montesquieu had celebrated the looseness of Parisian sexual *moeurs* as a sign of an overflowing fullness of self. The Parisian (or *parisienne*) knew who he was: his sense of identity did not depend on the undying love of another; he could play a plurality of roles, enter into many different relationships, and yet remain himself. Rousseau argued, on the contrary, that self-expression was precisely what was missing from the Parisians' sexual lives. "Since the greatest fear of these dissipated people is *ennui,* the ladies pursue not love but amusement. Gallantry and solicitousness are more important than love; so long as men are assiduous, it doesn't matter that they be passionate. The very words 'love'

and 'lover' are banned from even the most intimate intercourse between the sexes. . . ." (*Julie,* II. 21, 270) Subjected to a continuous bombardment of stimuli, seized by a
dizzying succession of changes, forced to constantly compete
for property, carried along by unpredictable ebbs and flows
of power, the individual could not focus his attention and
energy on a single object: his center could not hold. Thus
Saint-Preux feared that his love for Julie, up to now the
center of his life, was in danger of being swept away: "I'm
borne along from one caprice to another; my inclinations
are so enslaved to opinion that I can't be sure one day what
I'm going to love the next." (II. 17, 255) In a social system
animated by competition for property, the human personality was metamorphosed into a form of capital. Here it was
rational to invest oneself only in properties which would
produce the highest return. Personal feeling was a handi-
cap, since it distracted the individual from calculating his
best interest, and might pull him along economically
counter-productive paths. In an extremely fluid milieu, the
investor had to be prepared to change the objects of his love
from one moment to the next. Thus "The heart has nothing
to do with these liaisons, in which only external conven-
iences are consulted." Devoid of love, it was no wonder that
the institution of marriage was an empty shell. If infidelity
was pervasive, "what response could be more appropriate to
a bond in which the heart was never consulted? A man or
woman who marries only a fortune or a title has no personal
obligation to anyone." (II. 21, 271) In such a world the
whole basis of personal obligation and commitment seemed
to disappear: the human personality was no end in itself,
but merely a means; merely a valuable property, a competitive asset in the endless struggle to accumulate more.

Rousseau had looked for *l'homme*—a type of free man,

unfettered in body or mind—in the center of modernity, the Parisian metropolis. But he had found in the metropolis a vast market place in which all things were defined as property, all energy and activity devoted to acquisition, and all human relationships essentially competitive. At first Rousseau had condemned modern men for a Machiavellian insincerity which, he felt, cloaked an immoral selfishness. Later he came to blame the whole structure of modern society for forcing men to act insincerely and immorally in order to survive. Sometimes, however, when his critical insight was most penetrating, he realized that insincerity was not the real problem for modern man. The notion of insincerity presupposed the existence of a "real" identity, a "true" self, which the individual could then conceal. But modern society had made the very self-identity of the individual deeply problematical. Who were these modern men? Alas, they themselves could not say. The "social man" of modern times, Rousseau argued, "knows only how to live outside himself, in the judgment of others: indeed, it is only from the judgment of others that he gains consciousness of his very existence." He and his audience alike "always ask others who we are; we never dare to ask ourselves. . . ." Earlier, Rousseau had spoken of a gap between appearance and reality; now he judged that "everything is reduced to appearances, everything becomes factitious, just a game [*joué*]: honor, friendship, virtue, and even vice. . . ." (*Inequality*, 193) The men of the metropolis seemed to lack the basic equipment for insincerity: they had no selves to conceal. If their social roles and forms of behavior were masks, there seemed to be no faces underneath.

In deriving their whole sense of identity from the judgment of others, modern men were by no means unique. In traditional society, too, as Rousseau himself experienced it, men defined themselves in terms of the recognition which others conferred on the roles they played. But traditional forms of identity were ascribed to men on a permanent basis: on one hand they were virtually impossible to escape or transcend; on the other hand, they gave the individual a very secure sense of himself—though this security was based on self-deception. In any case, the relationship between every individual and the "other" who recognized him was stable, reflecting the general stability of the traditional power structure. In the stream of modern society, however, where the distribution of power shifted radically almost from moment to moment, the identity of significant "others," too, was necessarily in perpetual flux. Because the process of recognition was so volatile, the identity of every individual remained fundamentally elusive. A man was forced constantly to seek out new sets of "others" to ask who he was. Montesquieu had celebrated the human flexibility which metropolitan life had produced. Rousseau saw that men had become all too flexible here: they had no permanent sense of themselves to give them ballast and direction in the Heraclitian flux into which they were thrown. At the core of their being, where their consciences should have been, there was nothing at all. It was precisely this inner emptiness that liberated them from all moral inhibitions, and made all things possible for them.

One image of Rousseau's brought out very vividly some of the ironies of modernity. With each new human contact he makes, Rousseau said, the Parisian "must leave his soul, if he has one, at the door, and take up another with the colors of the house, as a lackey puts on new livery; when he leaves he can put on his own again, if he likes, till he makes a new exchange." (*Julie*, II. 14, 234) Rousseau himself had experienced the degrading condition of a lackey: of a man who, from being treated as a machine, tends to become one. This situation, endemic to traditional society, was decisive in motivating Rousseau to leave that society. In what sense could the free men of the metropolis—indeed, *all* the men of the metropolis—be described as lackeys? Servitude in traditional societies was essentially personal: each individual servant was bound to a particular master; the dominant or submissive roles in any human relationship were clearly marked and more or less permanent. In modern society, by contrast, a man at the bottom seemed as free as the man at the top. Nothing but the vicissitudes of fortune held him down, and the distribution of power could be radically altered at any time. However, because he experienced an inexhaustible "multitude of new needs," every modern man was "subject to all nature, and especially to his fellow-men." As the distribution of power grew less stable, and competition for it more intense, any man might find himself dependent on any other man—as ally, or enemy, as paean or obstacle. These modern men, then, were *servants without masters.* No man was bound personally to any other *man;* but all men were bound to an impersonal *system* which forced all their thought and action to serve its end.

In the maelstrom of modernity, as Rousseau saw it, a man could keep afloat only by reducing himself to "an image of fashion" [*simulacre de la mode*], and allow himself to be carried along by its ebbs and flows. (*Julie,* II. 21, 273) Here "You don't have to know the *character* of men, but only their *interests,* to figure out what they're going to say about anything." (II. 14, 233) Where a man's "interests" might change from moment to moment, anything so solid as a "character" would be a dangerous liability that could drag him down. All one could do, it seemed, was to accommodate and adapt oneself to the demands of the milieu in which one found oneself at any given moment—transient as these demands, and that milieu itself, might be. *"One must do as others do* is the first commandment of wisdom here. *This is what's done, that is what isn't done,* is the supreme basis of decision, from which there is no appeal." (II. 17, 250. Rousseau's emphases) In modern society the categories of the market had come to circumscribe all human experience. Inevitably, "Man is the cheapest commodity on the market; and among all the important rights of property, the rights of the individual are considered least." (*Emile,* IV. 211) The market defined the individual in terms that were purely relative and constantly shifting, as a function of his competitive relations with others: as a rich man or a poor man, as a prestigious or an inexpedient match, as a citizen of a conquering or a conquered nation, as a winner or a loser, as a master or a slave. It thus defined the human *self*— as a constant, underlying force which organizes and unifies all personal experience—out of existence.

The Paradox of Modernity

> The hand that inflicts the wound is alone
> the hand that can heal it.
>
> HEGEL

ROUSSEAU, like Pascal before him, described a world in which men were alienated, not only from one another, but from themselves. But where Pascal had depicted self-alienation as static, permanent, built into the human condition, Rousseau insisted that it was an historical peculiarity. In his model of Natural Man (which will be discussed at length later on), Rousseau portrayed a non-alienated state of being: the natural man "lives within himself," "always has all his powers at his disposal," "carries himself whole and entire about him." Thus, "it is by no means the original state of man, but merely the state of society, and the inequality which society engenders, that alter and transform man's natural inclinations," and shatter his original unity and wholeness of being. (*Inequality*, 136, 192–3) The psychological *malaise* of self-alienation could be understood only through an historical examination of its social functions. All through his writings Rousseau showed how both the ascriptive statuses endemic to traditional society and the achieved identities of modernity kept men from being themselves, and how both forms of self-alienation supported and legitimized the inequalities on which these societies were based. But the perspective and moral imagination which enabled him to grasp the historicity of alienation also gave him insight into its unique human value.

Pascal's idea of self-alienation emerged most vividly in his exploration of the phenomenon of *discontent,* the inability of men to remain at rest. For Pascal, it was man's inability to face himself that made the present unbearable to him: he needed constantly to escape into nostalgia or hope. The present only served as a springboard to project him backward or forward, always away from himself. Pascal saw this unrest as perpetual, but perpetually unproductive. It only led man down an endless series of blind alleys, from one transient *divertissement* to another. But Pascal's analysis of unrest was purely formal. He observed only that all forms of life were transient, that men sooner or later rejected everything; he never examined the particular contents which filled these forms of life, never delved into men's reasons for rejecting them. Thus he saw no order or rationality in the series of human preferences: reverie and activity, trivial events and world-historical actions—"dancing, singing, playing the lute, making verses, trying to grab brass rings, fighting, making oneself king" (*Pensées,* 146)—were scrambled randomly together.

For Rousseau, discontent was not a constant force in human nature; it could be understood properly only through an historical perspective. At the beginning of man's history, its power had been practically nil. "Savage man, once he has dined, is at peace with all of nature, and the friend of his fellow-man." It was only through a long, gradual process of evolution that discontent had become man's most powerful motive. Rousseau was at one with Pascal in

146

his vision of contemporary man as a creature who "enjoys not a moment's relaxation" (*Inequality*, 203); who "is always on the move, sweating, agitated, tormenting himself in search of still harder things to do; [who] works himself to the point of death, or even seeks death, to put himself in a position to live, or else gives up life to gain immortality." (192) But Rousseau saw this need to constantly transcend oneself as the outcome of centuries of cumulative human development. The need for perpetual progress was itself a product of progress.

This need had grown out of the competitive struggle into which all men had been forced by the development of society. As competition for property had extended and intensified, men came increasingly to define themselves by what they possessed. The earliest mode of self-identity, based on what Rousseau called *amour de soi,* was absolute: "each man regarded himself as the only observer of his actions, the only being in the universe who took interest in him, and the sole judge of his deserts. . . ." *Amour de soi* was essentially static, oriented toward the goal of "self-preservation." The new form of identity, based on *amour-propre,* was "a purely relative and factitious feeling, which arises only in society, which leads each individual to make more of himself than of any other, which causes all the mutual damage that men inflict on one another, and which is the real source of what we call honor." (*Inequality*, 154, 219) This sense of self was purely competitive. Eventually, the medium of competition was bound to spread beyond the realms of land and money, into every sphere of human activity; in every sphere, accordingly, "the rank and position of every man [were] established." Rousseau understood that, by the same mechanism which first gave property its general appeal; once *any* area of life was defined as property, *all* areas of life would be

147

redefined as property. This meant that the full extent of human capacities were bound to be channeled into the acquisitive struggle; indeed, their presence would make the combat all the more subtle and deadly. At the same time, the pressures of competition would keep men from merely maintaining their faculties at a constant level. *Amour-propre* was inherently dynamic: it forced men to develop their capacities to unprecedented heights and depths. "Behold all the natural qualities of man put into action. . . . Behold all our faculties developed, memory and imagination in full play, selfishness [*amour-propre*] in operation, reason fully active, and the spirit almost at the highest point of its perfection." For the first time "wit, beauty, strength, skill, merit, talent" could come into their own—yet not for their own sake, but as valuable property; not for any intrinsic merit, but for their value as weapons against other men. (*Inequality,* 174) Thus the unfolding of man's most authentic impulses and powers had been actuated by his least authentic needs. Springing from dubious roots, the process of man's self-development had generated profoundly ambiguous results:

I could explain how much this universal desire for reputation, honors, and advancement which consumes us all exercises all our talents and powers, and holds them up to comparison; how much it excites and multiplies our passions; how, by making all men competitors, by forcing all aspiring mankind to run the same track, it causes failures, successes, catastrophes of every kind, every day. I could show how it is to this ardor for having oneself talked about, this furor for distinguishing oneself—which almost always carries us outside ourselves—that we owe the best and the worst things about mankind, our virtues and our vices, our discoveries [*lumières*] and our errors, our conquerors and our philosophers, in other words, a multitude of bad things and a few good ones. [189]

But although discontent had been forced on man from outside, by the exigencies of a competitive social life, it was not ultimately alien to human nature. "As soon as the potential powers of [man's] mind begin to function, imagination, more powerful than all the rest, awakens them and leads them on. It is imagination which enlarges the bounds of possibility for us, whether for good or ill, and . . . stimulates and feeds our desires by the hope of satisfying them." (*Emile*, II. 44) Thus man's unrest sprang from his deepest impulses. Indeed, its ultimate source was an impulse which Rousseau saw as most distinctively human of all: what he called *"perfectibility."* This was the quality that distinguished man most clearly from the beasts: for "an animal is at the end of a few months, what it will be all its life; and its species at the end of a thousand years is exactly what it was at the start." On the other hand, man's "faculty of self-perfection, . . . which is inherent in the species as well as in the individual, . . . draws him gradually out of his original condition, in which he might have glided through life serenely and innocently"; "with the help of circumstances, [it] gradually develops all his other faculties. . . ." Thus the capacity for change and self-development, which generated man's discontent, made him what he essentially was. For it was human nature precisely to resist and transcend any fixed, static nature: to be *historical*. It was only in modern times that man's stature and dignity as an historical being had clearly emerged.

Rousseau's celebration of man's historicity did not blind

him to the ambiguities of human history. He saw that perfectibility, "this distinctive and almost infinite faculty," was
also "the source of all man's miseries." In the course of centuries, it had generated "both his discoveries [*lumières*] and
his errors, his virtues and his vices; and at length it makes
him a tyrant *both over himself and over nature.*" (*Inequality*, 142) Thus the history of man's self-development was simultaneously a history of his self-alienation.

This ambiguity was especially vivid in the history of sexuality. Primitive men and women, Rousseau speculated nostalgically, had had no sexual problems. Sex for them had
been merely "a transient business deal [*commerce passager*]
required by nature"; "a blind propensity which, having
nothing to do with feelings of the heart, produced a purely
animal act. The need satisfied, the two sexes knew each
other no more." Gradually, as civilization progressed, a
"different kind of relationship, no less agreeable and more
permanent," developed. Men and women "began to perceive the difference between objects, and to make compari-
sons; imperceptibly they acquired the idea of beauty and
worth, which soon generated feelings of preference."
Through the ideas of beauty and worth, sexuality was transformed into love: now men and women, "seeing more and
more of each other, came to feel that they couldn't do without each other." With this a whole new dimension of self-
expression and happiness suddenly opened up for mankind.
Ironically, however, love soon generated and nourished its
own antithesis. "A tender and delightful feeling insinuated
its way into their hearts, and the least opposition turned it
into impetuous fury: with love rose jealousy; discord tri-
umphed, and human blood was sacrificed to the gentlest of
feelings." (*Inequality*, 164, 169) In Paris, the vanguard of
human development, love had been entirely drawn into *"le*

tourbillon social" (*Emile*, IV. 217)—a whirlpool of *amour-propre*, vanity, competition, aggressiveness, which seemed to devour all human feelings and actions. Here a man could not help but be "borne along from one caprice to another; [his] inclinations are so enslaved to opinion that [he] can't be sure one day what [he's] going to love the next." (*Julie*, II. 17, 255) Here even the desire for sexual pleasure had been overwhelmed by the will to social power: "in most affairs the lover hates his rivals more than he loves his mistress"; it was vanity rather than desire that urged him on. (*Emile*, V. 393) Bodies and souls alike had been commandeered as weapons in this state of war.

How far modern men seemed to have fallen from the total satisfaction which natural man could get, from the "equilibrium between desire and power" which he had enjoyed! "Lacking everything, [man was] never less miserable; for misery consists not in a lack of things, but in the needs which they inspire." (II. 44–5) And yet, this happiness, which mankind had lost forever, was somehow barren, sterile: it would "preclude the progress of our most excellent faculties," and leave the possibilities of human life unexplored. In the thick primeval forests "there would be no communication among men"; "each one, thinking only of himself, would be isolated from the rest." Like the man and woman who might meet, copulate and separate, they "would touch one another at many points, but wouldn't be united at any." Had mankind remained fixed at this point, "there would be no goodness [*bonté*] in our hearts, no morality in our actions." Moreover—and probably more important to the modern *mondains* Rousseau always addressed himself to—"our understanding would not have developed itself, we would've lived without feeling anything, and we would've died without having lived; all our happiness would've consisted in not knowing how miserable we really are." (*Manuscrit de Genève,* I.2, 283)[25] Thus modern society developed "our more excellent faculties"; it generated our ideas of beauty, worth, goodness, morality; it taught us to communicate and to unite with one another, to understand, to feel, to love, to be fully alive. Yet it kept us from using these faculties and expressing these feelings and working out these ideas in our own way; it turned them against us, and used our energy as its fuel.

Rousseau's natural man had been in full possession of himself, but a stranger and transient in the world. In the course of history men had gained both an inner and an outer world, but lost themselves. The very process that brought man's latent powers into activity forced them into rigidly defined channels of operation. Modern man could not feel at home in the world which his activity had conquered, because the range of possible human activity was circumscribed in both form and content by an acquisitive, competitive social system which he had never made. These contradictions reached their most radical extreme in the modern metropolis, where, "in the midst of so much philosophy, humanity, civilization, sublime morality, we have nothing but deceitful and frivolous appearances, honor without virtue, reason without wisdom, and pleasure without happiness." (*Inequality,* 193) In this metropolis, individuality was at once most thoroughly unfolded and most harshly repressed. Thus Paris was the ideal medium for the development of individual talent (*Julie,* II. 18, 259) or genius (*Emile,* IV. 307); perhaps more than any place in history, it was "full of original men"; and yet, "it's impossible to find

25 A preliminary, unfinished version of the *Social Contract,* written around 1756. Roman numbers designate the Book, Arabic numbers the Chapter and page. Pages are cited from *OC,* III.

them here, because no man dares to be himself." (*Julie*, II. 17, 250) The modern age was, above all, an age of paradox: an age in which the potentialities for the self-development of men had multiplied to infinity, while the range of their authentic self-expression had shrunk to nothing.

How could men break the chains of this paradox, and become authentically themselves? "What, then, is to be done? Must we destroy societies, abolish mine and thine, and return to the forests to live among bears?" Although nostalgia motivated and pervaded much of his greatest work, Rousseau understood that "for men like myself, whose passions have destroyed their original simplicity," it would be neither possible nor even desirable to roll back the wheel of history and restore that primitive unity of being which Natural Man enjoyed. (*Inequality*, 207) It was inevitable that, to a modern man, the static, narrow, isolated existence of the natural man should seem a living death. (*Manuscrit*, I.2, 283) Rousseau, although radically critical of modernity, always situated himself very firmly within it. It was essential, he believed, to "take men as they are and laws as they might be" (*Social Contract*, Introduction, 351): to accept and to work with the developments in human nature which modern society had brought about.

To be obliged to "take men as they are" must often have struck Rousseau as a death sentence on whatever hopes he had for man. The trouble was, as Judith Shklar formulates it, that

> if men were alone responsible for inventing and maintaining their own social misery, they could scarcely be expected to overcome conditions that they themselves had chosen to create. One could hardly expect that those who had devised their own chains would either

153

wish, or know how, to liberate themselves. If there was no need for cosmic fatalism, there was every reason to despair of mankind's own social powers.[26]

This specter has been haunting radicalism since man left Eden. Social scientists today would call it the problem of transition—or, much more resonant in French, of *"passage."* In the language I have been using up to now, how could men whose whole lives were systematically inauthentic be expected to leap into authenticity? Sometimes Rousseau hoped that this question could be avoided through reforms from above: through the actions of great men, heroic legislators, enlightened despots, philosopher-kings. However, the hold which these benevolent despots exerted on their subjects' selves was precarious and transient (Shklar works this out); more important, even if their reforms could succeed, they would bring about the repression rather than the liberation of the self. (This aspect of Rousseau's thought will be discussed in a later section, "The Politics of Inauthenticity.") Rousseau often predicted imminent, cataclysmic upheavals from below. But he did not expect that the revolution would generate any significant human progress. In the concluding pages of the *Second Discourse* he portrayed an endless cycle of "quick and frequent revolutions," of despotisms and counter-despotisms, in which the rule of naked force would be interrupted only by equally brutal counterforce. Rousseau called this situation "a new state of nature," a nightmarish parody of the first: here all individuals would

[26] "Rousseau's Images of Authority": *American Political Science Review*, LVIII, 4 (December, 1964), 919–32. Shklar's bleakly pessimistic image of Rousseau contrasts very strikingly with mine. Both, I think, are real. (Rousseau is large, he contains multitudes.) Some of these contradictions will be explored and analyzed later on. Cf. also Shklar, "Rousseau's Two Models: Sparta and the Age of Gold," *Political Science Quarterly*, LXXXI (1966), 25–51.

"become equal once again, but only because they are nothing." This would be "the extreme point that closes the circle, and meets the point from which we set out." (*Inequality,* 191) The image of the closed circle is terrifying: it means No Exit for man. As Jean Starobinski says, this sort of revolution might indeed bring "a kind of end to history, but a chaotic end: mankind would be immersed in evil without hope." (*Rousseau,* 33–6)

If there was to be any hope at all, it would have to focus on the paradoxical idea of reform from within. This meant that modern men, men without selves, would have to create selves for themselves. Yet, in Shklar's phrase, how could they "either wish, or know how," to create themselves? And, moreover, what could they possibly create these selves out of? In fact, Rousseau believed, some of modern man's most destructive and self-destructive impulses contained a hidden potential for both individual and social good: thus he thanked that obscure providential power ["*celui*"] which "enabled our happiness to be born of those very sources [*moyens*] which seemed likely to make us most miserable." (*Inequality,* 127)

One of these sources, whose importance in the modern world Rousseau was the first to understand, was *anxiety.* Modern civilization was permeated by universal and perpetual discontent. Strangely enough, however, this pervasive anxiety, rather than threatening the social structure, seemed to hold it all the more firmly together. These desperate men, grasping wildly, blindly at once for self-recognition and for self-transcendence, clashing endlessly and fruitlessly with one another, expanding and expending their spirit in vain, were playing precisely the roles their social system meant them to play. Their frenzied energies helped modern society consolidate and expand its power, in preparation for the day when it could force the whole world into its mold. Just as, in the theoretical models of eighteenth-century ideologies, private vices were metamorphosed into public virtues—

> All discord harmony not understood,
> All partial evil universal good . . .

so, by the same logic or magic, private anxiety seemed to generate public health.[27] In any case, it produced public wealth: the most highly developed sectors of the European economy prospered and expanded throughout the eighteenth century. Personal insecurity seemed only to drive men harder to attain social "success"—a goal which, since it was understood as purely relative to the success of other men, could never be securely attained—and so, to integrate them ever more perfectly into the social system. How, then, could all this anxiety, which seemed so conveniently "functional" within the system, help men to outgrow and eventually overthrow it? This could happen only if modern men came to feel that their society could not possibly fulfill the needs which it itself had instilled in them. Then their anxiety and

---

[27] According to Ernst Cassirer, Rousseau "placed responsibility [for evil] at a point where no one before him had looked for it. He created, as it were, a new subject of responsibility. . . . This subject is not individual man, but human society. [*The Question of Jean-Jacques Rousseau*, translated and edited by Peter Gay (New York: Columbia University Press, 1954), 75.] The first sentence, so far as I know, is true, but the whole is misleading. The early English and French political economists all posited some sort of social system, operating under laws of its own, which circumscribed and to some extent determined the actions of individuals: that is the whole point of the "invisible hand" metaphor so dear to the classical economists. This is the leitmotif in Elie Halevy's study, *The Growth of Philosophic Radicalism*, translated by Mary Morris (London: Faber and Gwyer, 1928.) Rousseau was original in exploding the economists' belief that this system was inherently beneficient, in exposing and explaining some of its most monstrous results.

their desire to perfect themselves would drive them harder than ever to change a world which they had not made and did not want.

In order to give modern men a sense of *systematic* discontent, a feeling that their self-perfection was being blocked by the whole structure of their society, Rousseau appealed to a quality which the generation after him would call the moral imagination. This quality had grown out of and along with "this universal desire for reputation, honors and advancement which consumes us." (*Inequality*, 189) The moral imagination was a unique fusion of deep thought and deep feeling. It was what enabled men to develop ideas of good and evil, to create moral categories and codes, to identify themselves sympathetically with other men, to discern meanings and consequences, to make moral judgments in the concrete situations of their daily lives. Up to now, however, like all other human qualities, it had been channeled into the pervasive struggle for power. It had enabled men to conceive and develop their ideals of justice, honor, friendship, love, art, civilization, culture, humanity; but men had only used these ideals as *masks,* to conceal—both from one another and from themselves—the *amour-propre* that moved them all. Thus "notions of natural law . . . began to develop only after the prior development of men's passions had made its precepts powerless." (*Manuscrit,* 284) And yet, these ideals, much as men might exploit them in their actions, retained a latent and potential power in their hearts. Rousseau analyzed this in explaining why, to his initial surprise, *La Nouvelle Héloïse* had succeeded so splendidly in decadent Paris, which it denounced, but had been rejected so coldly in solid Switzerland, whose virtues it celebrated. "Do friendship, love, virtue, reign in Paris more than elsewhere? Surely not!" And yet, the Parisian metropolis developed in people "that exquisite *sensibility* which moves the heart when [friendship, love and virtue] are manifest, and makes us cherish those pure, tender and honest feelings in others which we no longer have ourselves." It was precisely this sensibility that separated him irrevocably from the Swiss peasants and burghers whose child he would often have liked to have been, and threw him back on the *mondains* of the metropolis which he tried so hard to escape: "It requires a *delicacy of feeling [délicatesse de tact] which can be acquired only through the education of the great world* to feel the fineness of the heart of which, if I may say so, *Julie* is full." The presence of this sensibility in Paris was no accident: it was integral to the character of modern man, indeed, necessary for his survival: "*Among so many prejudices and false [factices] passions, it is necessary to know how to analyze the human heart, and to disentangle the true feelings of nature.*" (*Confessions*, XI. 545–6) The very moral imagination which enabled men to use ideals to exploit one another, preserved for them a sense of what those ideals really meant. The insight which empowered them to see through one another today might drive them tomorrow to look into and see through themselves.

Rousseau's strategy, then, was to appeal to modern men on the basis of their own sensibility and awareness of life. This project was founded on the idea, not only that these men were less than perfectly integrated into modern society, but that this social system, in the course of its own development, had generated a mode of consciousness capable of transcending it. If this consciousness could be transformed into *self*-consciousness, then modern men—whose sense of themselves was inherently activistic, who strove constantly to transform their thought into action and their fantasies into realities—might be able to solve their deepest personal

158

and social problems through reforms from within. The solution which Rousseau was proposing was profoundly dialectical: he hoped to *"draw from the evil itself the remedy that can cure it."* The first step in this enterprise was negative: to "show [modern man], who thinks he's happy, how miserable he really is." This, as we have seen above, was the function of Rousseau's most penetrating psychological analysis and social criticism. The next step, which we will explore below, was positive: "to illuminate [*éclairer*] [28] his reason with new ideas, and warm his heart with new feelings, so that he'll learn that he can best *expand his being and multiply his happiness [félicité] by sharing them with his fellow-men."* Here Rousseau introduced the model of a *"Brigand feroce,"* an *"ennemi du genre humain,"* the worst of men. Even this Public Enemy might be made to understand "how *his own personal interest demands that he submit to the general will."* Then, "with a stout heart and a sound mind, this enemy of mankind would give up his hatred with his fallacies; *the very reason that drew him apart from humanity would lead him back to it.* Then he would become a good, virtuous, sensitive man. Instead of a ferocious outlaw, he would want to be the firmest pillar of a good society. "(*Manuscrit,* 286–9) Thus modern civilization could heal the worst wounds which it had inflicted upon itself.

[28] The verb *"éclairer"* could alternately be translated as "to enlighten." That would underscore the continuity, not only of Rousseau's own enterprise, but of all the Romantic thought that followed from it, with the eighteenth-century Enlightenment. I used "illuminate" above to emphasize the concreteness of Rousseau's imagery, the vividness of the light and heat which he felt within him at his most inspired moments, and which he hoped to radiate. In contemporary idiom, we might say: when he felt turned on, he wanted to turn on the world.

III

The Dialectic of Authenticity

A New Morality:
The Authentic Man

> Human nature is not a machine to be
> built after a model, and set to exactly the
> work prescribed for it, but a tree, which
> requires to grow and develop itself on all
> sides, according to the tendency of inward
> forces that make it a living thing.
>
> JOHN STUART MILL, *On Liberty*

The Tree on the Highway

FOR GENERATION after generation of political thinkers and cultural critics, since the Romantic era, the
symbolic antithesis of Machine and Tree has served to define the essential polarities and alternatives of modern life.
The Machine is understood to symbolize everything that is
rigid, compulsive, externally determined or imposed, deadening or dead; the Tree represents all man's capacity for
life, freedom, spontaniety, expressiveness, growth, self-
development—in our terms, authenticity. Rousseau, at the
very start of the Romantic age, was one of the first to use
this antithesis. But he understood, far better than most of
his Romantic successors—or, for that matter, better than his

anti- and "post"-Romantic successors—the complex and ambiguous relationship between its poles. Rousseau would certainly have agreed that man was essentially not a machine but a tree. However, he saw through the sort of naïve dualism that would simply reject the machine for the sake of the tree. He understood that the mechanical institutions and forms of behavior which modern men were coming increasingly to dread had been created, after all, by these modern men themselves. The paradox of modernity was that the machine was an outgrowth of the tree.

Rousseau tried to look this paradox in the face and live with it: to think it through, as we would say today, dialectically. He aimed neither to integrate modern men into the machine, nor to blow it up. He felt that, even when these men seemed completely within its grip—in the swing of things, as our own idiom puts it vividly—impulses and ideas were germinating within them which could burst the bonds that the machine imposed on them, and control its energy for their own happiness and growth. He articulated these impulses and developed these ideas with great originality and brilliance. The tree had generated the machine as an expression—although an ambiguous and dangerous expression—of the life within it; ideally the machine should not kill it, but help it live.

Rousseau's sense of what had happened to human nature in his time, and of what might happen to it in the future, emerges most vividly from the first page of the first book of *Emile,* a page that sets the scene, defines the historical framework, for his whole educational project. The book begins with the notorious maxim that "Everything is good as it comes to us from the hands of the author of things; everything degenerates in the hands of man." Rousseau goes on to qualify this: he does not mean to say that everything man has ever done is a mistake; but he does mean to focus on the innate human perversity that refuses ever to leave anything alone. Thus man "forces one kind of soil to nourish the products of another, one tree to bear the fruits of another. He mixes and confounds the climates, the elements, the seasons. He mutilates his dog, his horse, his slave. He doesn't want anything the way it was made by nature—not even man himself. He has to break himself in, as he breaks in a horse; he has to shape himself, as he shapes a tree in his garden." It is inherent in man's nature, then, to make all things new, including himself. This idea shatters the primitivist equation of man's nature with man's origin. To seek to make man natural simply by keeping him from developing civilized impulses—to educate "negatively," as Rousseau himself sometimes aimed to do—must end in disaster. At this point, Rousseau uses one of his profoundest images to formulate what is to be done:

> Man's nature is like a young tree which, by chance, has been born in the middle of a great highway. If it were left to itself the traffic would crash into its every limb, mutilate all its senses, and kill it before long.
>
> Tender, anxious mother, I appeal to you. You know how important it is to separate this newborn tree from the great highway, to protect it from the crushing force of social conventions! Cultivate and water the young plant before it dies; one day its fruit will reward your care. First of all, you must build a wall around your child's soul. . . . [*Emile,* I. 5–6]

The predicament of modern man is that of a tree on the highway. Man's nature, as Rousseau sees it here, has not been destroyed; but it finds itself thrown into a totally unnatural world. If human nature is to survive, it will have to learn to live in such a world, for this is now the only world there is. Indeed, it must learn to nourish itself on such a world, for its very roots are in the middle of the highway, the road which history has laid out.

"Tender, anxious mother, I appeal to you." It is important to understand whom Rousseau was appealing to, and why. Rousseau was sure that modern society was full of sensitive, tormented men and women who could respond to his ideas. But these men and women were scattered, isolated, fragmented individuals, devoid of collective power. Even if every man personally wanted to be himself, "Prejudices, authority, necessity, example, all the institutions in which we find ourselves submerged" would resist it. The only way to affect people, then, was to reach into the most hidden, most private corners of the self. Rousseau began with what he felt was the least socialized relation between people—and hence the most genuine one: the union of mother and child. "The laws, always concerned more with property than with people, because their object is peace and not virtue, give too little authority to the mother." In answer to conventional moralists, who claimed that mothers spoiled children with all their affection, Rousseau painted in lurid colors the social alternative to this natural affection:

> it's worse to deprave them, as you do. The mother wants her child to be happy, now, and she's right. . . . The ambition, the avarice, the tyranny, the mistaken foresight of fathers, their neglect, their cruel insensitivity, is a thousand times worse for children than the blind tenderness of mothers. [I. 5]

Rousseau hoped to reach this hypothetical mother at a moment when she felt farthest from the repressive norms of her society, closest to her deepest feelings—feelings not only for

166

her child, but for herself. At such a moment she would understand the need to "build a wall around [her] child's
soul," to "protect it from the crushing force of social conventions." Without this basic security, there would be no
way for the self to survive.

Thus it was urgent that a wall be built around the self.
The wall, however, was not meant to put the self outside
modern society, but rather to make the self strong enough to
live freely and fully within it. "Remember, first of all, that
when I aim to form a natural man, I don't mean to make
him a savage and relegate him to the woods." In the beginning, before highways and history, all trees grew in woods.
In the long course of history, roads and cities have been
built up where the woods used be. It would be fruitless to
pine for the old woods, because they are simply not there.
But it would be equally disastrous for the human tree to try
to find (or found) new ones, since that would mean, after
all, to pull up its own roots. Instead, Rousseau argues,

> The important thing is that, living in the whirlpool of
> social life [*le tourbillon social*], he should not let him-
> self be carried away by the passions and prejudices of
> men. Let him see with his eyes and feel with his heart;
> let no authority govern him except the authority of his
> own reason. [IV. 217]

The image of the whirlpool, like that of the highway, emphasizes the violent energy, at once creative and destructive,
of modern life. The highway can crush the self, the whirlpool can pull it apart or carry it away; but both can carry
man farther, faster, higher, deeper than he has even been.
Indeed, modern society forces men to become more distinctively individual than ever, simply in order to survive.
Thrown into a vortex, men must develop a deep and deli-

cate sensitivity to the forces that swirl around them; they must learn to feel and to understand, to respond and to interpret.

> This delicacy of perception engenders a spirit of discussion, for the more subtly we distinguish between things, the more things there are for us. This subtlety makes tastes at once more delicate and less uniform to the point where *there are as many tastes as there are people.* Through disputes over taste, insight and understanding [*lumières*] are enlarged; this is how men really learn to think. Thus it is the spirit of society that develops a thinking mind, and carries man's vision as far as it can reach. If you have a spark of genius, go spend a year in Paris: *you'll soon be everything you can be, or else you'll never be anything at all.* [IV. 307]

The climate of modernity at once threatens the tree of man with mutilation or destruction, and holds out a promise of unprecedented fruitfulness. Rousseau is terrified by this vast, ominous energy, but he does not want to flee it; he wants men to appropriate and absorb it for their own life and growth. But this can be done only if modern man develops an inner strength that will enable him to stand and to move on the highway, in the whirlpool, without being crushed or pulled apart or carried away: a strength that will be authentically his own.

> To be something, to be himself, and always at one with himself, a man must act as he speaks; he must always be decisive as to what course to take, he must take that course proudly and follow it to the end. [I. 8]

Authenticity, then, is what Rousseauvian education aims to teach.

"To be *something,* to be *himself*": why should these two ideas be first distinguished, then juxtaposed? The syntax of Rousseau's sentences, the sequence of his thoughts, can illuminate his underlying project by revealing the concrete historical situation in which it was conceived. Rousseau thought and felt and wrote at the beginning of an epoch which was engulfed by the first great wave of modernization. This was an age in which—to paraphrase Marx, who wrote as it neared its end—men suffered not only from the development of modernity, but also from the incompleteness of that development; not only from new forms of self-alienation, but from inherited forms that survived alongside them; not only from the living, but from the dead. Traditional roles and forms of identity were dying, but dying hard. The educational system which Rousseau confronted was still basically traditional: it raised each man to occupy a fixed social role which had been ascribed to him. This policy presupposed a static social order whose present alignment would last indefinitely. Rousseau admitted that, for all its repressiveness and cruelty, such a system might at one time have at least been feasible: "If men were born attached to the soil of their country, if one season lasted all the year long, if every man grasped his fortune so firmly that he could never change it, then the established method of education might have some advantages. The child, raised for his role, never leaving it, would never be exposed to the problems of any other." However, the course of history had not only exposed this policy as immoral, but made it unworkable:

Consider the mobility of human affairs, the restless and uneasy spirit of our times, when each new generation overturns the work of the old, can we conceive of any policy more nonsensical than bringing a child up as if he would never leave his room, as if he would always have his servants about him? If this wretched being takes a single step up or down, he is lost. [I. 10]

Writing out of his keen sense of the movement of history, Rousseau proclaimed a trenchant prophetic warning to the privileged classes:

You reckon on the present order of society, without considering that this order is itself subject to inscrutable changes, and that you can neither foresee nor provide against the revolution. In my opinion, it is impossible that the great monarchies of Europe should last much longer. [III. 157]

In the face of the coming revolution, not even those who stood highest in the traditional hierarchy were secure. Even the most well-born child would have to learn that "the fate of those unhappy people" in the lowest ranks of society "may one day be his own." The imagery of Rousseau's vision was extravagantly ominous: the privileged child's "feet are standing on the edge of an abyss, into which he may be plunged at any moment by a thousand unexpected but irresistible events." (III. 185) The great fortresses and dykes of social distance, which men of privilege had used for so long at once to insulate and to define themselves, were in the process of crumbling, and could never be put together again. Thus men in traditional societies were made of "something"—but the thing that they were made of was fatal in the modern world: unable to move as the ground shifted under their feet, they would be the first to sink into the abysses that were opening up.

Modern men had been relieved of this self-destructive

"something"—but, alas, had revealed nothing within. Thus Rousseau described "a man of our day" as "a Frenchman, an Englishman, a bourgeois: he is nothing." (I. 8) Stripped of the old forms, their personalities seemed devoid of content. More pliable than any ancient Alcibiades, they were totally susceptible to social forces: at best, reeds that bent with every wind, that could be carried along by every current, picked up and used as instruments of power, or crushed underfoot when there was nothing left to use them for; at worst, inner vacuums waiting to be filled, capable of holding anything. Thus the possible forms of identity seemed to be either "something" self-destructive, or else "nothing," no self at all. But if modern man could only discover and grasp "something" that belonged genuinely to himself, then "our happiness [could] be born of the very sources that seemed likely to make us most miserable" (*Inequality,* 127); then the threatening highway would become the way to freedom and fulfillment. "First of all, you must build a wall around your child's soul. . . ." Behind the wall Rousseau hoped to recover the buried roots of man, and to liberate the hidden sources of power that lay within the self. Within the protective enclosure of education, the underground work of excavation—and liberation—could go on.

What was the buried treasure that Rousseau pursued? He described concisely what he felt to be the secret of the self:

Life is not breath, but action; to live is to make use of our organs, our senses, our faculties, every part of ourselves which gives us the feeling of our own existence. The man who has lived longest is not he who has passed the greatest number of years, but he who has most felt life. [*Emile,* I. 9–10]

The essential thing was man's capacity at once to *be* alive and to *feel* alive: to fully "use every part of ourselves" and simultaneously "feel our own existence." This dual power had never asserted itself. Natural man had "carried his whole self around with him at every moment," but his self had been narrow, shallow, undeveloped, a paltry thing. Modern man had developed all his organs, his senses, his faculties, but knew only how to use them for alien ends; they had been cut off from "the feeling of our own existence." Rousseau hoped to teach modern men to use their vastly expanded minds and deepened sensibilities to *"feel life."* All of us, he said, must learn to "throw ourselves into every hour and everything. My only set rule would be this: wherever I was, I would . . . take each day as it came, as if there were neither yesterday nor tomorrow." (IV. 317) We must pursue an unprecedented fullness and wholeness of being.[1]

In order to be authentically "himself," Rousseau said, a man would have to be "always at one with himself." It was essential to unify all human faculties, to bring man's impulses and powers together. This ideal had radical force, for all previous forms of society had fostered and exploited man's inner division. In traditional societies (and in the contemporary enclaves where traditionalism survived), the sphere in which men could act freely was rigidly circumscribed. Here their thoughts and feelings were channeled into forms of abstract fantasy which were equally circumscribed, and totally cut off from any connection with their

---

[1] In his glorification of activism, and his demand for a total engagement and involvement of the self in the world, Rousseau parts company decisively from the Stoic moralists to whom he is in many ways indebted. Long before Rousseau, Stoical thinkers tried to liberate what they believed to be man's authentic self. For them, liberation consisted in isolation, detachment from an alien world. Rousseau, more paradoxically, seeks authenticity within this world.

actual lives. In such societies, like the one in which Rousseau grew up, the human imagination developed in a
strictly dualistic way: it generated visions of transcendent
bliss, which diverted men from their immediate misery; it
"liberated" the head by cutting it off from the body, which
could then be more effectively nailed down in its place.
Modernization brought this particular psychological split to
an end. In modern society the imagination became concrete,
and its fantasies emerged as ideas to be acted out in the
world. But modern men were divided against themselves
even more profoundly than before: their sensitivity and imagination, their thought and action, all were abstracted
from the feelings and needs of the self, and directed instead toward the ends which the marketplace imposed. Men
could think or do anything, if it helped them to acquire
money and power; but they could not think or do anything
that did not.

Rousseau believed that men were born with a unity of
self which conventional socialization beat out of them, but
which radical education could recover and reinforce. Observing the behavior of children, he saw that "Man's first
natural impulse is to measure himself with everything that
surrounds him, to discover in every object he sees all those
qualities which might concern him; his first study is a kind
of experimental physics for his own preservation." The
child, as he first came into the world, was uniquely fit to
perceive "the physical relations between things and himself." The immediate experience of children revealed that
"our first teachers are our hands, our feet, our eyes," indeed,
that "everything that comes into the human mind enters
through the gates of his senses," and that "man's first reason
is a sensuous reason [*une raison sensitive*]." If nature took
its course, this sensuous reason would "serve as the founda-

tion for intellectual reason." [2] Society, however, in its effort to constrict and condition its members, tried to destroy this natural form of reason and to "substitute books for senses." In fact this substitution "does not teach us to reason, it only teaches us to use the reason of others." (II. 89–90) The movement toward greater and greater abstractness was meant to accustom men to accept a whole system of socially approved norms and modes of behavior which were abstractly "given" to them but which their feelings would condemn. Behind the wall, Rousseau would work to keep the child's "sensuous reason" alive, so that the growth of his mind should stem from it. Emile would learn to develop his ideas out of his own experience; thus, at first, he would "have few ideas, but those few would be thoroughly grasped." His vocabulary would be limited; but he would not, like so many children of his time, "have more words than ideas" and "know how to talk about things that he doesn't know how to think about." (I. 40) He would "know nothing by rote, but a great deal by experience"; would "know how to speak only one language, but [would] understand what he is saying." (II. 124) The teacher should "follow rules which are just the opposite of the established ones: instead of taking your pupil far away—into other places, other climates, other centuries, to the ends of the earth, and even into the heavens—

[2] Rousseau believed that the man of genius developed precisely this way: the genius was he whose mind remained closest to nature. This idea became one of the fundamentals of romantic aesthetics in the generation after Rousseau. Here, as elsewhere, his horizon was wider than that of most of his successors: he saw the operation of "natural" genius most vividly in the "natural" science they despised. Thus "Bacon, Descartes, Newton, those teachers of mankind, themselves had no teachers. What guide could have taken them as far as their sublime genius carried them?" The genius taught himself as the child did: "It was from the obstacles they met with at first that they learned to exert themselves, and drove themselves to cross the vast spaces they covered." (*Arts and Sciences,* 29)

you should keep him to himself and to what affects him immediately. Then you'll find that he's able to perceive, to remember, and even to reason; this is the order of nature. As a sensuous being becomes active, he gains a discernment proportional to his strength." Emile should learn first of all to grasp what goes on around him, so that he knows how "to judge, to use forethought, to reason in everything that relates to him directly." He might "not know anything about the way things are done in the world, but he really knows about what touches him." His "mind and body [will] move together," reciprocally, "with each one guiding the other." Thus, "acting according to his own ideas, and not anyone else's, he unites thought and action." Every child, if he were only taught to explore and to penetrate his own immediate experience, could attain "what is generally thought to be incompatible, though in fact most great men have achieved it: a union of power in body and soul, the intellect of a sage and the vigor of an athlete." (II. 82–4) His ideas would always be in touch with his feelings, so that he could at once "work like a peasant and think like a philosopher." (III. 165)

No one understood better than Rousseau how important childhood experience could be in forming and orienting the mind of man. This meant, however, that the child's mind was in danger of becoming fixated on its formative experiences, and unable to respond to new demands and possibilities. The name of the danger was habit. The essence of habit was imitation; and "Imitation has its roots in our desire to escape from ourselves." (II. 68) This desire moved men to lock themselves into the most oppressive of traditional roles. Thus the typical peasant, exploited as he was, nevertheless "has always done what he was told, what his father did before him, what he himself did in his youth; he is the creature of habit, he spends his life almost like an automaton on the same tasks; habit and obedience have taken the place of reason." By contrast, Rousseau's ideal savage, bound by no traditions, confronting the problems of existence without any form of mediation, "is tied to no one place, knows no law but his own will. He is therefore forced to reason at every step he takes. He can't make a move, can't take a step, without working out the consequences." Exposed to a continuous succession of new challenges from his environment, the savage was actually forced to develop himself. Ironically, it was just this prototypically "natural" situation that could best prepare men for that most unnatural of situations, "the life of civil society [la vie civile]." Such a life "is so complex, so unnatural, so subject to accidents and revolutions, that it is dangerous to let a man grow accustomed to uniformity to the point where it becomes necessary for him. No doubt he must subject himself to rules. But the most important rule is this: be able to break any rule if the necessity arises." Hence the teacher who hoped to educate his pupil for modernity would "Leave him at first to the law of nature without hindrance; but never forget that under our conditions he will have to rise above that law. . . ." (94) By learning to act as if he were alone at the beginning of history, modern man could learn to keep himself together "under our conditions," at the climax of history.

In order to keep the child's mind from freezing itself into fixed, habitual patterns, the teacher would have to keep the environment as open and fluid as possible. "The only habit the child should contract is that of having no habits." From earliest infancy, therefore, regular schedules were to be avoided: "let him not want to eat, sleep or do anything at fixed hours, nor should he be unable to be left alone by day or night." A man who has been educated this way "doesn't know the meaning of routine, custom, habit. What he did yesterday has no control over what he is doing today. He follows no rule, submits to no authority, copies no pattern, and speaks or acts only as it suits him [*comme il lui convient*]." (II. 125) The present and the future of the authentic man would be freed from the burdens of the past, controlled entirely by the self's own desire and choice.

Children of the Future: Community Through Individuality

Rousseau's vision of a type of man who could change and evolve within a perpetually changing and evolving world, while sustaining a core of self-identity, became the basis of a new morality. One of the perennial objections to ethical individualism, from ancient times to our own, has been that it licenses each man to use and exploit other men as means to his personal ends. Against this objection, Rousseau advanced the idea that the cruelest things men did to one another stemmed not from "selfishness" but rather precisely its opposite: from an inadequacy, an emptiness of self. *"All wickedness,"* he argued, *"comes from weakness."* This connection was most clearly visible in the life of the child. "From his own weakness, the source of his first feeling of dependence, springs the later idea of rule and tyranny." (I. 33) The child was unable to fulfill his own desires; he could satisfy himself only through the mediation of others. His earliest relationship with adult authorities prepared him for the authoritarian society that awaited him when he grew up. "We do what he wants or we make him do what we want; we submit to his whims or we subject him to our own." Any child would quickly learn that "There is no middle course; he must rule or obey. Thus his earliest ideas

177

are those of domination and submission. He commands before he can speak, he obeys before he can act. . . ." (15–6) Rousseau hoped to provide a new way: *"Make man strong and he will be good. He who could do everything would never do wrong."* (33) If each man ceased to need other men to tell him who he was, one of the primary sources of conflict and aggression would be overcome. The closest communion among men, then, could be built not on self-denial but on self-affirmation, not on the individual's weakness but on his strength.

"Make man strong and he will be good." In order to make the child strong, it would be necessary to restrict him in certain ways at first; without the restrictions Rousseau proposed, the child's capacity for free expression and self-expansion would never be able to develop. It was essential to discourage "those wishes which [children] cannot carry out for themselves, those which others must carry out for them." This did not mean that adults should give nothing to the child, or do nothing for him. What it meant, in practice, was that "There is only one of the child's desires which should never be complied with: the desire to make men obey him. Hence, whenever they ask for anything, we must pay special attention to their motive in asking. So far as possible, give them anything that can give them real *pleasure;* refuse them everything they demand capriciously or for love of *power."* (II. 49) Rousseau drew a sharp line between pleasure and power, parallel to his distinction between self-love [*amour de soi*] and selfishness [*amour-propre*]; he insisted that the pursuit of power was hedonistically a dead end, in the short run as well as the long:

Self-love, which concerns itself only with ourselves, is content when our true needs are satisfied; but selfish-

178

ness, which compares the self with others, is never satisfied and never can be. That is because this feeling, which prefers us to others, demands also that others should prefer us to themselves, which is impossible. Thus all the tender and gentle passions spring from self-love, while the hateful and angry passions spring from selfishness. [IV. 174–5]

As Montesquieu showed in *The Persian Letters,* the pursuit of pleasure through power inevitably failed, because it destroyed the very thing it coveted: the authentic personality of another person. For the sake of their own happiness, Rousseau urged men to renounce a desire that was both insatiable and self-defeating. Or else, through the education of a new generation, it might be possible to keep this desire from ever developing: "The spirit of these rules is to give children more real freedom and less power, to let them do more for themselves and demand less of others. If we accustom them from the first to confine their desires within the limits of their powers, they will scarcely feel the lack of what is not in their power." (I. 35) Thus the child would lose the power to manipulate other people into doing things for him; but he would not miss this power if he learned to do things on his own.

When Rousseau exhorted men to "confine their desires within the limits of their powers," his advice often sounded like exhortation to contract the horizon of human possibility and withdraw into oneself. Indeed, as he grew older, and more isolated, Rousseau came more and more to feel that way. One of the central themes of the *Emile,* however, was that the limits of man's powers actually extended much further than they thought. Thus, throughout the book, Rousseau protested the restrictions and routines imposed on children, which stunted or warped the development of their faculties. It was essential to "Give children full use of such strength as they have; they will not abuse it." (I. 35) The child's body and mind, if left to themselves, would follow their own immanent principles of growth: "All their activities grow out of the need of their constitution to strengthen itself." Hence it was vital to unchain the spontaneous energy and activity of the child, "which springs from overflowing life." (II. 50) Rousseau embraced the modern idea that education should pursue the end of personal growth and self-development; but he deplored the means through which modern society promoted this end. If modern men developed themselves, it was because they were *forced* to develop themselves in order to compete successfully for power and property. To overcome this, Rousseau insisted that, after the child had begun to reason, "let there be no comparison with other children, no rivalry, no competition, not even in running races. A hundred times better that he shouldn't learn anything at all, than that he should learn jealousy or vanity." Instead, the child should be encouraged to *"surpass himself."* Hence, year by year, "I shall note the progress he has made. I will compare these results with those of the following year, saying, 'You have grown so much; that is the ditch you jumped, the weight you carried, the distance you flung a pebble, the distance you ran without stopping for breath, etc.; let's see what you can do now.'" Encouraged to surpass himself, Emile would be "stimulated to further effort without feeling jealous of anyone." (III. 146–7) Rousseau hoped to create an incentive for growth that should come from within the personality. The *Emile* showed modern men how to be more intensely and thoroughly alive than man had ever been before.

This fullness of self could bring men closer than ever to

one another. In modern society as it was, what passed for friendship and love was generally an ill-concealed mutual exploitation: people clung desperately to each other in the hope of proving themselves, only to discard each other when the operation failed, as it inevitably did. But if men could be brought up to feel secure in themselves, a lasting peace could be established among them, and out of this peace a genuine care and love could grow. Thus Rousseau argued that, in the rare cases of true goodness between man and man, the source of this beneficence was *"the power of an overflowing soul"* which *"identifies me with my fellow-man"* so that *"I care for him because I love myself."* What brought people really together was not their sense of personal weakness and inadequacy, but rather an abundance and plenitude of self: the "overflowing" of a fountain already full. Thus "The love of man, derived from love of oneself, is the basic principle of human justice." (IV. 196–7) This ideal of justice derived its authority not from its logical coherence (as Kant would argue), but from its emotional power; the ultimate source of that power was man's sense of himself. *"Extend self-love to others and it is transformed into virtue, a virtue that has its roots in the heart of every one of us."* It was the road of self-expansion, not of self-repression, that led to the palace of virtue. "The more we generalize [self-love], the more just it becomes; and the love of all mankind is nothing but the love of justice within us." Rousseau did not distinguish sharply between justice and love; rather, he saw them as continuous phases in the growth and fulfillment of the self. As each man learned to express and enlarge himself, his capacity for identification with other men would expand, his sympathy and empathy with them would deepen, and his feeling for them would radiate outward from defensiveness to indifference to scrupulousness to beneficence to love. An impulse toward mutuality had been present in human nature from the beginning, in the instinctive, undeveloped *amour de soi* and *pitié* of the Natural Man. For centuries, this feeling had been distorted, denied, driven underground, even as man's capacity for feeling was developing. Now, however, as the culmination of human development, the feeling of mutuality could come fully into its own. And self-interest, which had done so much to turn modern men against each other, could now bring them together. "The less [another person] is dependent on us, the less we have to fear from [his] self-interest." (215) If men were brought up to feel securely at home in themselves, their self-interest alone would lead them toward an enduring community. This ethical ideal runs through Rousseau's whole life and works. In his last, unpublished work he formulated it decisively: "It is power and freedom that makes excellent men. Weakness and slavery have only made wicked men." (*Rêveries* VI. 1057)[3] He who cared for his own authenticity could be counted on to care for the authenticity of others.

Rousseau knew how to evoke and to articulate the pervasive discontent that permeated modern civilization, but he did not know how to convert this personal discontent into the political power which alone could transform that civilization. He held up to modern men the ideal of a life that would be at once more individual and more communal, a life in which every man could best "expand his being and multiply his happiness by sharing them with his fellow-men." (*Manuscrit,* I.2, 288) But this ideal community seemed to have no prospects of becoming actual, unless perhaps in some vague future which could not even be imag-

---

[3] *Les Reveries du promeneur solitaire.* Roman numbers designate the chapter (promenade), Arabic numbers the page in *OC,* I.

ined, let alone anticipated. Rousseau's one clear hope was that, if modern men responded to his ideas, they might very gradually reform their society from within through the education of future generations. But serious difficulties lay in the way of anyone who would follow Rousseau's educational program. Emile and Sophie might be brought up to be themselves, but when they grew up they would grow into a society built on self-alienation. How would these children of the future live in the present? When the trees were grown, and the protective walls came down, the highway would still be as menacing as ever.

Survival in the Present: An Amiable Foreigner

In order to live on the highway, Emile would have to understand, first of all, the needs and motives by which other men were driven—needs and motives which drove them out of themselves. Thus an education for authenticity would have to be an education in inauthenticity. Rousseau explained this through another of his primary metaphors: the theater. When the child reached adolescence, and it was finally "time to show him the exterior of the great stage" of modern society, it was essential that he should "already know its hidden workings." If he only knew how to see through personal and social façades, to distinguish action from acting out, he would be able to take care of himself very well. Emile might be "led astray by his passions"; but this was far less dangerous to the self than being "led astray by the passions of others." (*Emile*, IV. 292) Rousseau believed that human passions could balance and regulate themselves from within—provided that one's passions were one's own. Emile would be safe on the highway so long as he went his own way. As a man, strong and secure enough that he had no need to compete, he would still manage to distinguish himself everywhere. Without accepting the norms or values of any social group, he would know how to create a place for himself within all. Feeling sure of his identity, he would not need to flaunt his individuality in order to prove himself to others. Nevertheless, it would be clear to others that

> Emile is not at all like everyone else [*comme tout le monde*]. . . . At first his idiosyncracies [*singularités*] will be excused with the phrase "He will learn" [*Il se formera*]. But after awhile people will get used to his ways, and, seeing that he doesn't change, they will excuse him, saying "He is made that way" [*Il est fait ainsi*].

In short, wherever Emile went, he would be *"an amiable foreigner."* (IV. 304) He might get involved in the society around him, but he would never let himself be dissolved in it.

"An amiable foreigner": this meant that Emile could never really belong both to his society and to himself. His predicament here was paradoxical. It was essential for him to resist the incessant changes of circumstance which forced his contemporaries to constantly change themselves. Hence, in addition to all the ordinary pressures which all modern men experienced, he would be subject to a whole new realm of pressures which they did not know. They had never built up any integrity in themselves; his integrity of self was in perpetual danger of being battered down. Sometimes he would have to stand and fight for his right to be himself; he would have to know how to make a stand. At other times, he would need to escape in order to survive; he had to know when, where and how to go. Consequently Emile would have to be even more mobile than the modern men whose

vast mobility he despised; he would need to be more adapt-
able than ever to the world outside, in order to keep himself
intact within. His second rule of the road, then, was: always
be prepared to move, and to keep moving. This imperative
sharply restricted the range of property Emile could possess:
the primary forms of property in modern society, land and
money, were both closed off to him. The landed proprietor, the free peasant or farmer, for instance, is "dependent
on his field, whose fruits are subject to the will of others. An
enemy, a prince, a powerful neighbor, a lawsuit, may deprive him of his field; he may be harassed in a thousand
ways." Free as he might fancy himself, he was essentially "a
slave." (III. 158) Money created its own form of dependence: the need for money drew men into an endless spiral of
competition and accumulation; everyone in this system
"wants to be master everywhere"—because the only alternative within the system was to be a slave—"and is never
happy where he is." Once a man started seeing things as
commodities, it would be difficult, perhaps impossible to
stop. Rousseau described the psychological process with a
metaphor that Marx would develop systematically: it
worked like magic; it was demonic. "The demon of property
infects everything it touches." Man himself had created this
demon; but once he let it possess him, it "forced [him] to
flee from himself." (IV. 319) With land and money excluded, the man who would be himself could call his own
only what he could carry with him—on his back or in his
head. Thus it was essential that he develop some basic skill,
the ability to practice some "honest trade," one with as few
tools as possible, so that he could "depend on his labor
alone," unmediated by things or by the men who might
control them. It would have to be a trade, moreover, that
was useful everywhere and not merely ornamental—it

"must be of use to Robinson Crusoe on his island"—so that Emile would be needed wherever he went. With this kind of property, he "is ready for anything," beyond the power of things or men or societies. "If he is treated badly, his bags are soon packed and he is on his way." Skilled as "both a worker and a thinker," he would be able not only to do whatever work was needful, but to decide for himself what work needed to be done. (III. 158–65)

The other sort of property which a man could carry in his head—a property on which Rousseau fell back increasingly as he grew older—was the power of imagination. At the end of Book Four of the *Emile,* we find a beautiful evocation of the freedom of fantasy. It is the freedom of a traveler on the open road, a drifter, a Chaplinesque tramp, dreaming about the great world that is opening up before him:

> I will take possession of everything in my neighborhood that catches my fancy; no conqueror is so determined as I; I even usurp the rights of princes. I take possession of every open space that pleases me, I give them names; this is my park, that is my terrace, and I am their owner; henceforth I wander among them at will. . . . No matter if I am interrupted by hedges and ditches, I take my park on my back and carry it everywhere; there will always be space enough for it near at hand. . . . This is the spirit of enjoyment; all else is illusion, chimera, foolish vanity. [IV. 319–20]

There is certainly something noble about this vision, which affirms so beautifully the strength and indomitability of the human spirit. And yet, the beauty is pathetic, the nobility ambiguous, and the victory of the spirit is simultaneously a catastrophic defeat for the self. This vision draws an absolute dichotomy between the spirit and the world, and enables Rousseau to assert his omnipotence in the imaginative realm only by withdrawing totally from and renouncing all his claims on the real one. This imaginative but imaginary "usurpation" would pose no threat to the "rights of princes," who would remain comfortably in control of things.[4] But in laying up all his treasure in his imagination, Emile would lose more than land. For Rousseau had conceived his Emile as a man whose life was "not breath but action, the use of his senses, his mind, his faculties, every part of himself that gives him the feeling of his existence"; a man who "acts as he speaks" and "unites thought and action"; a man who would completely "throw himself into every hour and everything, . . . as if there were no yesterday or tomorrow." For such a man, to live within his mind alone, to limit his actions to basically defensive reactions—possessing a place only until its "prince" came along, and then moving on—to renounce active participation in a world in which he was uniquely equipped to act, would be to paralyze his most vital powers, to impoverish his vast potentialities, to live a life in death. Such a life might make sense as a desperate last resort in a world where the self was totally powerless. But this shut-up-ness[5] could never consti-

4 Once again, the content of Rousseau's imagery is revealing. His powerlessness in the real world generates compensatory fantasies of a conqueror's—or, indeed, a Creator's—omnipotence. Here, as in his youthful wish for "the greatest castle in Spain," the structure of Rousseau's imaginary world is simply a mirror-image of the real world, which enables him to escape much of its pain, without transcending the categories and values which are the ultimate source of that pain. Rousseau's personal regression is also a historical regression: this abstract, compensatory, essentially conservative form of fantasy is characteristic of the traditional society which Rousseau grew up in and grew away from but never fully outgrew.

5 The term "shut-up-ness" is R. D. Laing's: *The Divided Self: An Existential Study in Sanity and Madness* (Baltimore, Md.: Penguin Books, 1965), 84-5. My discussion of inauthentic strategies and responses, here and in the chapters below, is deeply indebted to Laing's great work.

tute "the spirit of enjoyment" for a man who was truly himself. For such a man, as Rousseau himself imagined him, it would never be enough merely to imagine a world of his own: he would have to go on to create one.

But where could this new world be built up? It could not be done within the boundaries or roles of any existing society; the authentic man was of necessity a perennial "amiable foreigner." On the other hand, it could not be done alone; Rousseau was convinced that no satisfaction would be deep or enduring unless it could be shared. "Exclusiveness is the death of pleasure. Real pleasures are those we share with people; we lose what we try to keep for ourselves alone." (IV. 319) Authentic action would have to be interaction. Only through unity with others could the uniqueness of the self emerge. There was a profound contradiction, then, between the human need for mutuality and the social tendency to convert all human relations into mutual exploitation. Unless this contradiction could be overcome, authenticity would remain a vain and futile dream. The only way open to modern man, the only relationship which might bring people together without the destructive mediation of society, was *romantic love*. The tree could live fruitfully on the highway only if it intertwined itself with another tree.

Romantic Love: The Primary Community

Rousseau was not the first to feel romantic love, or to articulate this feeling: it was one of the most powerful impulses in the culture of the second half of the eighteenth century; it was expressed and elaborated in a vast and often brilliant literature of "sensibility." [6] Rousseau was original

---

[6] On this literature, see Hauser, *Social History of Art*, III. 29–30 and *passim.*, and Leslie Fiedler, *Love and Death in the American Novel* (New York: Criterion, 1960), especially 3–95.

and radical in infusing this pervasive yearning with a moral force, in deepening this passionate impulse into an ethical idea. No solitary individual, no dues-paying member of society, but only a man and a woman bound together by mutual love, could hope to become "a complete moral person." (*Emile*, V. 340) Each of the lovers would have to become the other's other half, so that, "if he must leave [her], he will feel that he is far from himself." (443)

How did romantic love sustain and nourish the self? Let us examine once again one of Rousseau's most concise formulations of what it means to be authentic.

> To be something, to be himself, and always at one with himself, a man must act as he speaks; he must always be decisive as to what course he should take, he must take that course vigorously and follow it to the end. [*Emile,* I. 8]

Consider, first of all, the expression "at one with himself." To be at one with oneself, rather than divided against oneself, means to accept all one's impulses and to unify them into a coherent whole, rather than try to repress or destroy some impulses which are branded *a priori* as evil. Perhaps the main force of this ideal in Rousseau's time among the *philosophes* and their sympathizers, was to legitimize sexuality as a valid and valuable area of human experience. We saw this earlier in our discussion of *The Persian Letters*. For all his own sexual fears and anxieties—indeed, perhaps because of them—Rousseau was basically sympathetic to the modern trend toward sexual liberation and expression. At the same time, he was alarmed at the shallow, compulsive, seemingly mechanical promiscuity of "liberated" Paris, where a man could not help but be "borne along from one caprice to another"; in such an atmosphere, Saint-Preux reported with alarm, "my inclinations are so enslaved to opinion that I can't be sure one day what I'm going to love the next." (*Julie*, II. 17, 255) Here sexuality operated not as a new medium for self-expression, but rather as another phase in the diffusion and ultimate disintegration of the self. Once again, a new area of liberation had only generated a new mode of alienation. Rousseau did not want to return to the old repression. He saw sexual desire, like all natural feelings, as basically good; "it must not be destroyed, it must be controlled." (IV. 299) The only authentic form of control, for Rousseau, was self-control. But the self-control that he had in mind here did not entail a reduction of sexuality. Rather, the mutual intimacy and trust and knowledge and tenderness of romantic love was a medium in which sexuality could flow more freely—and more deeply—than ever before.

> I am not afraid to encourage in him [Emile] that lovely feeling for which he is so avid. I will paint it as the supreme joy of life, as indeed it is. I will evoke it so vividly that he will give himself up to it; and then, by making him feel the charm which a union of hearts adds to sensual delight, I will make him digusted with loose living [*libertinage*]. Thus, in making him a lover, I will make him a good man. [292]

Sexuality would be intensified and deepened by the romantic relationship, and so best satisfied even on its own terms: its "control" would also be its consummation. Love would enrich sensuality by infusing it with tenderness, respect, beneficence. In this synthesis we can also see a union of *amour de soi* and *pitié*, the two impulses which Rousseau insisted were deepest and most authentic to man, and the basis of any legitimate morality. (*Inequality*, 126, 154, 219) Thus the unity and wholeness of being which the simple Natural

Man had enjoyed as a matter of course in his primitive forests would be experienced far more deeply and intensely by
romantic lovers who could achieve it in the midst of modern
society.

Romantic love was the source of another quality essential
to authenticity: *decisiveness.* "To be something, to be himself, and always at one with himself," one seminal passage
says, "a man must . . . always be decisive [*décidé*] as to
what course he should take, he must take that course vigorously and follow it to the end." There are two separate ideas
here: first, the decision itself; second, the confrontation and
working-out of its consequences. In love, the choice might
be made in a moment; its meaning took all one's life to
unfold. These reverberations were especially deep in the
case of first love: "the first love affair between a man and a
woman is bound to produce a chain of lasting effects on the
course of their lives, effects which might be imperceptible
over the years, but which end only in death." This was because first love generally occurred at a crucial moment in
the development of the self: "the most important and difficult part of all education, the crisis that constitutes the passage between childhood and manhood." At this moment,
the youth gained the power to extract himself from the
morass of "fear, envy, greed, pride, and all the emotions
that conventional education utilizes so well"—emotions
which animated his early adolescence, but which were ultimately alien to him. He could now throw himself into what
was probably "not only his first love, but his first real passion of any kind."

> It may be the only great passion he will ever know, and
> on it depends *the final form of his character.* His mode
> of thought, his feelings, his tastes, *fixed by a lasting pas-*

sion, are about to acquire a *firmness* [*consistance*] that will be *incapable of further change.* [V. 378–9]

The youth's physical and mental energy, scattered and diffuse until now, were suddenly focused and concentrated on his beloved; all his thoughts and feelings crystallized (to borrow a metaphor of Stendhal's) around their love. He found himself faced with the most important decision he would ever have to make, one which would define the range of all his later decisions: whether or not to commit himself totally to another human being. Love alone could fuse all his feelings and powers, could pull his personality permanently together.

Finally, the romantic dyad would enable its members to "act as they speak," to be *sincere* with one another. Here we encounter again one of our central themes. I argued earlier that Rousseau's most radical indictment of modern society was not that it forced men to be insincere, but rather that it broke down that personal identity on which sincerity and insincerity alike were based. Throughout his works, most systematically in the *Emile,* Rousseau tried to show how the modern men of his time could recover the integrity of self which the simple, uncultivated Natural Man had once possessed, without giving up their own acquired feelings and powers, without retreating from the vastly expanded (and constantly expanding) horizon of their being. Only if this recovery were possible would the problem of sincerity become meaningful again.

It is precisely because Emile and Sophie are children of the future, at once thoroughly cultivated and fully in touch with their deepest feelings, that the question of sincerity arises from the very start of their romance. Thus, when boy and girl fall in love at first sight, "There is no man in the world less able to disguise his feelings than Emile. How

could he conceal himself in the midst of the greatest upheaval in his life?" But suddenly he is alarmed to feel himself
exposed to these others: "confused, embarrassed, afraid, he
doesn't dare to look around him, for fear that he'll see
himself being watched." Indeed, he'd like to make himself
invisible. Why is Emile so afraid of what Sartre calls "the
look of the other"? It is because, although he has been
brought up to feel deeply and to express what he feels, he
has also learned that the world around him is profoundly
threatened by feelings, so that it imposes drastic penalties
on them (even feelings which go unexpressed are punished
internally by pangs of guilt and anxiety), seeks to drive
them underground or destroy them entirely. Up to now he
has led a sheltered life; he is just beginning to feel himself
as a man in the world, in a world ruled by "the crushing
force of social conventions." Now, unexpectedly, in a
strange place, among strange people, he is overwhelmed by
the force of his feelings. His defensive armor drops; his
coeur is *mis à nu*. Naked, he is more vulnerable than ever
before; if he is penetrated, will he be destroyed? His desperate fantasy of invisibility is a hope for the best of both
worlds: to shed his normal inhibitions without giving up
the protection they normally afford.[7] In fact, however,
Emile need not worry, he is among friends. Indeed, it is
precisely the overflow of his feeling for Sophie that gives her
the confidence and courage to express her own feeling for
him: "she is reassured by his anxiety; she sees her triumph,
and she enjoys it." At this point, the initiative lies with
Sophie. If she wants their relationship to develop, she must

---

[7] This fantasy at least as old as Plato's tale of the ring of Gyges, has
been worked out in Ralph Ellison's *Invisible Man*, (New York: Random
House, 1952.) Ellison understands the tactical advantages that invisibility may sometimes confer, but also its ultimate psychic cost: the
invisible man cannot be loved, or hated, or recognized in any way at
all, for himself; he can give little, and can receive even less.

expose herself to him, as he has just exposed himself to her. The next morning, instead of appearing for breakfast elegantly "dressed up" [*ajustée*], she dresses plainly, casually, even carelessly [*négligée*]. The tutor-narrator, initially surprised, soon understands that she is expressing "the coquetry of true love," far more subtle and delicate than the common coquetry that "desires only to please." Her carelessness is a sign that she wants Emile to like her "not merely for her clothes, but for herself." (V. 377–9) Indeed, Sophie may even be (consciously or unconsciously) testing Emile, to ensure that it is really "herself alone" that he loves. Emile passes the test, and their romance progresses toward marriage. Suddenly the life of stern, rugged independence which he has so painstakingly built up for himself is overthrown. His tutor and companion in celibacy laments: "O Emile! what art thou now? Is this my pupil? How thou art fallen!" (394) And yet, even the tutor, sad as he is to see Emile slip out of his reach (and the author, reluctant to see his fantasy almost ended), must admit that this is where his education for authenticity has been leading: "Is he really changed? No, *he has all the more reason to be himself.*" (396) Romantic love would give recognition and support to authenticity at its most precarious moment. In the world of I-and-thou, visibility, exposure, nakedness of the self—total sincerity—would be loved and rewarded most. This prospect moved Rousseau so deeply that he could describe it only in an eschatological language which he rarely used: "I have often thought that if the happiness of love could be prolonged in marriage, we would have paradise on earth." (440)

There might seem to be some inherent tension between this paradisic idyll and the modern world Rousseau actually lived in. If modern men and women were open, fluid, dynamic, infinitely expansive beings, how could they live monogamously? Was it not both unrealistic and humanly destructive to expect such permanence in a world that was a whirl of change? It was for just such a world that Rousseau's ideal of romantic love was conceived. This sort of love could help to anchor the personality in a world that threatened to sweep it away; once anchored, the self could explore the possibilities of modernity without being pulled apart by it. Moreover, belonging to each other exclusively, and being together alone, could enable men and women to get into one another—and hence into themselves—more deeply than they could otherwise do. Thus Saint-Preux writes Julie: "My love for you must grow and expand incessantly as I discover more of your charms; you are an inexhaustible source of new feelings which I could never have imagined! What new delights my heart has experienced through you." Again, "let us animate all nature; it's dead without the fires of love." (*Julie*, I.38, 115–17) The image of spreading fire here, like the image of flowing water elsewhere in Rousseau's writings, emphasizes the elementally, organically dynamic character of love. This inherent dynamism marks Saint-Preux's love as archetypally modern. Rousseau believed that the self, every individual's self, bore infinite, inexhaustible riches within it. Only by being together alone could men and women create the climate of mutual trust and intimacy that the self needed before it would give up its buried treasures.

Rousseau was well aware that romantic love, as he understood it, would inevitably bring the lovers into conflict with their society, which had plans of its own for them. But while most romantic writers understood this conflict as a clash of love and duty, Rousseau insisted that love generated its own form of duty. He had argued, first of all, that the root of virtue was love of oneself; and secondly, that the romantic dyad was the form of human association which brought the self most fully into activity. It followed from this that romantic love was the primary source of moral obligation, and that the mutual commitment which lovers made to one another, and to their relationship, was the first and most binding social contract. This idea emerges most vividly in the *Nouvelle Héloïse*. After the young lovers have secretly slept together and pledged themselves to one another, Julie torments herself with guilt; to atone for her supposed sins, she contemplates rejecting Saint-Preux, the man she loves, and marrying Wolmar, the aristocrat her father is trying to force on her. Saint-Preux insists that her guilt is misplaced: their love is expressive not of immorality, but rather of a new morality.

> Be more just to yourself, my darling, and see things with an eye less prejudiced against the sacred bonds which your heart has made. Weren't you following the purest laws of nature? Didn't you freely enter into the holiest of engagements with me? It was no crime to have consummated [*fait*] your love, but it would be a crime to violate it. The only offense against honor which you could commit would be to marry another man. Be mine forever, and you will be innocent. The tie that binds us is legitimate; the only crime you could commit would be the infidelity that would break it. From now on only love can guarantee your virtue. [I.31, 100]

"Only love can guarantee your virtue": the noblest virtue, then, was loyalty to love, fidelity to a mutual commitment freely and lovingly made. It was essential to be faithful to "the sacred bonds which your heart has made" in order to be "just to yourself"; and the self was where justice as well as love began.

If the romantic lovers could stay together, they would

196

support and sustain each other's authenticity against all the pressures of a hostile world. But even if they were pulled apart, it was vital for them to remain separately loyal to their love; only by continuing to affirm this love could the self uphold its integrity alone. Julie not only rejects Saint-Preux, but works hard to blot her feeling for him out of her mind (we will examine her project in detail later on); her lover, however, refuses to make it easy for her. He makes it clear where he stands in a way that forces her to come to terms with what she has done—done not only to him but to herself. "Julie, can you have forgotten my vows along with your own? *I have lost everything; only my good faith remains to me;* and I will preserve it till the day I die. I could not live for you; I will die alone and free." (VI.7, 679–80) Saint-Preux, as we see him here, at the end of the story, is not a happy man—but he is his own man; he has no place in the world, but at least he knows who he is; deprived of his woman, he is naked with himself, but he is not ashamed. His love has brought him a dignity which the loss of his loved one cannot take away.

From Mystique *to* Politique

If the lovers managed to keep themselves together, their problems would be only just beginning. Where would they go? What would they do? True, they could live like foreigners or fugitives for a while, drifting and driven on the open road. But as soon as they felt the need to stop running and settle down, they would have to confront a society whose structure negated everything they hoped to do and to be. They were surrounded by "civil relations which place you at the discretion of others, and which force you, in order to escape from scoundrels [*fripons*], to become a scoundrel yourself"; they were in constant danger of becoming "dependent on men whom you despise." The corrupt and self-destructive relationships they feared permeated trade, finance, the army, the civil service, the whole social system: there was "not one [vocation] that does not place Emile in a precarious and dependent position, and force him to regulate his morals, his feelings, his conduct according to the examples and prejudices of others." This bleak prospect might well move Emile to renounce the vast possibilities of the modern world, and to aim only "to live in independence with the woman I love, gaining health and a good appetite by my day's work." He might decide that "the only property I desire is a little farm in some quiet corner. . . . Give me Sophie and my land, and I will be rich." But even then, his tutor warned him, modest as these goals might seem, "such treasures are rarer than you think." There was no corner so quiet that the problem of authenticity would not arise in it.

A field of your own, dear Emile! Where will you find it? In what corner of the earth can you say "Here I am master of myself and of what belongs to me"? . . . Who knows where to live independent and free, without treating other men badly and without being treated badly oneself? Do you think it is easy to find a country where one is always allowed to be an honest man [*honnête homme*]? If there is any safe and lawful way of living . . . without dependence on others, it is, I admit, to live by the work of our hands, by the cultivation of our own land; but where is the state in which I can say, "The earth I dig is my own"? Before choosing this happy spot, make sure you will find the peace you desire; beware lest an unjust government, a persecuting religion, perverse customs, should disturb you in your home. . . . Take care that you can live right without having to pay court to bureaucrats, to judges, to priests, to powerful neighbors, to scoundrels of every kind. . . . Above all, protect yourself from annoyance by the rich and great; remember that their estates may anywhere adjoin your Naboth's vineyard.

Emile stood at a crucial point in his life. He was finally *"tout formé,"* "master of himself," "master of his own person." He and Sophie were about to find themselves "alone in society," thrown back on their own resources. It was imperative now to "know what manner of man [*quel homme*] you want to be." At this moment, however, Emile learned that he was not yet equipped to make such a decision, that there was a whole dimension of human life which he knew nothing of: the *political.* For it was only a political community, a just state, that could give him the protection he needed to live a life of his own. But what sort of political institutions did the state require in order to serve this end? Exactly what was an individual entitled to claim from the state as his right? What was the state entitled to expect in return? How could this ideal state be brought into existence? Rousseau had begun his educational project by avoiding politics and appealing to isolated individuals in their private lives. Now, ironically, it turned out to be impossible for the individual to settle securely into his private life until, "after having considered himself in his physical relations with other beings, and in his moral relations with other men, he has learned to consider himself in his civil relations with his fellow-citizens." (*Emile,* V. 419–21) Thus the *mystique* of romantic love could be fulfilled only through the *politique* of the Social Contract. Two trees would stand no better chance than one, until the highway was made livable for all.

A New Politics:
The Authentic Citizen

> We must illuminate his reason with new
> ideas, and warm his heart with new feel-
> ings, so that he will learn that he can best
> expand his being and multiply his happi-
> ness by sharing them with his fellow-men.
>
> ROUSSEAU, *Social Contract,*
> original version

> Where the modern state has reached its
> fullest development, man leads—not only
> in thought, in consciousness, but in actual-
> ity—a double life. . . .
> Human emancipation will be complete
> only when the real individual man has
> taken back into himself the abstract citi-
> zen; when, as an individual man, in his
> everyday life, in his work and in his rela-
> tions with other men, he has recognized
> his own personal powers [*forces propres*]
> as social powers.
>
> MARX, "On the Jewish Question"

ROUSSEAU'S WRITINGS on the state are permeated
by radical contradictions which have perplexed readers for over two centuries. Sometimes he envisions political
life as a medium for self-expression; at other times, the pur-

pose of politics is said very explicitly to be self-destruction. Rousseau is often accused of being a theorist of totalitarianism, and indeed (as we shall see later in detail), he often *is* a theorist of totalitarianism; but his political theory just as often points in a totally opposite direction, toward a brilliant statement of what I have called the politics of authenticity.

Sometimes the extremes meet, and he seems to point in both directions at once. Thus, at the start of the *Emile*, we are told that the ideal man whose education Rousseau is about to describe is far from an ideal citizen; indeed, the only way to make him a citizen is to tear his manhood down. Between these polar antitheses "no harmony is possible. Forced to combat either nature or social institutions, you must make your choice between man and citizen, you can't have both." The alternatives posed here are stark and bitter. Political community can arise only over the individual's dead body—or, rather, his dead soul. Either/or: there is no third possibility.

> The natural man [*l'homme naturel*] exists entirely for himself. He is the numerical unit, the whole; he enters into relations only with himself or with men like him. The citizen [*l'homme civil*] is only the numerator of a fraction, whose value depends on the denominator: his value depends on the whole, that is, on society [*le corps social*] Good social institutions are those best fitted to make men unnatural [*dénaturer l'homme*], to take away his absolute existence and give him a relative one, to absorb the self into the communal whole, so that each individual no longer regards himself as one, but as part of a larger totality, and is aware only of the whole. A citizen of Rome was neither Caius nor Lucius, but a Roman. [I. 7]

The sensibility that underlies this passage is about as radically totalitarian as we are apt to find anywhere. It is so total that it thinks of everything: it makes a point, as ancient Rome would never have thought to do, of taking away an individual's very name. On the very next page, however, Rousseau seeks a way out of the dualism of individual *versus* community, a road to virtue that will not need to be paved with so much human sacrifice. Thus he characterizes the age he lives in as one in which every man is "always in contradiction with himself, always oscillating between his inclinations and his duties, neither man nor citizen, no good either to himself or to others. Such is the ordinary man of our day, an Englishman, a Frenchman, a bourgeois: he is nothing." Behind this formulation lies the idea that the unfitness of modern men for citizenship and their unfitness for manhood spring from the same source: the truth of their obsessive "selfishness" is an inner bankruptcy, an emptiness of self. Rousseau speculates that if these men can be renewed at the source, both their infirmities can be healed at once. How, he asks, "can a man live for others if he is brought up to live for himself?" His answer is that a man cannot genuinely live for others *unless* he is educated to live for himself. *"If these two aims could be united into one, we could resolve man's self-contradictions, and remove the one great obstacle to his happiness."* (I. 8–9)

Here we see Rousseau at his most insistently paradoxical. First he says that man and citizen, the ideal of individuality and the ideal of community, cannot be harmonized. Then, a moment later, he says that the only hope for man *or* citizen lies in a synthesis of the two; both individuality *and* community are essential to human happiness. This means that we need most to reconcile qualities that seem most incompatible; above all we must attempt what we are sure we cannot do. The task Rousseau set for himself as a political theorist was to imagine a community in which men could be freely and openly themselves, in which they could discover and express the fullness of their powers, and in which personal authenticity could be a politically cohesive force. If such a community could be formed, the wounds of modern history might be healed, and the liberating potentialities of modern life could begin to unfold.

The Maternal State: A Program for Radical Liberalism

When Rousseau was seeking to educate men to be themselves, he began by focusing on the bond between mother and child as the archetype of an authentic human relationship. In his attempt to work out a politics of authenticity, he returns to this image, and develops the vision of a maternal state. In the *Emile,* "The mother wants her child to be happy, now, and she's right"; she resists "the avarice, the tyranny, the mistaken foresight of fathers" who would manipulate the child. (I. 5) The article on Political Economy begins similarly, with a rejection of patriarchy as a political ideal. In the patriarchial family, Rousseau says, children have no rights, but only privileges granted by the father; they must subordinate their personal impulses and needs to "the principal object of the work of the whole house," which is "to preserve and increase the father's patrimony." [8]

---

[8] Rousseau was as deeply aware as anyone of the sins of the fathers. But he did not believe that their sinfulness was inherent in the human condition; rather, it was thrust on them by particular historical and social conditions. Because modern men could achieve a sense of themselves only through competition with one another, parents were forced to exploit their children as pawns in an unending struggle for power. But if a new, uncompetitive form of personal identity could be developed, parents would no longer need to manipulate their children in order to prove themselves, and the family would gain a new lease on life.

In an ideal state, on the other hand, "the wealth of the exchequer is only a means . . . of maintaining individuals in peace and abundance." (242) Such a state can be most vividly described through a maternal model:

> If children are brought up in common in the bosom of equality, if they are imbued with the laws of the state and the maxims of the general will, if they are taught to respect these above all things, if they are surrounded by examples and objects that constantly remind them of the tender mother who nourishes them, of the love she bears them, of the inestimable benefits they receive from her, of what they owe her in return, then they will surely learn to cherish each other mutually as brothers, . . . and to become in time defenders and fathers of the state whose children they will have been for so long. [261]

Thus the relation of these child-citizens to their mother-state will be direct and unmediated; it will express itself through an endless flow of nourishment, affection, love; there will be no threatening father-figure in the picture, no representative of a repressive society, to pre-empt the love of the mother and impose discipline on the sons; the children will not come into conflict with one another because the mother's bounties are infinite, there is more than enough to be shared by all. Most important, this relationship is reciprocal and dynamic: the state's overflowing beneficence will imbue its members with a basic security and strength of self that will enable them to grow up to be men; once grown, they will be ardent citizens, who will cherish and protect the mother who has made them the men they are. In the maternal state, then, the identity of citizen is meant not to abolish the power and dignity of a man, but to fulfill it;

men will not be denatured here, rather their nature will be more fully liberated and expressed than ever before.[9]

Rousseau's demand for a synthesis of man and citizen marks at once a crucial point in the history of liberalism and a breakthrough in the growth of modern consciousness. It is essential to remember that Rousseau was addressing an audience of liberals, men who regarded the state as essentially an instrument for helping individuals to fulfill their personal aims. These liberals believed that the state could best protect individuals by establishing a constitutional and legal framework within which they could all compete peaceably with one another and strive to accumulate wealth. Such a state would have to be absolute and comprehensive in its political powers, but it could afford to be limited and peripheral in its social functions. Ideally it would remain in the background, negative and invisible, guaranteeing peace and order, leaving all men free to pursue their individual ends within the framework of modern society. Rousseau was

[9] The bond between mother and child, which Rousseau never experienced, was one of the focal points of his rich and brilliant (though often anguished) fantasy life. His mother's death in childbirth engendered in him both a desperate need for maternal love and a paralyzing sense of guilt (as his mother's murderer) which often led him to abase and mortify himself before women who could satisfy this need. He addressed his first and deepest love, Madame de Warens, as "Mamma," and felt incestuously guilty about their sexual life. Moreover, he saw maternal love as paradigmatic of the relationship between man and nature. In 1765, when he was exiled and alone "like another Robinson Crusoe" on the island of St. Pierre, he exclaimed: "O Nature! O my mother! I am here under your sole protection! Here there is no cunning and rascally man to thrust himself between you and me." (Confessions, XII. 644) The Oedipal basis of Rousseau's hostility to the father-figure, only implicit in the Economy and the Emile, is embarassingly clear here. Also striking here is the child's passivity, and the static bliss he enjoys, protected by a benevolent mother nature from the cruel world of men. In the maternal politics of the Economy, however, the relationship between the mother and child is more dynamic, and the child plays a more active role: maternal love makes him a man, capable of engaging rather than escaping the world, and of taking care of his mother as well as himself.

205

very careful to spell out explicitly the assumptions and values which he shared with the liberals of his day. "What is the purpose of political association?" he asked in the *Social Contract*. His answer was brief and clear: "The preservation and prosperity of its members." (III. 9, 419–20) again, in his Encyclopedia article on Political Economy: "Far from each individual being obliged to perish for the sake of all, all [are obliged to] pledge their lives for the sake of each. . . . (*Economy*, 256) The benefits which the state owed its citizens were "rights of the state of nature" (256) which, "great as they are, belong to all men." (258) Thus Rousseau shared the liberals' view of the state as a protective instrument for individuals. Where he went beyond them was in his view of what it was that the state was supposed to protect. He insisted that in order for the state to give genuine "protection to its members," it would have to secure "respect for their persons." (257) This insistence had radical force because it opened up a vast range of problems which liberalism was reluctant to confront. It suggested that the thing which the liberals took most for granted, the integrity of the individual personality, was in fact most problematical, most in doubt. Rousseau's general theory of modernity showed that the structure of modern society, far from enabling individuals to express themselves, was itself the direst threat to individuality. This system forced all individuals to compete unceasingly for property and power, generated enormous inequalities between them, jammed them into rigid, polarized class roles, made them repress one another on pain of being repressed themselves. If liberalism wanted to be more than a screen for this repression, if it really meant to uphold the individualism which it claimed as its ground, it would have to extend itself into new, uncharted terrain. The liberal state would have to address itself to the anti-liberal society around it, and drastically reform that society from within. Political life, then, would have to be the medium through which every man could become and sustain and develop himself: a maternal state would give its children the nourishment they needed for organic growth. Such an ideal would enlarge the state's sphere far beyond what liberals had always regarded as its natural frontiers. Nevertheless, it followed legitimately from the liberal doctrine that a state's only claim to legitimacy lay in the benefits it could confer on individuals. If no previous state had demanded so much of its citizens, no state had ever undertaken to do so much for its men. Rousseau was the first theorist of radical liberalism.

For a mother who wanted her children to take care of her, it was essential that they should be able to take care of themselves. One of the most urgent aims of social policy in Rousseau's maternal state was to make its citizens economically self-sufficient. "No one who depends on others, and whose resources are not in himself, can ever be free." (*Corsica*, 903) [10] How such an economy might work was illustrated in the model, which Rousseau evoked with imaginative brilliance, of a Switzerland of bygone days. There, where men were "buried in snow for half the year," they were forced to labor with "an effort that made them robust." "Communications were always difficult, and when snow and ice cut them off altogether, each in his own hut was forced to be sufficient to himself and his family, which led to crude but happy industry. Each man in his own household practiced all the necessary arts and crafts; all were masons, carpenters, cabinetmakers, wheelwrights." (*Corsica*, 914) The exigencies of nature in effect forced men

[10] *Constitutional Project for Corsica,* in *OC,* III.

to be free, to be and to develop themselves far beyond the point they would otherwise have reached: *"each is everything for himself no one is anything for another."* (*Letter to d'Alembert,* 61) In such a setting every man, "living on his own land, succeeded in making it satisfy all his needs; being well off on what he had, he desired nothing further." This self-sufficiency liberated them from their most pressing needs for one another, needs which had generated all the most destructive and self-destructive relationships of modern social life—competition, inequality, exploitation, and total mobilization of every man's *forces propres* for a permanent state of war. "Since needs and interests did not conflict, and no one depended on anyone else, their only relations with one another were those of benevolence and friendship. . . ." (*Corsica,* 914) Once the state freed men from the worst pressures of modern society, and enabled them to be fully themselves, these men would come together far more cohesively than before.

To help its citizens help themselves, the state would have to assure their "social security," to guarantee their "welfare" [*salut*], to secure their "lives, liberty and property." In modern society as it actually operated this was a radical ideal, because it was precisely "the men in power" that these basic rights had to be secured against; it was "most necessary, . . . above all, to protect the poor from the tyranny of the rich." (*Economy,* 255–6) However, this tyranny was not the crime of a few particularly evil rich and powerful men. The source of the evil was a whole social *system* which forced all men into the roles of rich and poor, strong and weak, masters and slaves. (*Inequality,* 187) Hence, in order to provide self-sufficiency for its men, the state would have to take drastic structural measures to reorganize the economy as a whole. "It is one of the most important functions of government to prevent the extreme inequality of fortunes; not, however, by taking wealth away from its possessors, but rather by depriving all men of the means to accumulate wealth; not by building hospitals for the poor, but by securing all citizens against poverty." (*Economy,* 258) Rousseau did not want to effect this by seizing the property of the rich, for such a move would be directed only against individuals, not against the social system that was the real culprit. It would be better to leave intact the right of property—"the most sacred of all the rights of citizenship"—and redistribute wealth through progressive taxation. Rousseau particularly favored an expenditure tax designed to destroy the conspicuous consumption of the rich. (*Economy,* 263, 270–7) At the same time, the state could create incentives that would "encourage agriculture and the useful arts," while discouraging finance and commerce. It was important to do this because pecuniary wealth was "purely relative," attainable by any one man only at the expense of others; as such it generated competition and all its bitter fruits. Moreover, the value of one's money was inherently precarious; it fluctuated mercurially according to the infinitely complex movements of a vast world market that was totally beyond anyone's control. On the other hand, "natural goods" were "immediately useful to man," and so "always have an absolute value, which in no way depends on the operations of trade." (*Poland,* XI. 1007–8) By encouraging the small farmers and artisans who could produce these "natural goods," and orienting the national economy around them, an active and imaginative state could make independence economically feasible, and so enlarge vastly the space in which men might be themselves.

This desire to make men independent underlay Rousseau's demands for equality. After the French Revolution it became a staple of liberal rhetoric (and, occasionally, of liberal thought) to criticize Rousseau for having pursued equality at the expense of liberty. On his own testimony, however, he valued equality precisely as a means to liberty: "because liberty cannot exist without it." (*Social Contract,* II. 11, 391) This new equality was attainable only through "a total alienation of each associate with all his rights to the community as a whole," so that "since each man gives himself absolutely, the conditions are the same for all." In such a state "each one, in giving himself to all, gives himself to no one; and since there is no associate over whom he does not acquire the same right as he gives others over himself, he gains an equivalent for everything he loses, and an increase in power to protect whatever he has." (I.6, 360–1) However, it would be "vain and chimerical" for the state to guarantee every man equal protection of "whatever he has" so long as society was divided into haves and have-nots. Where economic inequality remained so great as to put some men's whole lives at the mercy of others, legal and political equality would never be more than a façade behind which the state could "take the part of the strong against the weak, and of him who has against him who has not. . . ." (*Emile,* IV. 198) Because "laws are always useful to those who have, and harmful to those who have nothing," legal equality would be a liberating force only in a social system in which "all have something and no one has too much." (*Contract,* I.9, 367) Thus Rousseau did not insist on any exact, quantitative equality of wealth; nevertheless, he sought to contain inequality within very strict and narrow limits. Wealth should be distributed, he said, so that *"no citizen should be rich enough to be able to buy another, and none so poor as to be forced to sell himself."* (II.11, 392) Inequality became destructive at the precise point where it forced men to lean on other men in order to take care of themselves.

In setting upper as well as lower limits to wealth, Rousseau recognized that inequality threatened the freedom of the rich as well as that of the poor. He had shown in the *Second Discourse* how inequality developed "as soon as men began to stand in need of one another." Once *some* men began trying to exploit their fellow-men, *all* men had to follow suit or else be exploited themselves. Rousseau hoped to use economic policy to bring men back to themselves, not only (as we saw above) by giving everyone the chance to be everything for himself, but also by depriving everyone of either the need or the temptation to be anything for another. Since wealth and poverty, "which are naturally inseparable, are equally fatal to the common good," the state would need to "bring these two extremes as near to each other as possible," so that society would contain "neither beggars nor millionaires." Then "Luxury and indigence would disappear imperceptibly together" and men would be simultaneously "cured of the frivolous tastes created by opulence, and of the vices that grow out of poverty. . . ." (*Contract*, II.11; *Poland*, XI. 1009) The pernicious needs which put men both onto and against one another, and so destroyed their independence, could be overcome by a policy designed to "bring all fortunes to that middle position which constitutes the genuine power of the state." (*Economy*, 277)

From Economics to Politics: Participatory Democracy

The reforms that would be necessary to give all men economic independence necessitated drastic restrictions on their economic freedom, the freedom of all men to compete

for wealth and power. Rousseau believed that these restrictions could be justified by a greater freedom for everyone
which they would bring about. This claim was based on his
analysis of the dynamics of competition. Once even one man
acts competitively, he argued, all the rest are forced sooner
or later to compete with him, even against their will, simply
to protect themselves. (*Inequality,* 164 ff.) In modern times
this predicament had been worked out to its dismal conclusion: "free enterprise" had generated a social system in
which everyone was perpetually coerced, subject to the necessity of dominating other men in order not to be dominated by them. In this state of war it would be suicidal for
anyone to disarm unless he could be sure that everyone else
would do the same; yet this certainty seemed impossible,
since everyone distrusted everyone else, and all were right;
thus everyone was caught in a fatal impasse which no one
wanted but which no one had the power to stop. Rousseau
thought that a democratic state could end the impasse by
moving all men simultaneously out of this competitive
structure, so full of pitfalls and booby traps, closing it off
forever, and opening up a new structure that would be safe
to live in. Thus radical liberalism would give legitimate
meaning to the notorious paradox: "In order that the social
compact should not be an empty formula, it tacitly includes
the agreement, which alone gives force to the rest, that whoever refuses to obey the general will shall be compelled to
do so by the whole body. This means nothing less than that
he will be forced to be free. . . ." (*Contract,* I.7, 364)

If these reforms could be put into effect, or even begun,
they would drastically slow down the metabolism of economic life. This very success would generate a whole new
range of human problems. When Rousseau set out to explain under what conditions power could be legitimate,
part of his definition of this enterprise was to "take men as

they are." (*Contract,* Preface, 351) It followed that any state from that point on which aspired to legitimacy would have to recognize and accept its citizens as the avid, restless, dynamic, perpetually striving modern men that they actually were. At the same time, however, it was essential for such a state to block off the main line of their striving: competition for wealth and power. What, then, was to be done with all the human energy that had flowed into economic activity? The solution Rousseau proposed was to create new channels for this energy, to displace and to redirect it from economic to political life.

"In a well-ordered city," Rousseau said, "every man flies to the assemblies; under a bad government no one is interested in what happens there." It was vital to create a political life that modern men would be happy to throw themselves into. In order to engage and satisfy these men, however, the state would have to give them some means of asserting and expressing themselves as individuals, "not with their purses, but with their persons." (*Contract,* III. 15, 428) Here was the one form in which Rousseau felt inequality could be justified: an "inequality of honor" that would be based on "merit and virtue," (*Poland,* III. 964–5) or, more concretely, on "actual services to the state." (*Inequality,* 222–3) Indeed, Rousseau even encouraged "competition and emulation" for civic honors. (*Poland,* IV. 968) He hoped the incentive of public honor and acclaim would encourage men to direct their individual aspirations and energies toward communal ends, to distinguish themselves in virtue. However, this inequality would have to be kept from spreading cancerously, as it would tend to do if left unchecked. Thus hereditary titles and distinctions were absolutely forbidden; (*Corsica,* 910) personal distinctions were to be made by "public acclamation" from below, not by appointment from above, so that they could not be dispensed as patronage; (*Poland*, IV. 967–8; XIII, *passim.*) political honors were not to be accompanied by financial rewards, lest men use them as springboards to consolidate just that form of power which they were meant to replace. (III. 964–5; XI. 1009) But the most crucial way in which the new competition for honors would differ from the new competition for wealth and power was that, in Rousseau's game, *everyone could win.* The success of some men was not predicated on the failure of others; there was no reason why all men could not reap the fruits of virtue. There was no guarantee that every man would become a good citizen. But there was nothing inherently exclusive about the identity of *citoyen,* nothing that would compromise the independence of any, nothing that could not be shared by all.

If men were to serve the state "not with their purses but with their persons," they would need the chance to participate actively in the governmental process. For Rousseau the most compelling reason for citizen participation was not efficiency but authenticity: to be oneself meant to shape one's destiny, to unite thought and action, to control the forces that control one's life. This is why Rousseau saw representation, even (perhaps especially) where it was truly representative, as slavery. (*Contract*, III.15, 428–30) He was never very specific about the necessary degree of participation, or about the institutional forms through which it could best operate.[11] But he left us some powerful and sug-

---

[11] On the one hand, Rousseau often distinguished the ultimate power of "sovereignty," which had to be popular, from the daily functioning of "government," which could best be left to an aristocracy. (Cf. Shklar, "Two Models," 38.) On the other hand, he circumscribed very narrowly the area of governmental discretion, and insisted that the people must give the government very specific instructions on all matters. He looked back nostalgically to the Greeks, who were "constantly assembled in the public square" (*Contract*, III.15, 430), but recognized the impracticability of such an arrangement in any modern society.

gestive images of participatory democracy. Thus he insisted
that citizens must have "enough of a share in the public
administration for them to feel at home [*chez eux*]."
(*Economy*, 258) The image of home was richly evocative for
Rousseau: home was a place where a man was always welcome, where he knew every inch and every corner inside,
where he could create a world that would be most fully his
own, where "each was everything for himself and no one
was anything for another." The other arresting image of
participation emerges vividly toward the end of the *Letter
to d'Alembert:* the public festival. Against the reality of the
modern theater, which divided people into active actors and
passive spectators, which isolated spectators from one another, which kept them all locked up, "fearful and immobile in silence and inaction," and which reinforced a repressive social and political order, Rousseau set the vision of a
spontaneous festival, in the open air, in the warm and clear
light of the sun, bringing all the people together, embody-
ing and expressing their freedom:

> But what will be the object of these entertainments?
> What will be shown in them? Nothing, if you please.
> . . . Plant a stake crowned with flowers in the middle
> of a square, gather the people together there, and you'll
> have a festival. Do better yet: *let the spectators become
> an entertainment to themselves; make them actors
> themselves. This way each one sees and loves himself in
> the others, and all will be better united.* [126]

Here a new kind of event, a new form at once in art and in
politics, came into being. Now citizens could contemplate
themselves in action, resolve the dualism into which their
faculties had been split, and achieve a new unity of self.
Each man, in expanding his personality and sharing his

215

whole being with his fellow-citizens, could see himself more fully and love himself more ardently than ever before. Here some of the most radical aspirations in both modern politics and modern art, the search for expressiveness, spontaneity, participation, community, could be fulfilled. Here, in such a community, a politically active man could *"play his own role,"* so that, *"the man and the role being the same, he is in his place."* (81) Here, finally, the two ideals of man and citizen "could be united into one," so that "we could resolve man's self-contradictions, and remove the one great obstacle to his happiness."

The synthesis of *homme* and *citoyen* was so important because, according to Rousseau, the personal needs and aspirations of the individual man could not be fulfilled except through political activity and involvement. But public life would not be able to satisfy these men unless they had a threshhold of private happiness to start from. Men whose lives lacked this happiness would be questionable political material: they would be tempted to exploit politics to settle their personal scores, or driven into apolitical apathy and despair.

> The position of the state is . . . solid only when each man feels in his place, and all cooperate for the public good, instead of wasting themselves against one another, as they do in every badly constituted state. . . . [126]

Thus, in addition to all its economic and political benefits, the maternal state would have to provide emotional and psychological benefits as well: it would have to generate sources of private "joy" which would overflow into political life and action. The one mode of happiness which Rousseau believed could generate virtue was romantic love.

216

When Emile and Sophie were ready to settle down together, the omniscient tutor warned them that they would never make it unless they belonged to a political community that could protect them from the pressures of the society around them. When Rousseau contemplated the actual prospects for romantic love in this society, the situation appeared even more dire: it was enormously difficult for romantic lovers to get together in the first place. Here, again, the paradox of modernity appeared: the very conditions which made love possible seemed to make it impossible.

> The trouble is that society, in developing men's personalities, creates class distinctions between them, but social distinctions do not correspond to personal ones, so that the more men are stratified, the farther they are pulled apart from one another. Thus we have so many ill-assorted marriages and all the evils that flow from them. Thus we can see that the farther we get from equality, the more are natural feelings altered; the wider the distance between great and small, the looser the marriage-bond; the deeper the gulf between the rich and the poor, the fewer husbands and fathers there will be. Neither a master nor a slave can belong to a family, but only to a class. [*Emile*, 369]

In the metropolis, where men were both more and less equal than ever before, the most intimate relationships were determined by calculations of advantage. Marriage was seen as an instrument with which to acquire, consolidate and increase wealth and power. Young men and women were treated—and were taught to treat themselves—as commodities for speculation in a human market. "Has my father sold me, then?" Julie cried. "Yes, he had made his daughter into a piece of goods [*marchandise*], . . . and profited at my

expense! He has paid for his life with mine!" (I.28, 94)
Thus marriage served to initiate innocent youth into the
primary experience of modern society. They began their
lives as adults by being sold; thrown into a universal market
place, they would learn gradually to sell themselves. Modernity had liberated the self, only (it seemed) to transform it
into capital. The modern development of individuality and
of *sensibilité* opened up new dimensions of personal intimacy and love; yet any genuinely personal relationship was
forced to go underground, and to define itself against all the
institutions and values of modern society. Social relations
were split into the dualism of "public" *versus* "private"; an
individual could be himself only by leading a double life.

Rousseau believed that the state could overcome this dualism by creating social conditions in which "the heart," the
source of man's most intensely and deeply personal feelings,
could express itself. This would entail, first of all, freeing
young men and women from the corporate will of their families, and giving everyone the liberty to love and to marry
anyone else. To facilitate this, Rousseau recommended festivals in which, under public auspices, the young could
come together, get to know one another, and fall in love.
"The inclinations of the children would be somewhat freer;
the first choice would depend somewhat more on their
hearts; the agreements of age, temperament, taste and character would be consulted somewhat more; and less attention
would be paid to those of station and fortune, which make
bad matches when they are satisfied at the expense of the
others." If individuals were free to marry their hearts'
choice, cutting across class lines, "these marriages, less circumscribed by rank, would prevent the emergence of parties, temper excessive inequality, and maintain the body of
its people better in the spirit of its constitution. . . ." The

218

happenings in which all men and women would show themselves to one another would "bring the people together not so much for a public entertainment as for the gathering of a big family." Thus, "from the bosom of joy and pleasures would be born the preservation, the concord and the prosperity of the republic." (*d'Alembert*, 130–1) In a maternal state, whose citizens were one big family, the dualism of private and public life could be overcome. If indeed "the only pure joy is public joy" (136), the only pure republic was one whose collective life arose out of the fullness of its citizens' individual lives. The strongest state, then, would be the one which enabled men to be most fully themselves. Rousseau was the first to understand that modern youth, who yearned so ardently for both individuality and community, for both private and public happiness, would be the ideal clientele for such a state, if only their romantic longings could be developed into political aims.

Rousseau's most vivid and concrete vision of such a community occurs early in the *Nouvelle Héloïse,* in Saint-Preux's idyllic account of a visit to the country of the Haut Valais, in a remote corner of the Swiss Alps. He soon discovers a society whose members enjoy an "equality of soul" [*égalité d'âme*] and radiate a "disinterested humanity" which he has never encountered in the cities of the plain. The economy of the region, he learns, is self-sufficient: there is very little money in circulation, but no need for it, because everyone's basic needs are fulfilled; for this reason, too, there is no motive for foreign exchange or trade. There is neither poverty nor luxury for anyone, but abundance for all. The people here experience their work as a pleasure. Satisfied with themselves, and with what they have, they are unavailable as a market, hence beyond the reach (and the temptations) of the bourgeois economy. Because they "know that no one could possibly be called here for business' sake," they are free of the pervasive suspicion and distrust that spread murkily over the cities below; accordingly, "anyone who comes here is welcomed." Class divisions continue to exist here, yet within a framework of equality; there are neither rich nor poor, and "servants eat at the same table with their masters." The basic social unit here is the family, but a far different sort of family from those below: here "children, once they have reached the age of reason, are the equals of their parents." The family is a vehicle for education and emancipation, not subordination and exploitation: "the same liberty reigns in the cottage as in the republic, and each family is the image of the state." Here, Saint-Preux believes, the romantic couple could settle down and be themselves. (*Julie,* I. 23, 80–1)

Once the lovers were free to live happily ever after, how would they live? Rousseau believed that, for one thing, the desperate intensity of exclusive love would gradually abate. As the lovers grew older, had children and then grandchildren, developed a widening network of group affiliations, their passion for one another would become less ardent and more gentle, and the horizon of their feelings would expand. After years of life together, Saint-Preux told Julie, "when age had calmed the first fires of our love, the habit of thinking and feeling together would generate a friendship no less tender to succeed our transports." In the course of time, "All good feelings [*sentiments honnêtes*], nourished in our youth with those of love, would fill the great void which love had left. In the bosom of this happy people [the villagers of the Haut Valais], inspired by their example, we would fulfill all the duties of humanity; we would unite in doing good; and we would not die without having lived." (83–4) Rousseau's biological image of *nourriture* emphasized the organic process through which he believed private self-fulfillment could generate public virtue. Lovers would come to care for their fellow-citizens by a natural growth and development of their love for themselves and for one another. Here, then, men could become both more private and more public than men had ever been before.

The politics of authenticity demanded radically liberal social reforms designed to make men free and equal, happy and beneficent. But these reforms were only a start; they would be valuable only insofar as they enabled individuals to express their authentic personalities, to develop all the latent spontaneity, individuality and creative power that lay within them. However, even the freest institutions might prove to be disappointing; ironically, they might even serve to repress the very human energy they were meant to release. Rousseau confronted this nightmarish possibility at the very end of his life, in the Sixth Promenade of his *Rêveries du promeneur solitaire.* He argued there that "all natural inclinations, including beneficence itself, change their nature in society, without anyone's intention or choice," and "transform themselves into new and onerous forms of subjection." It seemed that any human activity, as soon as men institutionalized it, was fixed, frozen, congealed, rigidified, compulsive. The idea of a free institution, then, was a contradiction in terms: institutionalization itself would destroy the very freedom it was meant to protect. In order for something agreeable, beneficence for example, "to give us pleasure, we must do it freely, without constraint. To take away the sweetness of a good deed, all you need to do is to make it a duty. The weight of duty makes a burden of the sweetest pleasure," and "is enough to destroy it, to change it into repugnance and aversion. . . ." (*Rêveries,* VI. 1052–3) There seemed to be a hard core of self-alienation which no amount of social reform could overcome. If this were so, then even the most authentic forms of being, even the best of all possible families, states, societies, worlds, were bound to turn sour for the self in the end.

> I have never fit properly into society, where everything is duty, obligation, constraint; my independent nature makes me incapable of the submission necessary for anyone who wants to live among men. So long as I can act freely, I am good, and I do nothing but good things. But as soon as I feel the yoke of men or of compulsion, I become rebellious—or, rather, resistant—and that is why I am nothing. [1059]

"The submission necessary for anyone who wants to live among men": this foreclosure on all utopian hopes reinforced the withdrawal and despair that marked Rousseau's last years; years in which he felt himself as a ghost in a machine, immersing himself in alienated labor while he yearned for mystical bliss.

Although the contradiction between duty and spontaneity often reduced Rousseau to despair, there were times when he tried to deal with it, to think about how it might be resolved. He understood that it was essential to develop some form of citizenship which a free man would not reject as an imposition on himself. Rousseau hoped to accomplish this by maximizing the opportunities for every man to personally *choose* the state to which he would belong.

But not even explicit consent was sufficient grounds for *unconditional* obedience: men were never authorized to give their government a blank check. "To renounce one's freedom is to renounce being a man, to surrender both the rights and the duties of humanity. Such a renunciation is incompatible with man's nature, since, in removing all freedom from his will, it removes all morality from his actions." But in order for a law to be genuinely *his* law, every man would have to prescribe it directly, by himself, not by proxy, through a representative; representation was "slavery" because it deprived citizens of the chance to make their own choices. (III.15, 428–31) This concern with personal choice also underlay Rousseau's ban on "partial societies within the state": his real objection to corporate bodies was that, in creating social roles which mediated between individuals and the state, they made it impossible that "each citizen should think only his own thoughts." (II.3, 372) It was one of the profoundest paradoxes of Rousseau's political thought that, although the general will represented the transcendence of individuality, it was only out of the free choices of individuals that the general will could arise. Indeed, he extended the realm of personal choice far beyond the limits set for it in the previous history of political thought. Not only the existing government, not only the constitution of the state, but the whole structure of society, the "fundamental compact" which generated all other obligations, was to be put up to all citizens, at least once a year, to be chosen and undertaken anew or dissolved forever. Rousseau defended this idea by drawing on an argument of Grotius' that "each man can renounce his membership in his own state, and recover his natural liberty and his goods on leaving the country." If, as was generally accepted, this were so, then "It would be absurd if all the citizens together could not do what each can do by himself." This meant that "there is in the state no fundamental law that cannot be revoked, including the social contract itself." (III. 18, 436) Thus it is unfair to say, as Shklar does, that "There is not much room for choice in [Rousseau's] system. . . ." ("Two

Models," 36) Rousseau in fact reserved to men the most crucial choice of all: the choice of the whole "system" itself. *Hommes* were *citoyens* only insofar as they chose to be; if they found the state wanting, it would have to go. Rousseau's search for personal authenticity led him to take more seriously than any thinker before him the idea that political obligation must be based on personal consent. In order for men to belong to a community without alienating themselves, the very existence of the community would have to remain permanently in doubt, a perpetually open question. A community of authentic men would have to dissolve and recreate itself again and again; the social contract would need constantly to be negotiated and affirmed anew.

Inner Contradictions of the Maternal State

Even if this ideal community could hold itself together from within, it would be bound to encounter enormous difficulties in coping with the pressures of the world outside. The danger it faced was not so much military conquest as peaceful erosion. As Stanley Hoffmann points out, the community could be gradually "diverted from the closed-circuit practice of patriotism into the open contest of ambition and vanity." In order to be secure against this form of corruption, "the small community ought to be not just self-sufficient, but *insulated*. Should its citizens have more than accidental or occasional contacts with foreigners, then the citizens may be tempted to revert to the evil practice of 'comparing oneself in order to know oneself.' " The Haut Valaisians were protected by geography: buried deep in the mountains, they did not need to worry about outside agitators coming in. On the other hand, their community might well worry, should they themselves, or their children, feel even an occasional impulse to get out. If they were free to leave

224

home, they might succumb to the world's temptations, and never come back; or worse, they might return, only to transform the mountain—perhaps even inadvertently—into the image of the plain. Intercourse with the world would cease to be dangerous only if "the whole world . . . [were] covered with such communities." (Hoffmann, "Rousseau on War and Peace," 330) Alas, the liberation of the whole world was not likely to occur soon, and Rousseau would have been the last to expect it. But if intercourse could be bad, isolation would be even worse. If the community remained in hiding from the world, it would be unable to draw on the vast human energy which could spring from its citizens' personal choice and commitment alone. This was so because choice and commitment could not be either psychologically or politically fruitful, could not generate either individual satisfaction or social solidarity, unless they sprang from real alternatives. Unless the people were exposed to genuine alternatives, they would slide inexorably into inertia and apathy, metamorphose into mechanical men, passively fulfilling their programs; the structure of the community might remain intact, but the life which that structure was meant to contain would drain away. Here another cruel irony emerged: if men were not given a real chance to be inauthentic, they could not really be authentic. Thus, by establishing itself with any degree of security, Rousseau's maternal state might defeat its own purpose; its success could dry up the deepest sources of its spirit. If it were not in constant danger of being destroyed from within, it would lose its inner meaning. In its very life and energy it seemed to turn against itself.

These contradictions emerge most concretely in Rousseau's most vivid respresentation of an ideal community, the Haut Valais. As Saint-Preux describes this country, which he has just discovered, he celebrates "the grandeur, the variety, the beauty of a thousand astonishing spectacles; the pleasure of seeing nothing but new things around you—strange birds, bizarre and unknown plants—to observe a new nature, to find yourself in a new world." (*Julie*, I.23, 79) Here an archetypally modern man is exalting an environment which he experiences as antithetical to the modern cities of the plain he has just left. And yet, paradoxically, the qualities he praises here are precisely those most endemic to modernity. He finds the Haut Valais overwhelmingly *new:* it expands the mind, enlarges the self, opens up new dimensions of possibility, makes life fuller and more intense. The irony of his vision is that the world he sees can be new and psychedelic only for one who confronts it as an *outsider;* its liberating character is a function of *distance.* As soon as Saint-Preux steps inside this world, and tries to experience it on its own terms, he finds that in fact its structure is totally hostile to those modern values which at first led him to idealize it. This mountain refuge has managed to protect its citizens from the destructive clash of self-interests that rages in the world below only by drastically enervating their selves. This world is so peaceable and harmonious only because, as Rousseau's startling image reveals, "All our desires which are too alive are deadened [*s'émoussent*]." The process of deadening "takes away that sharpness which makes our feelings so painful, and leaves only a light and gentle emotion in our hearts. Thus the passions which most torment men in the world below do most to make men happy up here." Since the Haut Valaisians are so feeble, their "pleasures are less ardent" and their "passions are more moderate," the greatest happiness possible for them is negative: "a peaceful tranquillity that makes them happy not through the enjoyment of pleasures, but through the exemption from pains." We can see now that this "new world" is not really so new after all. Those high mountains were no accident of geography: they place us at the height of an old, familiar symbolic hierarchy, in a Christian Heaven. "In lifting oneself above the level of men [*au dessus du séjour des hommes*], one leaves all base and earthly feelings behind; in approaching ethereal regions, the soul imbibes something of their unalterable purity." The creatures who live so happily here have little in common with men: many of their human feelings have been crippled, the rest destroyed: they are deadened souls. In the course of ascension, *"you forget everything, you forget yourself,* and you don't know where you are."(78–9) The price of heavenly happiness is high: life, feelings, pleasures and treasures within, all that makes one human, one's very self, "everything" must go.

Where are we now? We are with Saint-Preux, a modern youth, a tree on the highway, on a long and tortuous trip in search of himself. We have found, with him, that the individual needs a lover to sustain him in authenticity; that the romantic couple needs a political community to protect them from the pressures of the alienated and alienating society that surrounds them; and that the community itself needs protection from the societies and states it hopes to transcend. Saint-Preux has stumbled on an idyllic community behind the mountain walls of the Haut Valais. In many ways it looked like just the place he has been looking for. As we got deeper into the life of the Haut Valais, however, we saw that the walls we hoped would protect the tree have sealed it off from the light and air it needs to live; here it can live on only in a deadened state. Behind these walls we have experienced an abrupt, jarring reversal. Just as the self seemed about to be fulfilled, it has been emptied of its life and power. Just where it seemed most possible to unite man and citizen, we have been cut loose from "the level of men" altogether. The community which at first seemed ideally conducive to authenticity has turned out instead to be a setting for self-obliteration. If this state is maternal, its children are stillborn.

But what is most jarring about this reversal is the power with which it pulls Saint-Preux along, tempts him to reverse himself in accord with it. His prose glows with life as he describes the deadened state, he burns to live in it. "Ah, Julie, if only we could pass our lives together in this unknown place": this romantic wish now takes on a new, ominous meaning. It appears as a longing to escape: if only we could make a leap out of the real world and into a bodiless, weightless one, if we could somehow become less passionate, less ardent, less profound, less alive, less human, if we could just stop being ourselves—*then* we could be happy. Rousseau's politics of authenticity, at the point of its greatest depth and concreteness, has suddenly turned into its opposite. These polarities of impulse and idea coexist in deepest intimacy, and converge in a single, paradoxical point. It is this strange convergence which we must now try to understand.

IV

The Politics of Inauthenticity

The Life and Death of Julie

> My dear Julie, you were born to rule.
> Your empire is the most absolute conceiv-
> able: it extends even over the will.
> *La Nouvelle Héloïse*

> This was a post- and counter-revolutionary
> conservatism, a revolt against . . . liberal
> standards from the other end, not from the
> rear but from the front, not from the old
> but from the new. . . .
> THOMAS MANN, *Doctor Faustus*

> In the fight between you and the world,
> back the world.
> Two tasks on the threshold of life: the
> first, to narrow your circle more and more;
> the second, to make sure that you have not
> lost yourself somewhere outside it.
> KAFKA

ROUSSEAU'S IDEAS as to how modern men could become fully themselves form an intellectual achievement of the highest order, a triumph of the radical imagination. But this achievement also reveals some of the ominous
ambiguities of that imagination. For at the very heart of
Rousseau's project of self-creation, intertwined with it, we
find a radically opposite impulse: a will to self-alienation—
and, ultimately, to self-annihilation. In exploring this po-

larity, we enter a strange world: like a thick, lush, romantic forest it entices us and draws us in; but the deeper in we go, the darker it gets, and the harder it is to tell which pole is which. In the dark Rousseau, like Saint-Preux on the mountain, forgets everything, forgets himself, and loses touch with where he is; only after deep perplexity and long suffering does he find himself again. What colors his world so darkly is anxiety: he wants to blot out a situation he cannot bear to face. Ironically, this anxiety grows organically out of the search for authenticity itself. Rousseau understood that the more avidly modern men pursued themselves, the more they concentrated their will and energy on this goal, the more terrified they were bound to feel—terrified not only of failure, but, perhaps even more, of success. From their terror sprang a desperate desire to reverse themselves, to flee as far from themselves as they could get. Rousseau saw that they could succeed in this new, perverse project only if they managed somehow to turn the energy and dynamism of their own search for authenticity against themselves. At this point a new politics was born: a politics of inauthenticity. This politics appealed to the modern youths who cared most— and hence who feared most—to be themselves. It continued to speak the idealistic language of their search. But it sought to invert their desire for a fuller life into a longing for a new form of death, and to transform their radical insight into how the self could be found into knowledge of how it could be irrevocably lost. This inversion could work only with the help of new forms of false consciousness which could convince them that they were freest when they were really most enslaved, new self-deceptions enabling them to feel fully authentic even as they were alienated from themselves more totally than ever before.

These two radically opposite impulses converge and in-

tertwine tragically in *La Nouvelle Héloïse*.[1] In the life sto-
ries of the two young lovers, Saint-Preux and Julie, Rousseau dramatized the personal and political alternatives
which he believed modern men and women would have to
face. In the changes which he made them go through, he
showed how frightful this modern predicament was.

Authenticity, Guilt, Escape

As Rousseau's tale unfolds, we encounter the lovers at a
crucial moment in their search for authenticity. It is the
moment that he called "the most important and difficult
part of education, the crisis that constitutes the passage between childhood and manhood." Saint-Preux, who appears
with no fixed address, no point of origin, no personal or
social past, desperately needs such a crisis to give form to his
life, and comes through it easily and happily. For Julie, it
opens up problems far more complex, and forces her to
make a fearful choice. For the passion she feels in the present contradicts totally the aim and meaning of her past life.
Her whole education and upbringing have been designed as
means to the ends of her father's ambition. His social aspirations are typical of the European *haute bourgeoisie* at a
time when European society was not yet thoroughly *em-
bourgeoisée*. He wants to marry his daughter to the Baron
de Wolmar, a landed but impoverished member of the old-
est, highest nobility. In the terminology we used earlier, this
means changing his family's status from an achieved to an
ascribed one, transforming his descendants from persons
into institutions. It is a paradox endemic to bourgeois life
that this project of depersonalization is intended to be its

[1] The point of departure for my discussion of *La Nouvelle Héloïse*
below is Peter Gay's essay, "The Three Stages in Love's Way: Rousseau,
Laclos, Diderot," in *The Party of Humanity*, especially 135–146.

greatest personal achievement. Julie is perfectly right when she says that "he has made his daughter into a piece of goods, . . . and profited at my expense," that "he has paid for his life with mine," that he is reducing her to "a slave" (*Julie*, I.28, 94); but this enslavement is the natural culmination of his economic freedom. By treating his daughter as a commodity—as, after all, he has always treated himself—he hopes forever to remove his family from the fluctuating, unstable human market. Through a kind of social alchemy, he hopes to transform the basis of their identity from the fluidity of a commodity to the rigidity of a stone. In the course of her life Julie fulfills this design more thoroughly and profoundly than he could ever have imagined possible —only to see her new world come to an abrupt, catastrophic end.

In getting a liberal education from her tutor, Julie has learned to reject both aristocratic and bourgeois norms, in favor of a search for authenticity, which she finds in love. But the love of Saint-Preux is not enough: romantic love overflows beyond its source, into the world around it; it needs the recognition and support of a wider community. In the world as it is, however, there is no community that will provide this support, nowhere romantic lovers can belong authentically. Thus, if Saint-Preux and Julie are intent on staying together, they must either run away, and live like fugitives on the road, or else win some sort of minimal recognition from their own society. It is this latter course that Julie hopes to follow. She feels guilty for deceiving the world, yet ultimately justified—"*coupable mais non dépravée*"—in her secret love. Pregnant with her lover's child, she hopes to marry and settle down: hoping, as she says, "to draw from my fault [*faute*] the means of correcting it [*la réparer*]." Then the negative energy that has gone

into deceiving society can be changed into positive energy
that will support it, if only their illicit love can be legitimized, if their double life can be unified. Then, too, their
child, "the first fruit of our love would seal the bond between us." (III. 18, 344) To draw from the fault the means
of correcting it: this is precisely the dialectical solution that
Rousseau proposes for the faults of modern society as a
whole. If modern society can accept and recognize the romantic idealists who have grown out of it, perhaps it can
begin to heal the wounds it has made.

Alas, this society is not only unwilling to accept these
young idealists; it turns against them with unprecedented
ferocity, because it is terrified by the ideals they embody. If
Julie wanted only to marry beneath her, this one demand
by itself might be acceptable; the lovers could live happily
ever after and would never be heard from again. In fact,
however, Julie's objection to the marriage customs of her
society is only a small part of a total rejection of all its
standards and norms. She and Saint-Preux do not only want
each other: they want themselves. Moreover, they need to
belong to a community of selves—or to create one—because
their feelings for themselves and for each other are inherently dynamic, and need to overflow into the whole environment around them. But a society built on self-alienation
is profoundly threatened by such feelings; their overflow
could carry all its institutions away. To allow them a legitimate place within its borders, then, would be to open the
floodgates; and this it will not do.

Julie's father, who incarnates the power and authority of
society, declares war on her feelings and needs. At first he
uses the Calvinist language and imagery of her childhood to
make her feel filthy and depraved. But the sexual guilt he
elicits only strengthens her resolution: she understands that

the sexuality he reviles is integral to the selfhood she is seeking; the intensity of his abuse assures her of her success in being the person she wants to be. Next he appeals to her sense of family honor: he has promised her to the Baron; would she have him disgrace the name they share by reneging on his vows? But she has promises of her own to keep; a name that negates her needs loses its power over her. For a while there is an impasse between them; it appears that neither father nor daughter will give way, and that the lovers will go their own way, living like fugitives or gypsies, unfulfilled but authentic, rejected by the world but accepting themselves and each other. In such a case the sphere of authenticity would be small but irreducible.

But Julie's father and society have more power over her than she thinks, power to crush even this limited sphere. Thus, in desperation, her father escalates the war: defeated in religious and social struggles, he now turns to a total psychological warfare. He tells her (whether truthfully or not is never made clear) that the recent, sudden death of her beloved mother was caused directly by her discovery of Julie's secret affair. He then throws himself on his knees, bursts into tears, and implores her to consider his old age and precarious health: "don't send me to the grave, dead of sorrow, along with the woman who carried you inside her. Julie, do you want to kill your whole family?" This appeal is melodramatic and outrageous, but emotionally it hits home. Her father defines her as a commodity (admittedly, a precious one), himself as its owner. His whole identity, emotional as well as economic, is based on his proprietary relationship to people. To recognize her as a human being with independent and valid needs of her own would wreck the whole basis of his life. Thus, in order to be true to her lover—and to herself—she must be emotionally prepared to commit the most hideous crime she can imagine, the murder of her mother and father. The search for authenticity has brought her to this pass: in order to live in the present and the future, she must destroy those who have been nearest and dearest to her in the past. The authentic man, it would seem, must become a monster. This terrible polarity reveals how radical the search for authenticity really is. Modern society, we see, can adapt and modify itself so as to bestow enormous benefits on the individual; but the one thing its structure cannot tolerate is to let the individual be himself. The emerging desire of youth for self-fulfillment in the world has opened up a new, enormous gulf between the self and the world. Those men and women who want to be themselves now find themselves totally alienated from their society in a way that no men or women have ever been before. The price of authenticity turns out to be an unbearable loneliness and guilt.

Even in the best of circumstances, this would be a terrible burden for the self to bear. But there are undercurrents of feeling in Julie that make it harder still. As their romance unfolds Saint-Preux finds that, as united as he and Julie feel together, they are sharply divided in what they feel. Where his love flows like water, spreads like fire, animates the whole universe, hers is static, serene, the still point of a turning world. As they lie together after making love for the first time, he comes to rest in her aura. "What a difference between the frenzies of love and a situation so peaceful!" On getting up, he is attacked by "self-hatred and humiliation" for having ever disturbed her peace. He is tortured by "the suspicion . . . that you know how to love better than I do." He would immobilize his feelings, as she has done, and pursue happiness as she pursues it, wishing not that it should overflow into the future, but that it should be frozen in an eternal present. Seeing the world in her way, he becomes instantly nostalgic, looking backward rather than forward, though their love has hardly begun: his most intense wish is that their first night together "could have been prolonged forever." Before long, the flow of his own feelings returns; but this only makes him feel more vividly than ever the vast distance between them. In being himself, he is renouncing another form of being, which she embodies. He mourns the loss of something beautiful: "my transports are not equal to your *délicieuse langueur,* the emotion that is the source of supreme happiness." (I.55, 148–9) Modernity, it seems, has opened up a new world of happiness for man, happiness that is fluid, dynamic, infinitely expansive; but modern man can enter this world only by giving up another, older form of happiness, a happiness that seems solid, secure, eternal, that requires nothing of the self but relaxation, passivity, *langueur.* Those who seek authenticity must leave this languid peace, and all hope for it, behind. And yet, the more society resists its youth's desire for authenticity, the narrower its path becomes, the more drastic conflicts arise, the deeper and more desperate their need for this sort of peace is bound to be.

To protect herself against all this anxiety, and bring her peace, Julie gives way. "I was armed against your threats," she bitterly confesses to her father, "but not against your tears." In submitting to his plan for her, she is turning herself against the passion that is most decisive in making her the person she is. No wonder she tells her father caustically that "It's you who are killing me." (III., 18, 348–9) In fact, however, by refusing to accept the terrible burdens that authenticity would entail, she is killing herself. The rest of the book works out, tortuously but inexorably, the dialectic of her death.

In what sense is Julie killed by her submission? Obviously, she is kept from living the life she would choose for herself. And yet, demoralizing and oppressive as the wrong life with the wrong man would surely be, it need not be fatal. We might think that a Stoic attitude would be possible for her. Indeed, this is the way Julie herself at first tries to live. She tells herself that her father may have power over her body, her outward behavior, but not her heart, her inner life; the autonomy of inwardness should still remain to her. Alas, the wall she puts up between herself and the world soon falls. For she is a woman of modern times, and the inner world she lives in is poles apart from the dualistic universe of the Stoa. She has no distant but ultimate Reason to believe in, no transcendent Cosmos to cling to. For her, the world around her is the only one there is. In this world, she can fulfill herself only as a whole being, bringing all her feelings and thoughts together in action. Her deepest sense of herself draws her toward oneness, self-unification; divided, she will fall apart. Yet if she were to follow through the force of her feelings, where would they lead her? "In the end we would fall into an abyss; and when we arose, we would find ourselves covered with crimes—we, whose hearts were made for virtue." Hoping to escape the abyss of anger, violence, guilt, *Angst* that she feels well up within her, she makes a desperate leap. "My friend, let the veil fall! Is it really necessary to see the terrible precipice before us, to avoid falling in?" (353) *Let the veil fall!* Torn apart by inner conflict, Julie tries to hold herself together by blotting out her inmost feelings, perceptions, responses, ideas. She has pulled down a wall between herself and the world, only to build up an even thicker wall within herself: everything in her that conflicts with the role the world wants her to play must not merely give way, but disappear. Because she is

239

so deeply committed to living authentically, she cannot bear to divide herself. But this forces her to escape in a far more radical way: to actually negate herself. She creates a new kind of project, and consecrates herself to it: *to be inauthentic.* This perverse project grows out of the pressures generated by the search for authenticity itself. She has been forced into a fight to the death with the world; now, in a desperate struggle to survive, she has chosen to back the world. She hopes to keep alive by killing herself inside.[2] And yet, ironically, even as she systematically deadens herself, she struggles to keep the idea of the self's authenticity alive. The deeper she immerses herself in a life of total inauthenticity, the more she insists that this life in death has "restored me to myself" (365). From this point on, her life story becomes a nightmarish "experiment on what can be done to the self." [3]

[2] This is symbolized in a cruelly vivid way. In the course of putting pressure on Julie, her father knocks her down. This, we learn, kills the child she is carrying within her, the life she and her lover have created together.

[3] I owe this phrase to Erving Goffman, "Characteristics of Total Institutions," 12, in *Asylums*, 1–125. My interpretation of what is happening in Julie's world is deeply indebted to Goffman's vision. Also, to Sartre's discussions of "bad faith" in *Being and Nothingness,* (New York: Philosophical Library, 1956) and *Anti-Semite and Jew* (New York: Grove Press, 1962); to Erich Fromm, *Escape from Freedom* (New York: Rinehart, 1941); to Erik Erikson's 1950 essay, "Wholeness and Totality," reprinted in *Identity: Youth and Crisis* (New York: Norton, 1968), 74–90; to Barrington Moore, Jr., "Totalitarian Elements in Pre-Industrial Societies," reprinted in *Political Power and Social Theory* (Cambridge, Mass.: Harvard University Press, 1958), 30–88; to R. D. Laing, *The Divided Self;* to Robert Jay Lifton, *Thought Reform and the Psychology of Totalism: A Study of "Brainwashing" in China* (New York: Norton, 1961), especially 419–72; to Franz Neumann, "Anxiety and Politics," reprinted in *The Democratic and the Authoritarian State* (Glencoe, Ill.: The Free Press, 1964), 270–300; and, above all, to life in the twentieth century.

Conversion: The Counter-revolution Within

What Julie wants is self-contradictory and self-defeating. She wants to be what others want her to be, and not what she herself wants to be. She wants to be a self that is created and constituted by others, not one which generates its own identity. But her very desire stands in its object's way: self-negation is still the self's own project. She understands that non-being cannot come from within the self. She goes on to convince herself that it can be conferred on the self from without. In calling her by a new name, a name of its own, the world can magically recreate her in its own image. Thus she comes to see her marriage as such a miracle. The moment she was pronounced Wolmar's wife, "I suddenly felt a revolution within me. An unknown power seemed to resolve the disorder of my feelings, and reconstitute them according to the law of duty and nature." (354) The fact that this marriage was imposed on her now appears as an ideal expression of the world's power over her identity. The political metaphor of revolution is crucial here: Julie's feeling incarnates a peculiar kind of revolutionary spirit, the spirit that starts new calendars and proclaims that mankind's old needs and impulses have been annihilated along with the old institutions. The true model of this kind of revolution is a religious revival. "I felt genuinely transformed. What a torrent of pure joy flowed through my soul! What a sense of peace and inner serenity, so long gone from a heart stained with ignominy. I felt myself reborn, and beginning a new life." (355) The emotional form of her revival is Christian, Protestant, evangelistic; but its social content makes her more at home in this world than she has ever been before. Having embraced this world so ardently—and so desperately—Julie comes to conceive of it in its own way, as the

241

best of all possible worlds. "I believed I saw the instrument of Providence and the voice of God in the minister who was performing the ceremony." (354) She overflows with gratitude: "Eternal Providence, who makes the insect crawl and the heavens revolve, you who are watchful over the least of your works, you have recalled me to the good that you made me to love! Deign to receive from a heart purified by your care the homage which you alone render worthy to be offered!" (356) Behind Julie's intricate dialectic, a sacrament has indeed taken place: she has got herself reincarnated as someone else.

Who is this new person, this recent entry into the world? It is not a woman who has just renounced the great love of her life: after all, such a woman might (at least sometimes) feel tempted to renounce her renunciation and go back to where she once belonged. To fit into her new role, Julie rewrites the disturbing history of her past so that no future disturbance can possibly arise from it. According to the New History, there was never anything to worry about. Her entanglement with Saint-Preux was sordid from the start: pure "vice," "defilement," "corruption," contrary not only to duty, but also to nature, reason, the heart, the conscience, the judgment of all humanity, and the will of God. Her tyrannical father, whom she earlier rightly accused of trying to sell her like a piece of goods, is transfigured into "a father as zealous for his daughter's happiness as for the honor of his house." (IV. 12, 489) Moreover, when earlier he struck her down and killed the child within her, he was actually acting as the agent of God's just wrath: "Heaven refused to favor designs conceived in crime; I did not deserve the honor of being a mother. . . ." (III. 18, 345) In addition to transforming the present and the past, her new role also has the power to determine the future—not only her own future, but that of Saint-Preux as well. "Everything is changed between us; it is absolutely necessary [*il faut nécessairement*] for your heart to change. Julie de Wolmar is no longer your old Julie; a revolution in your feelings for her is inevitable." (363) Here she does not exhort him to keep his distance, or say that he *ought to* stop loving her. Her message is not *pre*scriptive at all, but rather *de*scriptive. She simply informs him of what *is* the case—that the old Julie has ceased to exist, and that another person, "Julie de Wolmar" is now lodged in her body; and she proclaims, redundantly ["*il faut nécessairement*"], that once this misunderstanding is cleared up, his feelings *will* change. She feels no need to persuade him, let alone to convince herself —indeed, she is able to deal with "herself" as a distant third person: her role, operating under its own power, will take care of everything. Love for Saint-Preux, hatred of an imposed role, have nothing to do with her; they are ascribed to some other person, only dimly recollected, probably dead.

Among the favors of Providence, it has delivered Julie from the prospect of marriage to a man she loved. Her husband has taught her that love, far from enriching marriage, is a pernicious obstruction to it. This is because the devotion of lovers to one another distracts them from the real business of marriage, which is "to jointly fulfill the duties of civil life, to govern the household prudently and to bring up the children well." Moreover, love focuses on shallow, transitory qualities—such as youth and physical charm— which are external to what a person ultimately is. Love, therefore, is inevitably effaced by age: when lovers confront one another with wrinkled faces and grey hair, "the idols that they worshipped will be destroyed." Only then, when they are devoid of feeling, will they be themselves and "see themselves and each other as they really are [*on se voit ré-*

ciproquement tel qu'on est]." Since Julie and the Baron feel no passion for each other in the first place (indeed, Wolmar feels no passion of any kind), they are privileged to immediately "see each other as we are." Finally, love infuses the lover with "a continual agitation of jealousy or privation" which is inconducive to the perpetual peace which marriage should be. Julie's loveless but perfect marriage, on the other hand, described by her, as usual, in the third person, is "a constant and invariable attachment of two good and reasonable people who, destined to spend the rest of their lives together, are content with their lot, and work [*tâchent*] to make themselves agreeable to one another." (III. 20, 372–4) When Julie celebrates the perfect mutual self-knowledge she enjoys, and indeed praises Wolmar for having "restored me to myself" (III. 18, 365), it is essential to understand the peculiar sense of self she has acquired. This is a self that strives with all its power to become the perfect incarnation of a social role—which it has itself assumed, yet depicts as its inexorable "destiny"—and to annihilate everything within itself that keeps it from sinking peacefully into the role forever, "content with its lot." Deep down, Julie turns out to be strikingly similar to the metropolitan *mondains* whom she self-righteously condemns, men and women who with every new connection they make "leave their souls behind, and take up another with the colors of the house, as a lackey puts on new livery. . . ." (II. 14, 234) She is trying to obliterate a whole dimension of herself: memories of the past, responses to the present, hopes for the future, all of her that cannot squeeze into the livery of the House of Wolmar. Her "new self" is really a new form of self-mutilation.

The Counter-revolution Without: The World of Clarens

If the people around Julie were authentically themselves, she would be constantly confronted with human possibilities which she wants desperately to forget. To avoid such an encounter, she fuses all her creative powers in a brilliant attempt to transform these people into *personae,* as she has supposedly transformed herself. She expands her role as lady of the manor on Wolmar's estate at Clarens into the vocation of ideal legislator and philosopher-queen. She creates a whole world in the image of her mutilated, deadened self. She makes herself perhaps the first theorist and practitioner of the politics of inauthenticity.[4]

The search for authenticity, as we have seen, led Rousseau to an ideal of personal independence plus romantic commitment. These could best be secured, he argued, in an egalitarian and democratic republic whose citizens participated actively in its affairs. The republic of Valais, as it is evoked briefly but vividly by an elated and hopeful Saint-Preux, embodies this ideal. The opposite ideal—a state designed explicitly to obliterate the selves of its sovereigns and its subjects alike—is fulfilled in the political system of Clarens. Like Valais, it appears to us through the eyes of Saint-Preux, but a Saint-Preux whose romantic hopes have been crushed, and who is drifting aimlessly. He is morbidly, masochistically fascinated by the life which his beloved has

---

4 Starobinski is the only commentator I know who gives adequate emphasis to the hypocrisy and self-deception at the core of the political system of Clarens. He is especially astute in analyzing the pseudo-egalitarian rituals which Julie develops (V.7, 607–11), and counterposing them to the honest and egalitarian rituals in the *Letter to d'Alembert* and elsewhere in Rousseau's work. (*Rousseau,* 121–7)

chosen in preference to life with him, and he describes it in minute detail, appalled but enthralled.

The most striking thing about the social system of Clarens is that it is an island of rigidity in a sea of fluidity. It is polarized into two static castes, masters and servants, separated by an enormous social distance. Yet it is no backwater of feudalism: the servants work for wages, and are free to come and go; the masters' claims to obedience have nothing to do with tradition. At first Saint-Preux is puzzled: "Servitude," he observes, "is so unnatural to man that it couldn't exist without some degree of discontent. Here, however, the servants respect their masters and say nothing." (IV. 10, 460) How can a feudal lord like Wolmar hold onto his servants in an age when men have become sick of feudal servitude, insistent on their natural rights, avid in pursuit of their personal interests? Saint-Preux's answer defines what Rousseau saw as the political alternatives for modern times:

> In a Republic, the citizens are kept in order by morality, principles, virtue; but how can one contain an army of servants and mercenaries without force and constraint? The whole art of a master is to hide coercion under a veil of pleasure and interest, so that they'll want to do what they're supposed to do. [453]

If the search for authenticity led to a free and democratic republic, the pursuit of inauthenticity points to an authoritarian state that is governed like an army. However, the avidly individualistic men of modern times cannot be forcibly conscripted into any state—certainly not into one that is even more repressive than the old feudal rule: before they can be treated like soldiers, they must somehow be convinced to enlist. The task of a modern autocrat is paradoxical: he must entice free men to freely renounce their freedom. Modern men can be governed only by their own consent; "the whole art of a master" is to manipulate and engineer their consent. Julie learns to practice this art magnificently. Having let the veil fall over her own self-awareness, she fulfills her role by pulling it over the minds of others. The veil replaces the scepter as the symbol of this new form of authority.

In the republic of Valais, social and public life were meant to secure and enrich a happiness whose deepest springs were individual and private. The society of Clarens, on the other hand, seeks to break down individual and private life altogether. One of the first steps in this project is to minimize (and, if possible, eliminate) the role of the family. Thus the servants are taken from their parental homes at the earliest possible age, before they have developed any sense of themselves, "in order to make them what [their masters] want them to be." (444) They become "members of the [master's] family"; they "change their father and mother, and get new, wealthier parents." However, as we will see, this surrogate family totally negates all the feelings and values which Rousseau believed a genuine family could embody. Julie and her husband, in their assumed roles as "new, wealthier parents," aim to freeze their "children" in a childish state forever: their status as servants, inferiors, will be permanent; their service with the Wolmars "should be their first, and if they're worth anything it will be their last." To ensure this, servants should be drawn from the country, not the city: the vast diversity of urban life styles and experiences might give them ideas about themselves. With rural boys, any servant who for whatever reason leaves the Wolmars' household will revert to his former status as a peasant. (445) This is because he will be incapable of imagining any alternatives. To destroy the human capacity to imagine alternatives is one of the fundamental aims of "the art of a master."

In addition to circumscribing the range of his servants' experience, the successful master will know how to keep them from getting together, forming small, intense primary groups, developing a common underlife. Saint-Preux observes that "Servants are hardly ever united, except at the expense of their masters. If they agree about anything, it's to rob in concert. . . ." (460–1) Julie attempts to conquer the servants by dividing them. She makes it in the interest of everyone to inform on all the others. She manages to "transform the vile role of an informer into a function of zeal, integrity and courage, as noble—or, at least, as praiseworthy —as it was among the Romans." Just as in Usbek's seraglio, competition, distrust and mutual enmity among the servants tie them all the more firmly to their master's favor, and hence to their own servile roles. Thus, "far from banding together against their master, they are united only to serve him better. No matter how much interest they may have in loving one another, they always have a stronger interest in pleasing him; and their zeal to serve him overwhelms their mutual good will. . . ." (463)

Because love rests ultimately on self-love, solitude is just as dangerous as intimacy; the servants must be kept at a distance not only from one another, but from themselves. Thus all recreation is programmed and supervised by Julie and her husband, so that the servants will "derive all their pleasures from their masters." They devise games, through which the servants can at once exercise themselves and compete with one another, making them doubly fit for their functions. Should it happen "that any of our people doesn't accommodate himself to our rules, and prefers the freedom to go where he pleases, on whatever pretext, we never deny him permission; but we see this licentious taste as very suspect, and we're ready to distrust anyone who feels this way. Thus the same amusements that furnish us with good servants also serve as a test for choosing them." (455) The system perpetuates itself by screening out anyone who shows any sign of being anything less than totally dependent on it.

Julie is able to create this total dependence because she knows how to engage not only men's self-interests, but their deepest emotional needs. Those who live in the world of Clarens are deprived of family, friends, lovers, of inner space. They are given no chance to feel themselves, to develop their own powers, to move and experiment, to grow. They have no basis for self-esteem—indeed, for any sense of personal identity—apart from the recognition their masters give them. Julie knows how to manipulate her emotions, to give or withhold herself, according to the needs of the system she serves: she compensates for having been used by using herself as a means for using others. By giving her love, she can make its object feel intensely, magically alive; by withdrawing it, she can make any man feel psychically dead. She plays the various servants and subjects against one another in competition for her favor. "No one can bear that his zeal should be compared with that of his fellows, and everyone wants to be first in favor, just as he feels himself as first in devotion. This is their only complaint, and the greatest injustice they feel." (460) Indeed, they are

> far less afraid of the grave reprimands of M. de Wolmar than of the touching reproaches of Julie. He, talking of truth and justice, humiliates and confounds the culprits; she, in making clear how she is forced to withdraw her kindness from them, *makes them despair of*

their whole being [leur donne un regret mortel de l'être]. She often draws tears of grief and shame from them, and she is sometimes moved herself when she sees them repent in the hope that she won't hold to her word. [465–6]

Julie's feeling for her subjects has all the emotional power of a mother's love for her children. In fact, however, it is a total inversion of the maternal love that Rousseau saw as one of the few authentic feelings left in the world. Julie hoped to be a real mother, to bring up the love-child she had conceived with Saint-Preux. If she had been allowed to live on her love, she could have infused her children with a self-confidence, a sense of basic trust and security, which would enable them to outgrow childhood and act on their own long after she was gone. But her society denied her: it killed the life she was carrying within her before she could bring it into the world, and left her feeling dead and empty inside. She has managed to live through this death by conceiving a frightful caricature of the family she was not allowed to have. The bond between Julie and her surrogate children does not flow from the fullness of her being; rather, it expresses her desire at once to forget and to exploit an emptiness of being. She does not want these children to be happy; she wants them to be obedient. She does not want them to grow up, but to be fixed in childish weakness and dependence forever. Her emotion is not spontaneous, but simulated; it comes not from her heart, but from her head; it is a power that can be turned on and off at will, according to her rational calculation of the interests of the House of Wolmar. She uses this power to keep her subjects in perpetual anxiety: her love must be earned, they must prove themselves again and again, by playing the roles and fulfilling the functions she demands. "The best subjects are those who are most afraid [alarmés]" (447)—most terrified of being left unloved and alone.[5] Clarens is a grotesque parody of the maternal state Rousseau hoped to create: it has all the suffocating enclosure that a mother can have, without any of the sustaining love.

Julie's genius for manipulation reaches its apex in what she calls her Elysium, a secret orchard which she creates as a private sanctuary. Saint-Preux, at the very end of his visit to Clarens, is initiated into its mysteries. He is alive to the sexual symbolism: he is getting into her at last, into the real core of her being, in a way that he never did during their love affair. The whole Elysium episode has a descriptive vividness and intensity, an analytical precision and brilliance, a symbolic complexity and depth that makes it one of the great moments of European Romanticism.

"This place," Saint-Preux writes, "although very close to the house, is so completely hidden by a covered walk that it's completely invisible. The thick foliage which surrounds it lets no eye penetrate within, and it's always carefully locked up." Because "the entrance was concealed [masquée] by alder and hazel-trees," Saint-Preux, once inside, can't find his way back to where he has come in. Wandering through the orchard, discovering layer after layer of its hidden depths, he lets his imagination carry him away. He suddenly feels as though he's been transported, dropped from the clouds to a desert isle. He is surrounded by lush

[5] Franz Neumann distinguishes "two fundamental types of identification [of masses with their leaders]: a libido-charged (affective) and a libido-free (non-affective)," and argues that "the non-affective identification with an organization is less regressive. . . ." This is because "Non-affective loyalty is transferable; personal loyalty is not. The former always contains strong rationalist elements, elements of calculability between individual and organization, and thus prevents the total extinction of the ego." "Anxiety and Politics," 278.

and exotic plants, by brightly colored wild flowers and strange birds, by bubbling streams and cataracts. "I felt that I was in the wildest, the most solitary place in all of nature; it seemed to me that I was the first man who had ever penetrated into this wilderness." He cries out: "O Tinian! O Juan Fernandez! Julie, the world's end is at your door!" By what magic is this possible? Julie explains calmly that, although "nature has done everything," it has done so only "under my direction," so that "there's nothing here except what's here under my orders." (IV. 11, 471–2) Saint-Preux is amazed that "a place so different from what it once was"—a barren, desolate spot, as Julie informs him—"can have become what it is only through great care and culture; and yet I can't find the slightest trace of cultivation." Everything here evokes "the idea of a desert Isle," [6] yet every detail has been planned and arranged. It is clear that the planners and the gardeners "have taken so much pain to hide from themselves [se cacher] the pain they have taken." What for? She enlightens him once again: after all, she says, "nature itself seems to want to hide [dérober] its true charms from the eyes of men"; therefore, in an environment which nature has endowed poorly, "those who love her are reduced to doing her violence," and "this can't be done without some degree of illusion." (479–80) That which displays the "true charms" of nature must "do violence" to nature: it must be illusory, hidden, disguised, masked, veiled. With brilliant sophistry, Julie has stood the meaning of nature on its head.

This argument serves symbolically as an apologia for the whole life she has created. For just as she has done violence

---

[6] This noun is capitalized by Rousseau. The fact that he rarely capitalizes nouns suggests that, as I am arguing, when he does so it is to emphasize the *Idea* of a thing, rather than a mere instance of it.

to nature, she has done violence to herself. She considers her orchard the one place where, at rare privileged moments, with servants and strangers excluded, "one says whatever one thinks, reveals all one's secrets, without restraining one's feelings; there one can give oneself up to the joys of trust and intimacy." There, alone, finally, "one is permitted to be what one is." (488) In fact, however, the self she reveals to her intimates within her sanctuary—Wolmar and, for a brief moment, Saint-Preux—is no more her authentic self than the sanctuary itself is authentic nature. In the sanctuary Saint-Preux beholds "not Julie as she was for me, and as I like to think of her"—not a woman who has always loved him, although she has renounced him out of fear and guilt—but rather Julie "as she shows herself to me every day" at Clarens: as "that chaste and virtuous woman surrounded by her entourage." She has surrounded herself, first of all, with "her three charming children, legitimate and precious token [gage] of conjugal union and tender friendship." Next is "the grave Wolmar, that Husband [once again capitalized by Rousseau] so dear, so happy and so worthy of happiness," whose "penetrating and judicious eye pierced to the depths of my heart, and made me blush again." Finally, there is Fanchon Regnard, the servant who initially betrayed the young lovers, "living proof of the triumph of justice and humanity over the most ardent love"; "what guilty feeling," Saint-Preux asks himself, "could penetrate to Julie, through such an inviolable guard?" What Julie has revealed here is a purely *official* self, an incarnation of a social role, in a full panoply of psychic armor. This epiphany is meant not to elicit his deepest feelings, but to suppress and paralyze them; indeed, his response is to guiltily "kill [étouffer] the vile transports of a criminal passion" in himself, rather than "soil such a beautiful tableau

253

of honor and innocence." Saint-Preux concludes from this scene that Julie would never have chosen the name Elysium if she had had a troubled conscience, and that "peace must reign at the bottom of her heart, as it does in the asylum she has named." (486–7) Here, thinking and feeling as she wants him to, he makes the same mistake about her as she makes about herself: he takes the wish for the actuality. Just as she has effaced the natural growth of the countryside and put in its place what she considers the "true charms" of nature, "the idea of a desert Isle," so she has tried to efface her personality as it has actually developed and put in its place the *persona* she would like to be.

What kind of society, finally, is Clarens? Where can we place Julie's Utopia in the history of political thought? Saint-Preux understands it as a kind of benevolent despotism: "How powerful and lovely is the empire of a beneficent beauty!" (IV. 10, 444) He goes on to doubt that "even the monarchs of Asia are served in their places with more respect than these good masters in their own houses." (459) With this, we seem to have come full circle: in the most advanced sector of modernity we suddenly find ourselves face to face with the most primitive form of power, Oriental despotism. If we look more closely, however, we can see that Clarens is intellectually as well as sociologically far beyond the politics of the seraglio, that it is governed on principles that are distinctively, insidiously modern. *The Persian Letters* grows out of an historical context in which the human possibilities of modernity were just coming to light. In Montesquieu's imaginative world, neither master nor slaves are initially aware of themselves as unique, autonomous beings. It is only through their pursuit of happiness that they discover themselves: they learn gradually, in very different ways, that the only deep and lasting satisfaction available to man is *self*-satisfaction. The protagonists of *La Nouvelle Héloïse,* on the other hand, have a thoroughly modern sensibility from the start: they crave authenticity, but also fear its immense emotional costs. Usbek's power is undermined and eventually destroyed by human needs—both his wives' needs and his own—which he does not understand. His personal needs make him dependent for satisfaction on other persons; and this means that he cannot satisfy himself except by treating others *as* persons. The message of *The Persian Letters* is that the personal needs of modern men place inherent limits on their political power. Julie, however, has got the message, and tries to go beyond it. She is fully conscious of these needs; she aims consciously to channel and manipulate them in others, to repress them in herself, to treat both herself and others purely as means for fulfilling the needs of the system. Thus we might say that while *The Persian Letters* is a pre-revolutionary work, *La Nouvelle Héloïse* is intellectually (though not, of course, chronologically) post-revolutionary—and counter-revolutionary. Usbek only gradually discovers himself; Julie feels and knows herself, but is filled with fear and horror by it, and tries to pluck it out. He has not yet reached authenticity; she wants to escape it.

It is the peculiarly modern character of Julie's despotism that makes it so dangerous. Rousseau saw that traditional roles and ascribed modes of identity were breaking down in the modern age. Men would no longer accept any authority simply because it was there; they would be loyal only to such rulers and institutions as could satisfy their personal interests and needs. At the same time, modern society had created human needs which it could not satisfy. It had encouraged (indeed, compelled) men to expand and develop all their powers, but only as weapons in an incessant struggle for power over one another. It had enabled them to achieve their sense of identity, but only in a form that was purely relative, nothing an individual could call definitively his own. It had elaborated ideas of personal honor, loyalty, trust, friendship, love, but only in an appearance, as masks for manipulation. Meanwhile, however, the pressure of the competitive struggle itself had generated "a delicacy of feeling which can be acquired only through the education of the great world," a sensibility which alone could "feel the fineness of the human heart." (*Confessions*, XI. 546) The freedom and generosity of spirit these men displayed were indeed masks for compulsive manipulation; but their underlying toughness and cynicism too were masks. Beneath both there was a third dimension: a hunger, a yearning for the realities they had feigned. Their needs, refined and developed by culture, were more intense than ever before. The institutional roles which had always mediated their feelings were collapsing around them, and the inner defenses which these roles had reinforced were giving away. At this historical moment they were exceptionally open and vulnerable to anyone who understood them. Julie, offering love and acceptance in exchange for voluntary submission, holds out the promise of a "new self" for modern men: a form of identity that will be free from the insecurity and anxiety that pervade modern life. But the promise is never fulfilled: their needs are only exploited, their anxieties only channeled, coordinated and played against one another, to keep them in line. "My dear Julie, you were born to rule. *Your empire is the most absolute conceivable: it extends even over the will.*" (IV. 2, 409) A modern awareness of how the self can be built up may also be utilized to tear the self down. In turning her self-awareness against itself, Julie has initiated a new phase of modernity: on the

256

ruins of a barren feudal estate she has built up an efficient, perfectly functioning totalitarian state.

The world of Clarens is a work of creative—and destructive—genius, one of the perverse triumphs of the modern imagination. Rousseau, thinking his way into the mind of a self-conscious and sensitive person who is forced to renounce everything closest to herself, constructs a whole new world for her in which self-renunciation is not only palatable but beatific, the summit of virtue and happiness. Within herself, Julie transforms a marriage imposed by social and emotional pressures into one that has been freely and gladly chosen; a cold, unfeeling, manipulative "Husband" into a warm, tender, loving man; another man, who genuinely devotes his life to loving her, into a cynical, degenerate criminal. In the society around her, she builds up a radically new, magnificently coordinated form of despotism. Within her and without her, she creates a universe which she can totally dominate.

The Crumbling of Clarens

But the structure of this new world is less solid than it looks. Paradoxically, it can stand only so long as she "takes pain to hide from herself the pain she has taken" in creating it, the violence she has done to body and soul. It will collapse as soon as she discovers its foundations in herself. Indeed, it is crumbling at the very moment when Saint-Preux is so struck with its apparent strength. The fact that he is there in the first place is proof of how precarious it really is. For Julie has sought to convince herself that her new role has obliterated all her old feeling for her lover, and all the feeling for herself that fed her love. But she has found that she cannot convince herself without convincing Saint-Preux as well. Thus she has summoned him halfway across the world to her side to prove to him that she no longer needs him. Indeed, to show him that he is an outsider to her, she has invited him into her sanctuary, her most intimate inner space. But his presence within her space has reawakened the very feelings which she hoped to prove were no longer there. Her love for him, which she has repeatedly pronounced dead and buried, is in fact very much alive; her need to make him countersign the death certificate has itself revealed this buried life.

This discovery fills her with panic. She writes a desperate appeal to friend Claire to come and supervise her life, to leave her no freedom, to become *"my continual safeguard against myself."* In order for her to fulfill her role—a role which she once thought had "restored me to myself"—even the pretense of an autonomous self now must go. Why, however, should the discovery of conflict and ambivalence within her evoke so much dread, and call forth such draconic measures against herself? The answer lies in the nature of her role, and of her whole new world. The role of "Mme. de Wolmar" cannot endure underlying conflict because it denies the possibility of anything underlying itself: it prescribes total self-absorption. Julie implores Claire, who she says has "delivered me so many times from the traps of my heart," to "protect me again from those of my reason." She once thought that it was only the body and its passions that she had to fear; she now finds the heart and its capacity for feeling, the mind and its power to reason, equally dangerous. They have turned out to be such a threat because, ultimately, feeling and reason alike emanate from and belong to an individual: they are *her* heart and *her* mind. "How can I depend on my feelings, when they have so abused me? I have lost the right to depend on myself." By the standards of Clarens, her feelings and freedom were abused simply by being used: any form of self-assertion is *ipso facto* self-abuse. "If only I had acted less according to my lights [*moins compté sur mes lumiéres*] in the past, I would find less to blush about today." (IV. 12, 489, 499) Inner light is a source of power independent of the new system. But the existence of an independent source of power refutes that system's fundamental claim: its claim of totality, of the power to make the personality anew. In creating a new world, Julie has left its creator, herself, outside.

This failure to include herself in her new world eventually leads her to catastrophic, fatal self-defeat. It is a defeat that emerges from what, at first, feels like victory. After Saint-Preux departs, and Julie's life resumes its routine, she recollects, and relives, a magic moment during his visit when she experienced the perfect peace and static equilibrium which she had always craved.

> I am surrounded by everything and everyone I care for; the whole universe is here. . . . My imagination has nothing more to do, I have nothing more to desire. To feel and to enjoy are one for me now; I live in all I love, I am filled with happiness and with life.

But what sort of life is this? No sooner does Julie sink beatifically into it than, like an undertow, something in it pulls her away from it, toward death:

> Come, death, when you will, I'm not afraid of you any more. I have lived . . . ; I have nothing more to feel or know, and you have nothing more to hide from me.

Commentators on *La Nouvelle Héloïse* have always piously celebrated Julie's death as a transfiguration. But she herself is not so inclined to celebrate it; her wish for death in the midst of life instantly alarms her.

Can any woman be more susceptible [to happiness]
than I am? Can she love her father, her husband, her
children, her friends, her relatives, more than I do? Can
she do better beloved? Can she enjoy better health?
. . . And yet, with all this, I am constantly uneasy
[*inquiète*]; my heart is ignorant of the very thing it
lacks, it desires something without knowing what. . . .
Everything around me gives me only a cause for contentment, yet I am not content. A secret languor has
insinuated itself into my heart: I feel it empty and
puffed up [*vide et gonflé*]. . . . This pain is strange, I
know, but no less real for all that. My friend, I'm *too*
happy: *happiness bores me.* [VI. 8, 689]

Fixed in one still point, Julie's happiness at Clarens is also a
Punkt, a period, a dead end. It has made her happy by cutting her off from her body and its passions, her heart and its
feelings, her mind and its thoughts; it has drained away her
memories of the past, her perceptions of the present and her
hopes for the future; it has left her *gonflée* on the outside
but *vide* within. The apparent fullness of her role as Madame de Wolmar disguises a profound emptiness of being, a
vacuum where the self should be. She has struggled to recreate herself in the world's image; but this act of creation has
turned out to be possible only *ex nihilo.* In the fight between herself and the world, she has backed the world;
when the world finally wins, its victory is pyrrhic. There is
no one left to play its role; it has won only an empty stage.

If Julie is down, Rousseau nails her down in an Author's
Footnote that oozes *Schadenfreude* for her—and, of course,
for that part of himself which had created and identified
with her. "Such contradictions, Julie! I am afraid, my charming devotee, that you are no longer in accord with yourself.

Indeed, this whole letter looks to me like a swan song."
(693–4) Julie has been *une fausse dévote* of her own ideal
of authenticity; she has betrayed herself to *une mauvaise
foi,* a life of self-deception and now, of self-destruction. She
undertakes to force her whole being into a social and psychological niche; but the ineradicable fact that she is there,
willing and doing the forcing, ensures that, as close as it
may fit, she will always be just a little too big. "If only I had
acted less according to my lights. . . ." She fails to see that
the power which animates her attempt to turn off her inner
light is that very inner light itself. Meanwhile, however, her
zeal against herself, which forces her alienated powers to a
brilliant climax in the creation of an alien world, eventually consumes the power, puts out the light, and destroys the
world. Thus, very shortly after Julie speaks of her deathwish,
she plunges into the water to save one of her children from
drowning. The child survives and recovers before long, but
the mother inexplicably begins to waste away. The doctor
says there is nothing somatically wrong with her; her family
and friends tearfully try to summon her back to the life she
has left; but she is determined to die. The fruit of her success is her suicide. And Rousseau, who has been so enthralled and so abased by her, is glad to see—indeed, to
make—her go.

Julie's suicide is not only a crime of passion but a political assassination. In the footnote where Rousseau points out
her self-deception and announces her impending death (or,
we might say, pronounces his sentence of death), he goes on
to make a political analysis of the verdict:

It follows from this that all princes who aspire to despotism aspire to the privilege of *boredom.* In every
kingdom in the world, if you're looking for the most

bored man in the country, go directly to the sovereign, especially if he's absolute.

Julie, as we have seen, is the most absolute kind of despot, because she knows how to manipulate, not only people's behavior but also their emotional responses and needs, and not only other people's but her own as well. Her personal *malaise,* like Usbek's, stems not from insecurity, but rather from security itself. The very totality of her power over herself and others has left her in a state of total equilibrium, with nothing further to desire. But this state, which at first appeared beatific, is in fact disastrous: "Woe to him who has nothing left to desire! He will lose everything he possesses." Indeed, "any other privation would be more bearable" than to be deprived of *"the pleasure of desiring."* Only now is Julie coming to realize how important this pleasure is to her. "So long as man desires," she sees, "he is happy; he focuses himself on the future. . . . Thus this state is sufficient unto itself, and the restlessness [*inquiétude*] it brings is itself a kind of joy, which compensates for the defects of reality." The power of the imagination is so great that "we enjoy less what we obtain than what we hope for, and we're happy before we're happy." Particularly for a modern woman like herself, in whose life restless desire has become the primary force, to live without desire or hope *"is to be dead."* (VI. 8, 693–4) Julie has frozen herself and all those around her into static roles, devoid of desire—of any passion, tenderness, hope, love, for one another or for themselves—of anything that might propel them beyond what is given. "What need have I to think or imagine," she asks herself, "at a moment when all my faculties are alienated [*alienées*]?" (695) But only the need to think and imagine can generate the energy which any modern man or woman needs in order to act and move and live. As a stagnant being whose faculties are alienated, whose impulses are pro-grammed and circumscribed by her role, whose will to self-improvement and self-development has been turned off, who is emotionally locked up in a world she has made, with nothing to live for, she has no way to live. She has become the first casualty of the peace she has made with herself; she has built a fortress against herself, only to suffocate within its walls.

With herself as with her sanctuary, Julie "takes pain to hide from herself the pain she has taken," the violence she has done in the process of destruction and creation. But in trying to destroy her love for Saint-Preux, she has under-mined her love for herself, her *amour de soi*, the deepest source of her life. In drying up this source, she empties her-self of vital energy; once empty, she is soon dead. On her deathbed, however, she lifts the veil which she has lowered over herself, and confronts the feelings she has suppressed for so long. Her inner light flares up for a moment before it goes out:

For a long time I have deceived myself [she writes Saint-Preux]. But my illusion was salutary for me; and it destroyed itself the moment I no longer needed it. You thought that I was cured of loving you, and I thought that you were cured of loving me. We should be thankful that our error lasted as long as it was useful to us; if I'd seen how close I was to the abyss, who can be sure that my head wouldn't have been turned? How hard I tried to stifle that feeling that inspired me with life, but it concentrated itself in my heart. It arises now again, when there is nothing more to fear. It sustains me as my powers depart; it stirs me up even as I die. . . .

Farewell, farewell, my dear friend. My life ends as it

began: it was through you that I began my life; it is
through you that I end it. Maybe I am saying too much
at a moment when the heart disguises nothing . . .
but why should I be afraid now to express everything I
feel? It's no longer me that's talking; I am already in
the arms of death. [VI. 12, 740, 743]

Julie realizes now that she has failed to become another person; she has succeeded, however, in becoming herself, in
establishing the integrity of the person she has been all
along. Her final consciousness of herself is honest, lucid, in-
cisive, but bleak. "How hard I tried to stifle that feeling
that inspired me with life, but it concentrated itself in my
heart. It arises now again, when there is nothing more to
fear. It sustains me even as my powers depart; it stirs me up
even as I die. . . ." She dares to plunge into being herself
only at the moment she ceases to be.

Thus authenticity is an abyss, inauthenticity a dead end.
Julie's life and death reveal the alternatives which modern
men are still forced to confront. The conflicts and pressures
that arise out of Julie's desire for authenticity drive her into
a new life of total inauthenticity; but the persistence of her
desire undermines the self-deceptions she would need to
survive such a life. The very energy and fullness of self that
lead her to crave the inert security of Clarens make that
security so psychically destructive for her. Ironically, then,
the search for authenticity both generates its antithesis and
makes that antithesis unviable, even fatal, in the end. We
must get out of this bind somehow if we want to write a
happier ending.

More Escapes from Freedom

A young man's worst enemy is himself.
The life of a good woman is a perpetual
struggle against herself.
There is no subjection so great as that
which preserves the forms of freedom: this
way we captivate the will itself.

Emile

. . . now, today, people are more per-
suaded than ever that they have perfect
freedom, yet they have brought their freedom to us and laid it humbly at our feet.

THE GRAND INQUISITOR

JULIE'S ATTEMPT to seal herself up in selflessness
finally sealed her doom. But her death was no final
solution to the fears and needs that gave her project life.
Throughout his life Rousseau was filled with dread by the
idea of being himself—an idea whose reality he understood
perhaps more profoundly than any man. Again and again
he sought a way out; he continually rebuilt Clarens in his
head.

The Price of Potentiality

The paradox of modernity, as it was emerging in Rousseau's time, was that men were at once unhappier and po-

tentially happier than men had ever been before. Their innate need for perfectibility, which had generated the whole structure of modern society, was beginning to generate an awareness of how imperfect a structure this society was. The insatiable needs with which this society had infused its members had developed an economy that was capable of giving them genuine satisfaction. The anxiety that had driven them to create and sustain a competitive and acquisitive social system was making them anxious about the value of this system itself. The sensitivity that enabled them to survive by seeing through one another was enabling them to see through themselves. The *amour-propre* that had brought them together in an illusory community had given them a vague but powerful feeling for what a real community could be. The development of human faculties and talents, which had proceeded through systematic self-alienation, was opening men's minds to the desire for a further development that would reclaim all this energy and power for the self's own needs. Thus the most inauthentic social system in history had generated the ideal of authenticity. The hand that had made the wound of modernity was the hand that could heal it. This was a possibility that Rousseau was the first to see.

But Rousseau's very awareness that the wound could be healed only made its persistent pain harder than ever to bear. Much of the pain of modern life stemmed from the awakening of every man's imagination, which in modern times had become the crucial force in the development of the self. It was only through the growth of the imagination that the self could emerge as a distinct and vital power, organizing the individual's life actively and dynamically from within, propelling him beyond whatever social roles and realities he might be "given." At the same time, however, this inward dynamism propelled man beyond some of the profoundest experiences and the most intense forms of happiness he had ever known. Never again could he recapture the childlike joy of "the primitive state," a joy that flowed from "a *perfect equilibrium* between our desires and our powers." This was the happiness of a closed world, of a world that could enclose its inhabitants in a perfect security of timeless being. Such a stable equilibrium was beyond the scope of modern men; the world they lived in seemed to have opened up irrevocably. In this new world

> the object which at first seemed within our grasp flies from us faster than we can follow; just when we think we have grasped it, it transforms itself, and once again is far ahead of us. We no longer perceive the country we have travelled through, and think nothing of it; that which lies before us becomes vaster, and stretches on before us without end. Thus we exhaust ourselves without coming to an end; and the more enjoyment [*jouissance*] we get, the farther away happiness [*bonheur*] gets from us. [*Emile*, II. 44]

Was this loss of a stable *bonheur* really worth it? It all depended on the intensity and depth of the *jouissance* that modern times could provide. If men could live authentically now, they would be able to utilize the quick changes endemic to modernity for their own personal growth. On the other hand, if they were doomed to imagine authenticity without being able to achieve it, and meanwhile to be driven forever in every direction by social forces which the self could comprehend but not control, then the whole modern experience would seem to be nothing but a nightmare meant to make men miserable. And those who, like Rousseau himself, felt and understood all that modernity could be, would be most miserable of all.

In *La Nouvelle Héloïse* Rousseau had tried to think through to the end the problem of how it might be possible for modern man to live a life of his own. In the end, alas, it did not seem to be possible at all. Modern society was clearly unwilling and probably unable to reform itself so as to live up to its own potentialities. It looked as if any tree that tried to live on the highway was doomed to be cut down. How could men escape this nightmare? Only, it seemed, by destroying their capacity to dream.

> The real world has boundaries, the world of the imagination is infinite. Since we cannot enlarge the real one, we must restrict the imaginary one, since all the suffering that makes us really miserable arises from the disparity between them. [45]

In other words, *if* (as Rousseau believed to be the case) we cannot enlarge the real world so that it will fulfill the ideals that we imagine, *then* we must contract the scope of our imagination so that we will not want more than the world is apt to give. Instead of trying fruitlessly to change a society that does not do enough for us, we must change ourselves so that we will not ask too much from it. Rousseau understood how far such a change would have to go: the life and action of "man's potential powers," and of "the imagination, the most active of all, [which] leads all the rest," was inherently open-ended and inexhaustible; and this infinite power was crucial to the whole structure of the self. Thus his campaign against the imagination was bound to escalate into a war against the self. And there was no way of limiting this war: the only way to restrict a force that was inherently infinite would be to destroy it. This was the source of what I have called the politics of inauthenticity, a body of schemes and fantasies which Rousseau cherished and elaborated all his life.

Rousseau never really expected to escape his sense of himself; but he did hope to seal other men off from the hope for authenticity which plagued him endlessly. He longed to be an ideal legislator, one whose "intelligence would be wholly unrelated to [the people's] nature, while knowing it through and through"; whose "happiness would have to be independent of [the people], and yet ready to occupy itself with [theirs]"; who could begin works in one century which could not be fulfilled until the next; who, finally, would be like a God, distant from the men he saved, not participating in their bliss. (*Contract*, II. 7, 381) If men could be protected from the dream of being themselves, they would not despair at the gulf between this dream and the reality of the world they lived in. If their ideals could be formed to fit existing realities, they might find a peace and equilibrium that Rousseau had never known.

Wherever the imagination was freest and the self most fully developed, the politics of inauthenticity would have to be most relentlessly total. This meant that the most drastic repression would have to be directed against men like Rousseau himself. He recognized that men like himself, who dreamed of an authentic world, were completely unfit to live in an inauthentic one; in backing the world, he hoped to help it exclude such men, or at least prevent any more like them from coming into being. Thus he used all his imaginative powers to imagine a political and social system that could legislate imagination out of existence. If Rousseau's politics of inauthenticity could ever be put into practice, it would instantly define him as public enemy number one.

The first premise of the politics of inauthenticity is that

what cannot be realized must not be idealized. The first application of that premise is that the ideal of authenticity must go. We must "restrict the world of the imagination" so as to eliminate this ideal. Once such a restriction goes into effect, the self is visible only in its bourgeois form, as *amour-propre; amour de soi* disappears without a trace because there is no trace of a *moi,* an authentic nucleus of a self, to love.

> It is too late to change our natural inclinations once they have taken their course, and selfishness [*amour-propre*] is confirmed by habit. And it is too late to lead us out of ourselves once the human self [*le moi humain*], concentrated in our hearts, has taken on that contemptible activism which absorbs all virtue and constitutes the whole life and being of petty souls. [*Economy*, 260]

Perhaps the most significant thing in this passage is what it leaves out, what Rousseau takes for granted and feels no need to say: that bourgeois "selfishness" is the only mode of expression available to the self. *Amour de soi* and *pitié,* which Rousseau has again and again described as the core of *le moi humain,* are simply non-existent here. Rousseau shows the same failure of imagination here which he himself exposes in the followers of Hobbes: "in speaking incessantly of need, oppression and avidity, they have transferred to the state of nature ideas which they have acquired in society. . . ." (*Inequality*, 132) According to this view, the competitive and aggressive behavior of men is not imposed on them by historical forces or social institutions, but "concentrated in our hearts," an expression of man's innate "natural inclinations." Here Rousseau perceives no latent depths or repressed possibilities beneath the manifest behavior; he is deaf to the profound longings and aspirations which, in so much of his work, he was the first to articulate. The static antithesis of Man and Citizen negates any idea of man's evolution in the past, and rules out any hope for further development in the future. The self is permanently stained by something very like Original Sin; a political life that will "lead us out of ourselves" is the closest these fallen men can come to unmerited grace.

Totalitarianism, Ancient Style

The existence of the self, from this perspective, was the fruit of a kind of fall. But this did not make the human condition hopeless: there were still survivals and intimations of a pre-lapsarian state. Many ancient societies, Rousseau imagined, had been governed in such a totalistic and repressive way that their members had never developed any sense of self. His most concrete models of classical totalitarianism were Sparta and republican Rome; but he felt that their example might still be applied to undeveloped areas of Europe, such as Poland and Corsica, where the process of modernization and individuation had not yet begun. The mythical Lycurgus, he said, had understood perfectly how to create and hold together a society of citizens without selves. He had

imposed an iron yoke on the Spartans, the like of which no other people ever bore; but he attached them to and identified them with the yoke by keeping them occupied with it all the time. He kept the fatherland constantly before them in their laws, in their games, in their homes, in their festivals. He never gave them an instant to be alone with themselves. And out of this perpetual constraint, ennobled by its purpose, was born that ardent love of country that as the strongest passion of the

Spartans—or, rather, their only passion—and which turned them into beings above humanity. [*Poland* II, 957]

Rousseau's point here was that repression could be effective in generating social cohesion and solidarity only if it were total. It would be possible to "attach men to and identify them with the yoke by keeping them occupied with it all the time," by leaving them nowhere else to turn. Like Montesquieu's model order of monks (*Spirit of the Laws*, V.1–2, and pages 40–41 of this book), this sort of republic could make its citizens virtuous by repressing all other possible outlets for their energy, thus leaving "love of country" as "their only passion," forcing all individual energy into political channels. The most important alternative for such a society to seal off was individuality itself.

This classically totalitarian ideal could be realized only through the most complete control by the state over the lives of its citizens. Rousseau understood that this control could be established most effectively not over men's bodies but over their hearts and minds: the state would have to monopolize spiritual as well as economic and social life. In ancient times this had been done through control of religion. But in the modern age, an age in which religion (even the sort of civic religion which Rousseau proposed in the *Social Contract*) was clearly peripheral to men's lives, the most important spiritual activity for the state was public education. In the *Emile,* and throughout his work, Rousseau explained how crucial education was in any attempt to strengthen the self; but he understood equally well how crucial it could be in keeping the self from developing. Thus, for Poland,

Education must give the souls of men a national formation, and direct their opinions and tastes so that they'll

272

be patriotic by inclination, by passion, by necessity. When an infant first opens his eyes he ought to see the fatherland, and up to the day of his death he should see nothing else. Every true republican has drunk in love of country—that is to say, love of law and liberty—along with his mother's milk. This love is his whole existence; he sees nothing but the fatherland, he lives for nothing else. When he is solitary, he is nothing; when he has ceased to have a fatherland, he no longer exists; and if he isn't dead, he's worse than dead. [IV, 966]

It would be safe to let citizens leave the fatherland, if they had first been conditioned to feel that outside the fatherland they did not exist; it would be safe to let them alone if everyone had been infused with the sense that "When he is solitary, he is nothing." Here, as at Clarens, the greatest danger to the social order was the aloneness of the individual with himself. Public education had to see to it that cultivation of the self was repressed early in life. Thus "children must not be allowed to play alone, as their fancy dictates, but all together and in public, so that there will always be a common goal toward which they all aspire. . . ." (968) The state would produce citizens who were totally committed to it only if it could totally fill their inner space.

If such a state could operate freely, it would mold its people as a potter molds his clay, and would recreate them in its own image, animate the clay with its own breath. Instead of "following the lines of least resistance, and shaping the government to fit the people," it would "do something far better: namely, shape the people to fit the government." (*Corsica,* Preface, 901) Rousseau knew how resistant the human material was bound to be: the self's own natural rhythms of life flowed through its whole being. Hence the transformation would have to be total and absolute; the state would have to fill its citizens with a new life.

> He who dares to undertake the making of a people's institutions ought to feel himself capable, so to speak, of changing human nature; of transforming each individual, who is by himself a complete and solitary whole, into a part of a greater whole, from which he receives his life and being; of altering man's constitution for the purpose of strengthening it; and of substituting a partial and moral existence for the physical and independent existence which nature has conferred on us all. It is necessary, in a word, to take away from man all his own powers [*ses forces propres*] in order to give him new ones which are alien to him [*qui lui soient étrangères*], which he cannot use without the help of others. The more completely men's natural powers are annihilated [*mortes et anéanties*], the greater and more lasting are those which he acquires, and the more stable and perfect are the new institutions. Thus, if each citizen is nothing and can do nothing without the rest, and if the power of the whole is equal or superior to the sum of the powers of all the individuals, we may then say that legislation is at the highest possible point of perfection. [*Contract*, II. 7, 381–2]

Here, as Judith Shklar says, we have a vision of "the perfectly socialized man, the citizen whose entire life is absorbed by his social role." Here "the individual loses his personal identity"; "the group absorbs all his resources, emotional as well as physical"; "the *moi humain* really is crushed by the *moi commun*. And this is the very essence of the psychological transformation of man into a citizen." ("Rousseau's Two Models," 33–5) Indeed, a transformation

274

of this magnitude would have to be even more than psychological. If Rousseau really meant to empty every individual of everything that was individual about him, and to arrange things so that no one had any impulses or powers that were naturally his own, so that each could literally do nothing without all the rest, he would have to annihilate not only human psychology but human biology as well. He would have to transform these human beings into a species of machines, whose powers would flow only when all together were connected to a central circuit. "A citizen of Rome was neither Caius nor Lucius; he was a Roman." When Rousseau spoke of the Spartans as "beings above humanity," his rhetoric was more serious than it looked; the desire to annihilate humanity, both other men's and his own, was one of the strongest and deepest undercurrents in the stream of his consciousness.

If the ideal state were one whose citizens were machines, the best form of social and economic activity would be the one that tended most to make men mechanical. This, for Rousseau, was the life of the inert traditional peasant. Men whose whole lives were mechanical in this way would make the ideal constituency for a classically totalitarian state. If such a state could find or create such a people, if it could entrench itself among them deep in the mindless inertia of traditional rural existence, if it could insulate itself totally from modern life, it would be able to generate a constant, uniform, static, automatic peace.

Peasants are much more attached to their soil than city-dwellers to their cities. For those who know nothing else, the equality and simplicity of rural life have an attractiveness which leaves them with no desire to change it. Hence that contentment with his station in life [*contentement de son état*] which makes a man peaceable; hence that love of country which attaches him to its constitution. [*Corsica,* 911]

. . . the whole basic tendency of our new constitution is to make this calling [agriculture] happy in its mediocrity, and respectable in its simplicity. Satisfying all the needs of life, providing all the means of gaining social recognition and fulfilling public duties, and all this without sale or traffic, it will leave men incapable of even imagining a better or nobler way of life. [925]

But, alas, even if this sort of paradise could ever be established, it would not last. Its citizens would remain happy with it only so long as they "know nothing else" and "are incapable of imagining a better life." However, so long as they remained men and not machines, their imaginative powers could not be turned off; the imagination might be put to sleep, but eventually it would be bound to awaken. So long as modern cities existed anywhere, they would exert enormous pull on the imagination, like trees of knowledge rich with forbidden fruit. Although Rousseau saw the modern city as a menace to this sort of state, "an abyss" that "breathes forth a constant plague which saps and finally destroys the nation," he had to admit that, as soon as its citizens discovered that the abyss was there, they would be irresistibly "drawn into the cities by the hope of finding a better occupation [*un meilleur métier*]." (911–2) In fact, even if they were totally sealed off from all existing alternatives, they would spontaneously generate new alternatives from within; they would grow their own trees of knowledge. If cities did not exist, farmers would invent them. Thus "The very success of this new constitution will force it to change." Rousseau explained that

Cultivation of the land cultivates the spirit. All agricultural peoples multiply; they multiply in proportion to the product of their soil; and when their soil is fertile, they finally multiply to such an extent that it is no longer sufficient to support them; then they are forced either to found colonies or to change their form of government.

When the country is saturated with inhabitants, the surplus can no longer be employed in agriculture, but must be employed in industry, commerce or the arts; and this new system demands a new type of administration. Let us hope that the institutions Corsica is about to establish will soon require her to make such changes! [906–7]

"Cultivation of the land cultivates the spirit": this meant that even the most idyllically static society contained the seeds of its own destruction. Neither individuals nor social systems could be frozen forever in a state of perfect innocence. Thus any classically totalitarian state was doomed to be swept away by the dynamism of social development, which flowed irresistibly on through the modern age, inseparable from human life itself.

Totalitarianism, Modern Style

Rousseau realized in the end that his longing for perfect inauthenticity was at least as hopeless, as extravagantly utopian, as his desire for authenticity. But he conceived of another alternative for modern men, less ambitious but more realistic than either of these extremes: a modern form of totalitarianism which could both control and satisfy men by "leading us out of ourselves." The secret of modern totalitarianism was that *"The most absolute authority is that which penetrates into a man's inner being, and governs not*

277

so much his actions as his will." (*Economy,* 251) Instead of
trying vainly to tear down and reconstruct the personalities
of his subjects, the shrewd modern legislator would "penetrate into a man's inner being": he would work with their
character structure as it was, and look for needs and impulses within this structure which he could utilize, so as to
manipulate and control them while leaving them as much
as possible as they were. This new form of totalitarianism
could save its subjects from the emotional pain and violence
of a confrontation between social norms and individual
needs. It could make it easy for them to accommodate themselves to the life of their times, renouncing the hope of self-
fulfillment which the dream of authenticity had opened up
to them, but escaping the despair which the defeat of that
hope would be sure to bring. The best way to lead modern
men out of themselves would be to recognize that in fact
they were out of themselves already: to accept historical
progress and capitalize on the forms of self-alienation that
were already present in modern life. The politics of inauthenticity had a dialectic all its own.

The forces that alienated modern men from themselves
were enormously powerful. All the institutions of their society forced them to compete against one another in order to
succeed; the only form of identity they knew was based on
amour-propre, entirely relative and invidious, inherently
aggressive. Instead of resisting the power of *amour-propre* in
its subjects, Rousseau argued, the state should encourage
and cultivate it, while channeling it toward public rather
than exclusively private ends. It should "offer a road for
their ambition" (*Poland,* XV. 1041), without struggling
against that ambition itself. It would then

> arrange things so that every citizen will feel himself to
> be constantly under the eyes of the public; so that no

one can advance or succeed without public approval; so that no post can be filled except by the will of the nation; and finally, so that, from the lowliest nobleman, even from the lowliest peasant, up to the king himself, if it is possible, everyone will be so dependent on public esteem that nothing can be done, nothing acquired, no success achieved without it. [XII, 1019]

If men could be induced to compete for public esteem and political power instead of private profits, this would "transform into a sublime virtue that dangerous disposition which is the source of all our vices." (*Economy*, 260) The state would transform *amour-propre* by nationalizing it, by integrating it into the political system.

This policy of nationalization would have to be comprehensive and complete; surprisingly, however, the state did not need to do very much in order to carry it out. It was essential to the state that children should play together in such a way that "there will be a common goal to which they will all aspire, and which will excite competition [*concurrence*] and emulation." Public education had to "accustom them to equality, to competition, to living under the eyes of their fellow-citizens, and to desiring public approbation." (*Poland*, IV. 968) But the competition, the emulation, the striving for approbation, all this would be going on anyway, independently of the state, as part of the pervasive process of socialization that integrated the children into modern society. The state did not need to teach them to fight against one another; all it had to do was to coordinate the multitude of separate contests under its own auspices.

When the children grew up, a complex, minutely graded hierarchy would be there waiting for them to grow into. I would be a distinctively modern kind of hierarchy. All feudal privileges and traditional ranks would be wiped out:

"all men must be equal by right of birth." (*Inequality*, 222-3) Status would no longer be hereditarily ascribed; it would be based strictly on competitive achievement, in a competition that was open equally to all. Performances would be exhaustively ranked and rewarded by the state. Here, ironically, Rousseau rejected the essential modern standard for success—wealth—because it wasn't invidious enough: it was "insufficiently public," it "fails to make a continuous impression on the hearts and minds of men," it "disappears as soon as it is awarded" and "leaves no visible trace to excite emulation by perpetuating the honor that should accompany it." As an alternative, he "would like all ranks, offices and honorific awards to be distinguished by external signs, so that no public figure would ever be able to go incognito; his rank or dignity will follow him everywhere." The public display of his status would not only "make the people always respect him"; it would penetrate his inner being, and "make him respect himself." That men should derive their self-respect (or lack of it) from their competitive performance was nothing new: as Rousseau saw, as we have seen, it was endemic to modern life. What *was* new was the stage on which their performances were to take place: it would shift from society to the state, from economic to political life. Thus everyone "would be forced to serve his country in order to cut a figure in it, to be a man of integrity for reasons of ambition." (*Poland*, XI. 1007; cf. III. 964-5)

The most decisive and energetic actions of such a state would be transitional: they would coordinate and synthesize existing forms of competition into a totally competitive social system. To create such a system necessarily meant to destroy any social forces that stood in its way. The most formidable obstacle Rousseau could see was the new plutocracy, which threatened to establish a monopoly of power that would bring all meaningful competition to an end. Thus the state would have to break the power of the pluto-crats. The most effective way to do this might be simply to expropriate them. But Rousseau rejected this option, first, because it would destroy the generality of the law, and make the state an agent of some interest groups against others; (*Contract,* II. 4, 373; II. 6, 379) second, because it would de-stroy "the right of property," which "is the true foundation of civil society," "the most sacred of all the rights of citizen-ship, and even more important in some ways than liberty itself." (*Economy,* 263) In a system based on the universal pursuit of power, it was symbolically crucial to preserve the idea of property; it was politically legitimate, however, to radically alter the reality. The state could do this through shrewd manipulation of its taxing powers and fiscal policies; under cover of a taxation it could carry out virtual expro-priation.

> You'd be astonished at all the resources the rulers can make use of for fulfilling public needs without trespass-ing on the goods of individuals. Since they are masters of all the commerce of the state, there is nothing easier than to direct it into such channels as will provide for every need, without appearing to interfere. [267]

"Without *appearing* to interfere": just as in the modern metropolis as Saint-Preux discovered it, appearance and re-ality were at opposite poles.

> The greatest talent a ruler can have is to disguise his power, so as to render it less odious, and to conduct his state so peaceably that it will seem to have no need of conductors. [250]

281

Such a ruler, like Julie de Wolmar, would replace the scepter with the veil. His guiding hand would be most powerful when it was most invisible.

The primary function of this state, then, was to create a society that could function without it. Once that social system was running smoothly, the state could retreat from the foreground to the background of human life. If a ruler could only "arrange things so that all citizens did what they were supposed to do, then there would be nothing left for him to do; and the crownng achievement of all his labor would be to be able to remain unemployed." (*Economy*, 250) Here "what they were supposed to do" would be precisely what they would in any case be inclined to do: to compete aggressively against one another for power. The "things" which the state would have to "arrange" would be, essentially, the rules of the game. The state would make and enforce the rules, and would serve as the ultimate judge of victory and defeat. It would prevent men from becoming so powerless that they would be effectively excluded from the competition, or so powerful that they could win it definitively; in other words, it would keep the game open equally to all. Such a state would be startlingly similar to the liberal radical state which Rousseau designed to maximize authenticity. It would be thoroughly egalitarian and democratic, and yet, paradoxically, it would also be more profoundly authoritarian than ever before. It would incarnate concretely the abstract paradoxes of which Rousseau was so fond. It would "secure each citizen against all personal dependence," but at the same time "give him to his country"; (*Contract*, I. 7, 364) however, "each, in giving himself to all, gives himself to nobody." (I. 6, 361) "Each citizen would be perfectly independent of all the rest, yet excessively dependent on the *Cité*." (II. 12, 394) It would "subjugate men in order to make them free"; it would "confine their will by their own consent"; it would arrange things so that "all men obey, yet none commands, and all men serve, yet they have no master." (*Economy*, 248) It is striking that Rousseau should describe these ideal citizens with the very image he used to describe the corrupt *mondains* of Paris: they were servants without masters. Thus, despite vastly increased equality and democracy, the structure of authority in modern society would remain intact: men would be protected from any sort of *personal* dependence, yet all would be totally dependent on an abstract, impersonal *system*. The state that kept such a system going would be able to satisfy the wills of its citizens by providing outlets and rewards for their *amour-propre;* at the same time, it would be able to control their wills by defining and demarcating the channels through which *amour-propre* could legitimately flow. This sort of state could afford to allow its citizens the fullest collective participation in the decision-making process, knowing all the while that they would limit their freedom and restrict their power within the limits it prescribed. Thus private interests and public power would coincide.

> Out of the effervescence excited by this mutual emulation will arise that patriotic drunkenness [*ivresse patriotique*] which alone can raise men above themselves, and without which liberty is but an empty word and laws a chimera. [*Poland,* XII. 1019]

The strongest fortress of such a state is the *amour-propre* of the people. So long as modern men remain alienated from themselves, they will stand in need of a state to tell them who they are. "The best subjects are those who are most afraid [*alarmés*]"; and the most successful government will be the one that can manipulate most skillfully its subjects' fears and anxieties. Such a state must know, above all, how to monopolize the sources of identity, to separate its citizens from the means of psychological production, to make it impossible for men to find or to create themselves.

Education for Inauthenticity: Emile, Sophie and Us

In order to attune men to modern totalitarianism, it is essential to begin early in childhood, before a person's sense of self is fully developed, while it is still weak enough to be broken down. Thus Rousseau addresses his *alter ego,* Emile's tutor:

> Isn't this poor child, without knowledge, strength or wisdom, entirely at your mercy? Aren't you master of his whole environment? Can't you make of him what you please? His work and his play, his pleasure and his pain—he doesn't know it, but aren't they all in your hands? Certainly he should do only what he wants, but he should want only what you want him to want. He should never take a step that you haven't foreseen, or utter a word that you couldn't foretell. [II, 85]

Here Rousseau's educational methods, so effective for building up the self, turn out to be at least as effective in tearing it down, or in keeping it from ever coming into being.

No one understands better than Rousseau how important it is to create an atmosphere of personal trust and intimacy between teacher and pupil. Trust and intimacy will help the child feel comfortable and secure with himself. At the same time, an atmosphere that encourages him to expose his deepest feelings and express himself may also give his master, who creates this atmosphere, enormous power to manipulate those feelings and repress the self. As Rousseau says, once the child trusts you, "you can surround him with all the lessons you would have him learn, without awakening his suspicions." (85; cf. 283) He then constructs scenarios for typical lessons. In the first scenario, the boy disturbs his master's sleep at night, and rushes wildly about the room, demanding recognition and attention. The proper response, Rousseau says, is to simply look through the child, turn one's head to the wall and pretend to sleep. The more hysterical the boy becomes, the more adamantly impassive the tutor must be, acting as if there is no one at all in the room with him. "I saw that, although he knew how to cope with scolding or anger, he was quite unprepared for total indifference [ce grand sang-froid]." If "my little rebel" [mon petit mutin] persists, and the tutor is forced to acknowledge his presence, he will lock the child up in a dark room alone. He may scream and shout at first; but fear will paralyze him before long, and reduce him to the silence and docility his master requires. (86) Rousseau has argued that wickedness comes from weakness; here he responds to childish wickedness by showing the child how weak he really is. Out of the terrors of the night the boy cried for love and care; by withholding the reassurance he needs, by treating him as if he doesn't exist, by cutting him off from the whole world around him, his master has plunged him into a darker night than he ever knew, and made him feel that his whole being is far more precarious than he dreamt.[7]

In the next scenario, the child learns that, if his home is a

[7] In an earlier episode, Rousseau prescribes a similar treatment for a very different offense: if your pupil goes around breaking windows, try locking him up for a few hours in a dark and windowless place; don't let him out until, terrified, he swears never to break a window again. "If I'm not greatly mistaken, there isn't a child in the world who could resist this treatment—unless he's utterly spoiled already. . . ." (63–4) By such means, young people are to be taught the meaning of property.

place of fear and insecurity, the world outside is even worse. Here the tutor provokes his pupil into disobeying him by venturing out of the house alone. But he has arranged the environment so that the youth will not get far. First of all, the neighbors have been alerted, and assigned parts to play. They line the streets as the boy goes by, and remark to each other in stage whispers that he looks like *"un petit libertin* who's been thrown out of his own house because he's good for nothing"; sadly but righteously, they say that such a boy will get no help from anyone, and will deserve whatever dire fate he meets. If he thinks he will get a more friendly response from boys of his own age, they too have been enlisted for the occasion: they lay in wait to taunt and attack him. Indeed, the tutor recollects with a gloating complacency, "the further he went, the more trouble he found. Alone and unprotected, he discovered that he was the plaything of the world"—a world whose coldness and hostility, bad enough in the ordinary course of events, have been artificially intensified to break his will. At this point, a friend of the tutor, who has been watching and waiting in the wings, comes onstage and offers to act as the boy's guardian angel: "he made him so aware of the imprudence of his exploit that in a half hour's time he had brought him home to me, distraught and afraid to look me in the face." Finally, "to complete the disaster of his attempt," the boy is confronted by his father, who tells him coldly: "If you want to go out by yourself, you are your own master; but I don't want a bandit[8] in the house; so when you go, make sure that you never come back." Crushed by this final threat of total parental rejection, on top of all his other fears, the child throws himself on his tutor's mercy. The next day the

---

[8] Barbara Foxley, Rousseau's Victorian translator, shows a degree of political awareness rare for her when she translates *bandit* as "rebel."

tutor takes him for a walk, a ritual procession meant to show the world that he is back in his old, subservient role. As if by magic, everyone's attitude toward the boy has changed completely: "I saw that he passed in triumph with me among the very same people who had mocked him the day before when they'd met him alone. You can be sure he never threatened to go out without me again." (88–9) This lesson has made the growing boy's life a nightmare; as old as he may grow, he will never fully awake. He has learned that the slightest attempt to assert himself in the world, to confront it on his own, will lead him to inexorable destruction; on the other hand, if he goes along with authority, and moves in the grooves it has laid out for him, he will meet with instant, painless success. After this, he will be happy and grateful never to go out alone; he will carry authority with him, at his side or in his head, wherever he goes.

When Emile approaches puberty, and Rousseau begins to talk about sex, we suddenly find ourselves plunged into another nightmare world of terror and anxiety. "Under my care Emile has remained in a state of primitive innocence, but now I see this happy time drawing to a close. Surrounded by ever-increasing perils, he'll escape me the first chance he gets, and that chance won't be long in coming. He will follow the blind instinct of his senses, and the odds are a thousand to one he'll ruin himself [*se perdre*]. I've studied the morals of mankind too much not to be aware of the irrevocable influence of this first moment on all the rest of his life." (IV. 282) The teacher's task is to hold back that moment indefinitely, to preserve Emile's virginity at any cost. The growing boy must be made to feel that there are only two alternatives for him: either total chastity, or else "the horrors of debauchery, its stupid brutality, and the imperceptible downward path by which a single misstep [*dé-*

sordre] leads to every kind of evil, and in the end drags anyone who takes that first step to his ruin." (289) The adolescent's world is a cruel one: his most persistent and pressing desires are pushing him toward inexorable doom. Once again Rousseau is seized with a vision of the abyss: Emile, going through changes he does not yet understand, is "like a sleepwalker [who] walks along the edge of a precipice, which he'd fall off if he suddenly woke up"; the most urgent task at hand is to "pull him back from the edge." (284)[9]

What is the abyss that so terrifies Rousseau? To fear "the blind instinct of the senses" is quite conventional; in the context of traditional Western culture it needs no special explanation. In fact, however, it is not really the body he is afraid of, but a much more formidable power. Indeed, he insists, against all common sense, that "sexual desire is not a *physical* need at all." The true source of sexuality, he says, is *"the imagination alone,"* which "awakens the senses" and makes them active. This paradoxical idea is unraveled in a passage which works out in a few lines, with obsessive brilliance, the total logic of repression. How, Rousseau asks, can we fight off the adolescent's sexual awakening? First of all, "By exercising his body with hard work, I can arrest the activity of the imagination, which is leading him on. When the arms are hard at work, the imagination rests. When the body is tired, the heart won't catch fire." The body, with its automatism and its limited capacities, turns out to be the censor's natural ally. His real antagonist is the "heart," the "imagination," the spirit. Here, as in Rousseau's model of a

---

[9] It is striking how closely Rousseau's sexual fears prefigure those of the Victorians. For an original, provocative study of the Victorian sexual and moral world, from which I have learned a great deal, see Steven Marcus, *The Other Victorians: Sexuality and Pornography in Mid-Nineteenth Century England* (New York: Bantam Books, 1967), especially 12–33.

stagnant peasant society, the function of enervating physical labor is to seal the body off from the spirit, to deaden it so that it will be impervious to the spirit's insidious appeals. However, this is only a beginning: the spirit has enormous secret reserves of strength. The tutor must protect Emile from all the experiences that might stir his spirit up: "reading, solitude, idleness, a soft[10] and sedentary life, the company of women and young people, all these are perilous paths for a young man, and will lead him into constant danger." Since most of these experiences are most readily available in the city, "I take him away from cities, far from objects that can tempt him." But a mere outward change of scene at this point in Emile's life would change him very little. First of all, since solitude is just as threatening as sociability, the country would provide no real protection, and the open spaces would make surveillance even harder. Moreover, Rousseau, always a subtle psychologist, realizes that "this isn't enough: in what desert, in what wilderness can he escape the images that pursue him? It isn't enough to remove dangerous objects if we don't also efface the memory of them." The fate of Julie made it clear to Rousseau how humanly destructive and ultimately futile the attempt to efface disturbing memories could be. Even if the work of repression were technically feasible, however, it could not begin until the site for demolition was located, until "the images that pursue him" were traced to their source. The possible sources in Emile's life are disturbingly few. He has never seen a city, or any other form of society. He has never

---

10 Softness and tenderness are particularly dangerous. Emile is encouraged to take up hunting because it "hardens the heart as well as the body; it accustoms us to blood and cruelty. Diana has been represented as the enemy of love, and the symbolism is apt: the languors of love are born of soft repose, but tender feelings are stifled by violent exercise." It is love, not lust, that is the source of all this anxiety.

289

been intimate with his parents. He has no friends. He has had only the most fleeting, evanescent contacts with strangers. Except for his tutor—an important exception, which Rousseau seems to blot out of his mind—he has had no relationships with other people. The one great relationship in his life has been—with *himself*. But it is precisely this relationship that makes *all* his experience, past, present and future, a source of temptation and terror. Rousseau relentlessly presses the logic of repression to its conclusion: "If I can't find the art of *detaching him from everything*, if I can't *distract him from himself*, I might as well leave him where he was." (284–5) In all human experience, the self is latently present. What sexual experience does is to awaken the whole range of human impulses—body and spirit, drives, feelings and ideas, memory and imagination, "everything"—to fuse and integrate them into a new synthesis: to bring the whole self into activity, to make man fully, authentically alive. We can see now that when Rousseau confronts sexuality as an abyss, it is the life and energy of the self he dreads.

How much of Rousseau's fear of sexuality is really a fear of the self becomes clear in his overwrought invective against the practice of masturbation. Once again, he is in accord with conventional morality. However, he depends neither on the older, theological convention that anathematized masturbation as a pollution of childish innocence, nor on the newer, pseudo-biological convention which claimed that it ruined the complexion, stunted growth and damaged the brain.[11] Rousseau's worries are more realistic and more profound:

[11] For the older belief, see Philippe Ariès, *Centuries of Childhood: A Social History of Family Life,* translated from the French by Robert Baldick (New York: Vintage Books, 1965), 106–19; for the newer one, Marcus, *The Other Victorians,* 19–25. For a more liberal and permissive

watch carefully over your young man. He can protect himself against all other enemies, but it's up to you to *protect him from himself.* Therefore, *never leave him alone,* night or day; at the very least, you must always sleep in his room. Never let him go to bed until he's sleepy, and make him get up as soon as he's awake. . . . It would be dangerous indeed if your pupil learned *to satisfy his senses by himself;* once he acquires this fatal habit, he is lost. . . .

If you must be a slave, Emile, I prefer to surrender you to a tyrant from whom I can rescue you. *I can free you far more easily from women than from yourself.* . . .

I would rather see him in the midst of the worst company in Paris than alone in his room or in a park, left to all the restlessness of his age. Whatever we may do, *of all the enemies that attack a young man, his most dangerous enemy is himself,* and this is *the one enemy we cannot avoid.* [298–9]

What Rousseau finds so dangerous about masturbation is its *inwardness,* its goal of self-satisfaction, its means of self-exploration, its expression of self-delight. His desire to suppress masturbation is essentially a desire to deny the youth any time or space—and, most urgently, to deny him any *inner* space—that he can call his own. It seems that Pascal's terror of the infinite spaces that surround him pales before Rousseau's fear of the infinite space within. The world, he is

---

view, based on the biological and medical knowledge of Rousseau's time but close in sensibility to our own, see Diderot, *D'Alembert's Dream,* in *Rameau's Nephew and Other Writings,* translated and edited by Jacques Barzun and Ralph Bowen (New York: Bobbs-Merrill, 1963), 169–71.

convinced, will not let the self expand to fill the vast spaces which its imagination has opened up; therefore, for the sake of its own happiness, let the self close down the scope of its being, before it collapses in despair.

Emile will be lost if he tries to satisfy his infinite desires by himself; but he will be in even worse shape if he focuses his desires on another. Emile is now subject not only to his own desire for Sophie, but to her desire for him. Because her love rewards him for being himself (396), their relationship brings his whole self most fully to life. But because her desires (like his own) are boundless, *"illimités," "sans mesure,"* they impose an enormous burden on him: he must be alive and full enough to satisfy needs that are inherently insatiable. Rousseau is terrified by the scope and depth of these needs; he fears the self will crack under the strain. As a man who never really felt secure in his manhood, Rousseau is particularly frightened by women's sexual desire for men. He sees their charms as a trap, a pit, a snare: if unsuspecting mankind let themselves be lured in, they will never get out. Nature has endowed women with "the power to stir a man's senses, to penetrate the depths of his heart [note the reversal in this image], to rekindle fires within him that are nearly extinguished"; if nature took its course, "the men, tyrannized over by the women, would at last become their victims, and would be dragged to their death, without the least hope of self-defense"; thus "the human race would perish by the very means established for its continuance." (322)

Because Sophie's feelings and needs are so malignant, it is especially urgent that she should learn to fear and hate herself. If she lets herself go in love, she will destroy the man she loves; hence her relationship with him must somehow be drained of self. This can best be done if she is taught that, as a woman, she is "specially made for man's delight," "made to please and to be in subjection to a man," (322) "at the mercy of man's judgment"; (328) that she exists only as a means, not as an end in herself. Thus "Girls should be accustomed as early as possible to restraint." It is legitimate, even beneficial, for these restraints to be arbitrary: "If they are always eager to be at work, they must sometimes be compelled to do nothing." She should be stopped even if she is performing her duties well; it is dangerous for her to learn to perform them in her own way. Under modern conditions, Rousseau explains, "the life of a good woman [*honnête femme*] *is a perpetual struggle against herself. . . ."* (332) This struggle must repress all forms of spontaneous activity. Even the most innocent action is potentially guilty if it is done spontaneously, for spontaneity enables the self to express its feelings and to develop inner rhythms of its own. To inhibit these feelings and rhythms, Rousseau plans nightmare scenarios for Sophie which are as lurid as those used earlier on Emile:

> Just because they have, or ought to have, little freedom, girls are apt to indulge themselves too fully with regard to such freedom as they have; they carry everything to extremes, and they devote themselves to their games with an enthusiasm even greater than that of boys. . . . This enthusiasm must be kept in check, for it is the source of several vices commonly found among women, caprice and that extravagant admiration which leads a woman to regard a thing with rapture today and be quite indifferent to it tomorrow. . . . Do not deprive them of mirth, laughter, noise and games, but do not let them tire of one game and go off to another; *do not leave them for a moment without restraint.* Train them to break off their games and return to

other occupations without a murmur. Habit is all that is needed, as you have nature on your side.

This habitual restraint produces a docility which woman requires all her life long, for she will always be in subjection to a man, or to man's judgment, and she will never be free to set her opinion above his. . . . [333]

Rousseau showed how our sense of justice is an expansion of our self-love; Sophie, however, is taught expressly *not* to love herself. Since woman is "formed to obey so imperfect a creature as man, a creature often vicious and always faulty, she should learn early to submit to injustice, and to suffer the wrongs inflicted on her by her husband without complaint. . . ." (333) In all respects, then, Sophie should be a perfect anti-self. Perhaps Julie de Wolmar failed to empty herself of selfhood only because she began too late; perhaps if the emptying process begins in the earliest stages of life, it can really work.

Rousseau means to make Sophie selfless, but not to make her mindless. If she were stupidly docile and submissive, Emile would soon grow bored with her, as the Persian sultans got bored with their slaves. Moreover, although Rousseau "would not altogether blame those who would restrict a woman to the labors of her sex and leave her in profound ignorance of everything else," such ignorance would be viable only amidst "a life withdrawn from the world." In modern society, however, "In great cities, among immoral men, such a woman would be too easily led astray; her virtue would always be at the mercy of circumstances." In order to "be able to resist temptation . . . she must know beforehand what she may hear and what she should think of it." (345–6) Thus Sophie should be intelligent and sensitive;

294

the only thing she must not be is imaginative. The inherent subversiveness of the imagination is revealed again in a strange, Pirandellian interlude that disrupts the narrative flow. Sophie is a character who has been created and given life for the purpose of becoming Emile's subservient and loving wife. Suddenly, however, she seems to break loose from her *raison d'être* and take on a life of her own. At the end of her adolescence, just when she should be looking for a husband to lean on, she forsakes social life, locks herself in her room, reads books, and pines away alone. None of the men, none of the prospects her society holds out, is good enough for her; she has gone on strike against her ordained destiny. Her parents are stunned, nonplussed: "How could such outrageous delicacy exist in someone who has been carefully taught from her earliest childhood to accommodate herself to those she must live with, to make a virtue of necessity?" Despite all the care they have taken in repressing her sense of self, they have been unable to destroy her capacity to imagine something better than the life she has been given. Thus she "couldn't be compelled to adopt [a] husband's way of thinking"; she seeks a man whose heart and mind would be at one with her own, with whom she could share rather than submit. This romantic idealism would be disastrous for Emile: his mate would be able to make demands on him, to judge him, to criticize him, if she had values of her own; she would cease to exist exclusively for his sake. At this critical point we encounter one of the most bizarre moments in all of modern literature: the author steps bodily into his story, seizes the character he has created, and tries to perform a drastic operation on her that will undo the damage he has inadvertently done: "let us resuscitate this sweet girl by giving her a less vivid imagination and a happier fate. I wanted to create an ordinary woman, but by giving her a great soul I have disturbed her reason; I have gone astray." He would create her anew with "a good disposition and an ordinary soul"; then she will fit her destined niche. (366–8) The reader is asked to believe that this emergency operation succeeds; minus imagination, Sophie is fully equipped to play the role she was made for, and the show can go on. But the absurd way in which the crisis is resolved betrays Rousseau's uneasiness about his whole project. He finds the self more resilient, and resistant, than he would have it.

If we assume that this strange form of brain surgery could succeed, and Sophie could be brought up with great intelligence and sensitivity but without any imagination or sense of self, how would she be likely to behave? Her submissiveness, we see, would be nothing but a mask. Thus "she is ashamed to be strong. And why? Not only to gain an appearance of refinement. She is too clever for that. She is providing herself beforehand with excuses, with the right to be weak if she chooses." (323) Rousseau explains that "A woman's real resource is her wit, . . . a wit that is adapted to her condition, the art of taking advantage of our position and controlling us through our own strength." (335) Women could harness men's strength by "making us desire what she can't achieve without us, and what she considers necessary or pleasing; therefore she must have a thorough knowledge of a man's mind. . . . By her own speech and action, look and gesture, she must be able to inspire men with the feelings she desires, without seeming to have any such purpose." (350) It would be wrong for a woman to "usurp her husband's rights and take the command upon herself"; on the other hand, it should never be necessary, because women can capture covertly all the power they want through their "natural gift for managing men." Here, as at Clarens,

Woman's reign is a reign of gentleness, tact and kindness; her commands are caresses, her threats are tears.
She should reign in the home as a minister reigns in the
state, by contriving to be ordered to do what she wants.
[370–1]

Rousseau understood that the authority of the veil could be
far more formidable than that of the scepter: power was
never more effective than when it was in disguise.

Thus Sophie would manipulate and control Emile, but
not for her own ends, since, as we have seen, she would have
no ends of her own. How would she decide what she should
do? By "accommodating herself to those she must live with,"
by "making a virtue of necessity." (367) In the climate of
modern society, the pressures of "necessity" were volatile,
and fluctuated mercurially; the identity of "those she must
live with" was always open to drastic change. Accordingly, it
was only appropriate that "her conduct is controlled by
public opinion" (340), a standard that shifted like the
wind. Sophie would be an agent of public opinion, to which
she would make Emile conform.

A woman's honor does not depend on her conduct
alone, but on her reputation, and no woman who per-
mits herself to be considered vile is really virtuous. A
man has no one but himself to consider. "What people
will think" is the grave of a man's virtue, but the
throne of a woman's. [328]

This vision had qualifications. Sophie was now told that in
cases of conflict she was entitled to put conscience above
public opinion (346); and yet, her own conscience would be
conditioned so that it could have no content apart from
this public opinion itself. So long as she was in charge, it

297

was certain that her family would never deviate from "what people will think" they should do or be.

The nightmares which Rousseau arranges for the education of Emile and Sophie crystallize his most distinctive contribution to the theory of totalitarianism: the idea that a little repression, if it is administered at the right time and place, can go on a long way. These traumatic lessons can be taught in a relatively short time, through a relatively low degree of control over the environment. If the teaching is effective, even these external controls can be dispensed with before long. "Once my authority is firmly established, my first concern will be to avoid the necessity of using it." (IV. 291) The powers that be will not need to use their authority because their subjects will have built up authorities far more effective within themselves. If their own selves become a source of terror to them, they will learn how to repress themselves so as to dispel the terror.

> I let him have the appearance of freedom, but he was never more under control [assujetti], because he wants to be. So long as I couldn't master his will, I kept control of his person; I never let him take a step by himself. Now I can leave him to himself, because I govern him continually. [298]

This internal and spontaneous repression eliminates the need for the sort of vast, expensive and unreliable machinery of violence on which any system of external coercion must depend. Moreover, it penetrates into the hidden depths of the self, where it can paralyze and punish forbidden wants and impulses as well as words and deeds. Finally, and perhaps most important, it is immune to the resentment and hostility, the sense of injustice and indignity, which any external form of authority inevitably creates in the men it rules. Indeed, it even enables the rulers to grant their subjects an enormous amount of political liberty, while resting assured that they will not use their liberty to step out of line. *"There is no subjection so great as that which preserves the forms of freedom: this way we captivate the will itself."* (II. 84)

Rousseau, the first and perhaps the greatest theorist of radical liberalism, saw clearly the ambiguities of the world that radical liberalism might usher in. This world held out hope of unprecedented happiness for modern men if their dream of authenticity should be fulfilled, but threatened them with total despair if their hope should fail. Rousseau looked long and hard at the world he lived in, and saw no hope for authenticity there. But if this was so, would it not be most genuinely liberal to protect modern men from the fatal lure of this dream, and from the inevitable bleakness of the morning after? Wouldn't a state that really cared about the freedom and happiness of its citizens do everything in its power to free them from this false and self-destructive hope? Rousseau often saw himself as the ideal legislator of a politics of inauthenticity. He theorized about how the state could divert men from themselves by maximizing rewards and incentives for its subjects' *amour-propre,* and creating a climate that would encourage them to aggress and compete within limits which it would define. He thought carefully about how men could be educated so that the hope of authenticity would disappear from their minds, or else be kept from appearing. Our discussion of Emile and Sophie in the chapter above suggests where these thought-experiments were apt to lead. Emile would no longer dream of authenticity because he would have only the most tenuous and fleeting idea of who he was: he would be terrified by every impulse or idea he felt within himself, and threatened by everyone and everything around him. Sophie, who had been emptied of her sexuality, her imagination and her sense of herself in order that she should not make impossible demands on Emile, would learn new demands that were far more cruel and insatiable than anything she could ever have asked for herself: in compensation (and perhaps in revenge) for the lifelong repression she endured, she would pursue power over the man who sought to keep her down, she would dominate and manipulate him mercilessly in the name of public opinion, she would drive him on unceasingly at once to compete and to conform. Totally alienated from themselves, they could both be totally controlled.[12]

All this showed how, with a minimum of trouble, a totalitarian political system could be constructed out of modern society as it was. Thus Rousseau was certainly a theorist of totalitarianism, but in a much broader and deeper sense than is usually thought. The fulfillment of his fantasies of total power and control should be sought not in the revolutionary extremes of France in 1793 or Russia in 1919, but rather in the ordinary, everyday workings of the typical modern states of our time. Like Rousseau's models, these states derive their power from the dynamism and energy of modern economic and social life, which they harness for their own ends; they keep their citizens in line by forcing them to run on an endless series of tracks in perpetual competition with one another. Moreover, his totalitarian models make clear the essential similarity of some contemporary systems which might seem to have little in common.

12 For startling similarities between Rousseau's ideal education for inauthenticity and real education in America today, cf. Jules Henry, *Culture Against Man* (New York: Vintage, 1963), especially 283–321, and Edgar Z. Freidenberg, *Coming of Age in America: Growth and Acquiescence* (New York: Vintage, 1967).

A political system built on *amour-propre* could be run as liberally and democratically as Athens or Valais—or the U.S.A.—and still have a structure of authority as total as Sparta or Clarens—or the U.S.S.R. Indeed, a liberal and democratic totalitarianism might be even more effective and powerful than cruder and more brutal forms, because it would be so subtly insidious: there would be no subjection so great as that which preserved the forms of freedom, because this subjection could captivate the self. The human costs of this captivity emerge clearly in the family life of Emile and Sophie. They are politically freer, yet psychologically more enslaved, than men and women have ever been.[13] The anxiety-ridden roles they play mark them as archetypal characters in a domestic tragedy that is still being played out in our suburbs today.

The catastrophic costs of such a system appear even more vividly if it is projected on an international scale. Rousseau hoped to "transform into a sublime virtue that dangerous disposition [*amour-propre*] which gives rise to all our vices." (*Economy*, 260) In fact, however, this nationalization of *amour-propre* would leave its psychological content intact; it would merely give that dangerous disposition a stamp of legitimacy. As Freud put it mordantly, "The state has forbidden the individual the practice of wrongdoing; not, however, because it wants to abolish wrongdoing, but because it wants to monopolize it, like salt and tobacco."[14] In such a system, politics would become the arena in which all men's most aggressive impulses could express themselves, and all their most explosive conflicts could be fought out. It

[13] This is the central theme in the tradition of social criticism that runs from Tocqueville's *Democracy in America* to Marcuse's *One-Dimensional Man*.

[14] "Thoughts for the Times on War and Death," 293, in *Collected Papers* (5 volumes, New York: Basic Books, 1959), IV, 288–317.

would replace economics as the primary ground on which men seek to prove themselves superior to one another. It would be invested with all the violence which Rousseau's contemporaries were putting into the struggle for economic power. Indeed, once *amour-propre* became transformed into "patriotic drunkenness," the modern state's power to concentrate power, to organize natural and human resources, would ensure that the scope and depth of violence would be vastly enlarged. International relations as Rousseau saw them were competitive and aggressive already; but in his day the enormous destructive potentialities of the politics of inauthenticity were only just beginning to appear. In the two centuries since his time, they have become far more real.

Dropping Out: Peace at the Bottom of the Abyss

Thus the vivid imagination that first generated Rousseau's search for inauthenticity, and then drove him to flee from it, finally showed him that, as terrifying as the search for authenticity might be, the politics of inauthenticity were even worse. The sort of social system that would be required to protect men from themselves could do its job only by marking men with psychic wounds far deeper than any it might avert, and carrying them farther than ever away from inward peace. Meanwhile, however, Rousseau's fantasies of a selfless world brought him alarmingly close to the realities of the world he lived in. Amid the movement of traffic on the great highway of modern society, the tree that was the self seemed only a stumbling block in the way. It seemed that the way would be clear before long. The roots of the self were drying, dying. Only drastically radical social reform could save it. But while nearly all modern men might wish in their hearts for such a reform, there seemed to be no class in modern society from which the will and the power for such a reform could come. If history took its course, the self would simply wither away. Only a still, small voice, pointing the way to the self's roots, proclaiming the dream of its freedom and fulfillment, stood against the flow of time.

In the last years of his life, Rousseau seemed to embrace an ideal of authenticity radically different from the one we have explicated up to now. This ideal was developed in the very last thing he wrote, the *Rêveries du promeneur solitaire.* Here he felt he could find himself by "circumscribing himself" as much as possible, by fleeing from everyone and everything, and retreating as deep into the woods as he could go. "Because there are no great highways in this happy place [the Swiss island of St-Pierre on the lake of Bienne], it's not much frequented by travelers; but it's ideal for the solitary and contemplative man who loves to get drunk on the charms of nature, and to gather himself together in silence. . . ." (V. 1040) If he managed to entrench himself so deeply that it was "impossible to get out," he could then be *"enlacé de moi-même,"* entwined with himself. (1042) Free from the sexual possibilities and problems of men and women, he could become fascinated by the sexual properties of plants; released from the demands of human political life, he could glorify himself as the founder of a colony of rabbits. (1043–4) Lying on his back in a boat, his eyes turned toward the sky, he could "let my mind wander freely, with no definite object, plunged into a thousand confused but delightful reveries, a hundred times sweeter than anything I have found in what men call the pleasures of life." (1044) By getting away from these pleasures, which required effort and action, and letting himself go passively, he would be able to "feel with pleasure my existence." (1045)

The pleasures of life diverted Rousseau from his existence because, he explained, "these brief moments of frenzy and passion, as vivid as they may be, even in their vivacity are only scattered points of light along the line of life." The trouble was that they were constantly "transient and changing too rare and too rapid to constitute a state. . . ." Like "everything on the earth," they were part of "a continuous flux," devoid of any "constant or stable [arrêtée] form." It seemed, then, that time itself was the enemy of authenticity. The self could feel itself only at "an instant when our heart could truly say to us: *I wish this moment could last forever.*" Passions would always pass away, but the authentic self endured forever.

But if there is a state in which the soul can find a resting place [assiette] solid enough that it can rest completely, and gather together its whole being, without any need to recall the past or extend itself into the future; where time means nothing to it, where the present lasts forever, with no duration or succession, without any other feeling—neither deprivation nor enjoyment, neither pleasure nor pain, neither desire nor fear —only the one feeling of our existence, and this feeling is enough: so long as this state endures, the one who experiences it may be called happy. Not with an imperfect, poor, relative happiness, such as we get from the pleasures of life, but with a happiness that is sufficient, perfect and full, and that leaves no emptiness (*vide*) which the soul feels the need to fill. Such is the state in which I often found myself on the island of Saint-Pierre. . . . [1046]

The self could achieve authenticity only when it felt "nothing outside itself, nothing except itself and its own existence," when it was "stripped of all other feeling." At such moments, totally naked, "one is sufficient unto oneself, like God." (1047)

The idea of nakedness, as we have seen, was always vivid in Rousseau's imagination as a symbol of the authenticity he sought. It appeared at the very beginning of his first work: "The good man is an athlete who loves to wrestle stark naked; he despises those vile ornaments which cramp the use of his powers, and which were probably invented only to hide some deformity." (*Arts and Sciences,* 8) Here it was desirable to be naked so that man's natural powers could express themselves freely in action. The nakedness Rousseau had in mind at the end of his life was far more stark than this: by then, it was these very natural powers themselves that Rousseau was seeking to strip away. Thus, after declaring his intention "to find consolation, hope and peace in myself alone," he vowed to do it by "separating my spirit from all the painful objects that have occupied it so unhappily and uselessly." (*Rêveries,* I. 999) He was equating the *self* with the *spirit,* a spirit that was fundamentally opposed to all flesh, including his own.

> . . . in the idleness of my body, my soul is still active; it still produces thoughts and feelings; its inward, moral life has grown through the death of all my earthly and temporal interests. My body is only an obstacle [*embarras*] for me, and I detach myself from it as much as I can. [1000]

Authenticity was a resting place, then, safe from the flow of sensation and duration; by getting out of his body and out of time, he could get into himself.

Georges Poulet, who has written sympathetically and powerfully about the world of the *Rêveries,* sees Rousseau's recollection of static, bodiless ecstasy as an ascent from psychology to metaphysics. "For the first time in literature a text appears which sets out to recount—not as a didactic development or a mystical vision, but as an experience personally lived—the common denominator of the Alexandrians and Scholastics." Stripped of all feeling but that of his own existence, Rousseau attained genuine "moments of grace." (*Studies in Human Time,* 169–71)[15] It is certainly right to connect this timeless ecstasy with the Platonic and Christian ideas that prefigured it in time. But there is a crucial dimension to Rousseau's experience that marks it off sharply from all the metaphysics and mysticism it resembles. All metaphysicians and mystics alike assert that there is a fundamental, ultimate dualism in the universe: there is evanescent, apparent false world, and an eternal, real, true world: this dualism is permanent, irreconcilable, inherent in the structure of reality. Rousseau, however, did not ascribe such a dualism to reality itself, but only to his own way of imagining reality. Unlike the mystics who see their ecstasy as a breakthrough to reality, Rousseau spoke of his own moments of ecstasy as moments of self-deception, when "I could no longer mark the point that separated fantasies from realities." (*Rêveries,* V. 1048) He felt that if he could see things as they really were, his happiness would not last. He recognized, moreover, that the dualistic world-view that underlay his ecstasy was not inherent in all human experience, but rather a product of particular experiences that had taken place in his own life. Thus, considering the life most men led,

15 *Etudes sur le temps humain,* 1950, translated by Elliot Coleman (New York: Harper Torchbooks, 1959); cf. especially 158–84.

it wouldn't be so good if men were to become avid for the sweet ecstasies I've had, and disgusted with the active life to which their self-renewing needs perpetually call them. *But an unfortunate man who has been cut off from human society, and who can no longer do anything good or useful for others or for himself, can find in this state compensation for all the human felicities that fortune and men have taken away from him.* [1047]

Compensation: in other words, it made sense to rejoice in his sheer existence if that existence held possibilities for so little else. It was rational to detach himself from his passions if there was no way to satisfy them, or if any satisfaction could at any moment be taken away. It was wise to bring time to a stop if time only focused his desires on "a future that often can never be" (1046), if time broke the promises it made. In resigning himself, Rousseau felt he was "submitting myself to my destiny, without struggling against necessity." It was not a destiny he sought or welcomed, but it was one that he felt he could not escape. He did his best to make a virtue of that necessity: "through resignation I found compensation for all my sorrows in the tranquillity it brought me, which I could never have achieved through the continual labor of a resistance that was as painful as it was unfruitful." (I. 996) He was so intent on separating himself from the world only because he was sure that "Everything is finished for me on earth." For the first time in his life he could feel "ravishing calm," stable equilibrium, perfect peace. But he recognized bitterly that it was the peace of total defeat: "here I am, tranquil at the bottom of the abyss." (999)

Unlike metaphysicians and mystics, then, Rousseau did

not believe that life in the world was empty of possibilities; what he believed was that his own life had been emptied of possibilities, that "all the human felicities" had been "taken away from him" by "fortune and men." (V. 1047) In his last years he often meditated on who or what had been responsible for the ruin of his life. Sometimes he concocted paranoid fantasies which put the blame on a conspiracy involving a host of anonymous strangers and all his nearest and dearest friends. In the *Rêveries,* however, his one cryptic explanation of his misfortunes was both more systematic and more sensible, but more sinister in the long run. Here there was no conspiracy, but something far more powerful: *"Individuals die, but collective bodies live forever."* (I. 998) The whole structure of society, it seemed, was rigged against him. Thus it was futile to hope for vindication when a new generation arrived, a generation free from the personal grudges, fears, jealousy and vindictiveness that were turned against him now. So long as the social structure remained as it was, "the most sociable of men" (995) would be sure to stay down and out. Nevertheless, although he might be buried, he would not die; he would create a new life for himself underground, at the bottom of the abyss. Rousseau knew that the self could thrive on the very repression that was meant to destroy it. Thus Sophie's powerful and subversive imagination was "an effect of her education" (*Emile,* V. 368)—an education designed to stifle her capacity for imagination. Like Sophie, the self, if deprived of space in the world, would still always be free to lock itself in its room and dream. And it would always have a room of its own, inside its own head, which not even the most repressive world could take away.

Rousseau was convinced that the estrangement and emptiness of his last years stemmed from a malignant destiny that was uniquely his own. But if he had remembered more of what he had seen and understood while he was still part of his society, he would have realized how much company he had. Thus, at the start of the *Rêveries,* he defined his sad fate: "Here I am, alone on the earth, with no brother, no neighbor, no friend. . . ." (I. 995) And yet, it could happen in Paris too: as Saint-Preux had written, "I am never more alone than when I am in the crowd." (*Julie,* II.14, 233) So much of human friendship here was a fraud, so much brotherhood a screen for otherhood; men were thrown together, yet set against each other; trust and mutuality were impossible, suspicion and anxiety were all men could really share. Again, driven from the world, Rousseau felt that he "could no longer do anything good or useful for others or for himself." (*Rêveries,* V. 1047) And yet, this too was a familiar predicament in a society where every man was "always in contradiction with himself, always oscillating between his inclinations and his duties, neither man nor citizen, no good to himself or to others. Such is the ordinary man of our day, an Englishman, a Frenchman, a bourgeois: he is nothing." (*Emile,* I. 8) In a world where one could be neither man nor citizen, where states and societies were taking more and more ominous measures to put the self out of the way, was not every man an alien? Rousseau had more *semblables,* more *frères* than he knew. So many since his time have tried to take his way out of time; they have gone their own ways away from the great highways, searching for space "for the solitary and contemplative man to get drunk on the charms of nature, and to gather himself together in silence. . . ." (*Rêveries,* V. 1040) Rousseau was the first to define the vocation, the life project which our own age has called Dropping Out. He understood only too well the limitations of such a life, a life at the bottom of the abyss. But he argued, with an unsurpassed clarity and brilliance, that in a time in which the politics of authenticity could not hope to succeed, it was only by dropping out that the self could hope to survive. Nevertheless, although survival was a victory, it was a sadly hollow one: a totalitarian society would welcome this project of dropping out, which could get its most authentic and hence most dangerous citizens freely and quietly out of the way.

Conclusion

My language, no doubt, seems new to you.
ROXANE TO USBEK IN PARIS

. . . therefore it is in everyone's power to
become what he is—an individual.
KIERKEGAARD

You may not be interested in the dialectic,
but the dialectic is interested in you.
TROTSKY

THIS IS A BOOK about a new language, a language
that has arisen out of the experiences and needs of
modern life. Its story begins in eighteenth-century Paris, a
time and a place in which a distinctively modern form of
society was just coming into its own. Industrialization had
not yet begun; nevertheless, within this metropolis, a dynamic, expansive economy and a fluid, open, pluralistic social life were beginning to emerge. Men were thrown *on
their own* in a way men had never been before. Human impulses and energies which had always been buried or rigidly
channeled were suddenly free to express themselves in the
open. A whole new world of possibilities, both exhilarating
and terrifying, was coming into being. The ideal of authenticity, as we have explored it here, articulated men's deepest
responses to the modern world and their most intense hopes
for a new life in it.

The eighteenth century inherited and developed two rival forms of political thought: natural-rights theory, whose political goal was a maximum of *freedom,* and utilitarianism, which aimed for the greatest possible *happiness.* Montesquieu and Rousseau understood that neither the natural-right theorists' idea of freedom nor the utilitarian concept of happiness was adequate to express the needs and aspirations of modern men. Amid the fluidity and intensity of the life of the metropolis, men would no longer be content to receive and ingest their pleasures in an essentially passive way; these new men could find their greatest happiness only through a direct, active engagement of their whole personalities. Moreover, traditional, static, repetitive pleasures were deadening to them; they demanded new forms of happiness which would enable them to enlarge and expand themselves. Each individual, now, in order to maximize his happiness, required freedom to discover or to create a happiness that would be uniquely and fully *his own.* At the same time, a type of freedom which merely protected men from overt restraint or coercion would never suffice. Such protection was certainly indispensable; but by itself it provided only what Hegel called a "freedom of the void." This was not enough because modern men were not the complete, self-contained monadic units which alone could be fulfilled in a void. Their personalities, like their cities, were radically dynamic and expansive; if they lacked the means to express and develop themselves through activity in the world, their deepest impulses would be thwarted and their most vital capacities suppressed. Any adequate notion of freedom would have to include the individual's power to experience, to change and to grow in pursuit of his greatest happiness: in other words, the freedom *to be himself.* Thus the idea of authenticity both deepened and synthesized the traditional conceptions of both freedom and happiness, and made it clear that only through such a synthesis could either of these ideals be realized.

When the ideal of authenticity was held up to the eighteenth-century world from which it arose, two things happened. At first the ideal served as a trenchant critical tool against the traditional social structure which, although ideologically on the defensive, retained vast political power throughout Europe. This structure, the legacy of feudalism, ascribed rigid class identities to all men, forced them to act out the roles of *personae* in a ritual drama which had been cast—and caste—for all time. Montesquieu's *Persian Letters* and many of Rousseau's greatest writings figured as weapons in the century-long struggle of *philosophes,* bureaucratic reformers, and bourgeoisie against monarchic absolutism, aristocratic and clerical privilege: a struggle which, in 1789, finally brought the old structure crashing down. But the new urban, bourgeois social structure which was ascendant throughout the century, and which was eventually buttressed and sanctified by the liberal, constitutional *République,* was just as destructive to human authenticity as the system it replaced—in a sense even more destructive, because it promised men so much. The opportunity and the means for every man to be genuinely himself, extended with the left hand, were taken back by the right. Rousseau showed with brilliant and depressing lucidity how, in place of traditional identities as stagnant and rigid as stone, modernity had provided a form of identity as transient and insubstantial as the wind. Modern man's sense of himself was entirely relative, a function of his momentary success or failure in competition for property and power against his fellowmen. His body, his mind, his soul, all his faculties and capacities, appeared as nothing but competitive assets, to be invested prudently for a maximum return; he was forced constantly to develop and perfect himself, yet unable, even for a moment, to call himself his own. The demand for authenticity, then, proved to be radically subversive of that peculiarly modern society out of which it grew. It generated a new form of radicalism, profoundly *dialectical:* a radicalism that aimed, not to abolish the ideals and possibilities of modernity, but rather to fulfill them.[1]

This new radicalism produced many striking images and ideas of what an authentic life could be—images and ideas still relevant in our time. Montesquieu explored brilliantly the psychology and sociology of domination and freedom. He showed how all authoritarian systems and relationships labored under an inherent disability, that they were incapable of satisfying even the men who controlled them; that people could get satisfaction from one another only when they reciprocally recognized one another's individuality and freedom. He emphasized the importance of sexuality, not only in giving pleasure, but in establishing and expressing the power and autonomy of the self. He criticized the subjection of women, and argued that this impoverished the lives of men as well, and the life of society as a whole. Indeed, he insisted that the liberation of all oppressed groups—sexual, religious, political—was vital to the happiness of the rulers themselves. He suggested that everyone would be happiest in a society where every individual would be free to express himself and to control his life. This radically individualistic ideal was embodied concretely in Montesquieu's vision of the Parisian metropolis. Here was a medium both dense and fluid, full of opportunities for action

---

[1] Perhaps not so new after all, considering that this admirable formula is plundered from the Sermon on the Mount (*Matthew* 5: 17). I hope to examine Biblical forms of radicalism and dialectic in a future study.

and interaction—economic, intellectual, erotic—ideally conducive to individual self-expression and growth.

Rousseau penetrated beneath the dazzling surface of modern city life, and brought out into the open the contradictions at its core. The great flow of newly liberated human energy was being rigidly channeled, forced into a constantly expanding and unending war for wealth and power. It seemed that men were free only to exploit one another, or else be exploited themselves. Rousseau understood that the frantic and brutal economic activity of modern urban men sprang not from any excessive "selfishness," but rather from a desperate poverty, a profound emptiness of self. These men were driven by the hope that, by triumphing over one another, they could somehow prove themselves. Of course their hope was futile: no amount of wealth or power could ever be "enough" to fill up men who felt like vacuums inside. But their inevitable failure only drove them on to work for more. If men had never been so free as they were here, it was equally true that men had never been so repressed, so totally out of touch with their feelings and needs, so alienated from themselves. Moreover, the whole of modern culture—legal and political institutions, artistic and scientific and intellectual activity, sexual and social life—only reinforced and legitimized this alienation. Nevertheless, Rousseau believed, "we must draw from the disease itself the remedy that can cure it." (*Manuscrit,* I.2, 287) The contradictions of modern life could be resolved only through a more penetrating and profound modernity. The way out was the way in.

Two of his most strikingly original images pointed that way: the Tree on the Highway and the Maternal State. At the root of both images was the idea that, "taking men as they are and laws as they might be," (*Contract,* Introduction, 351) it was possible to use the institutions of a modern democratic state to transform modern society radically from within, so that its liberating potentialities could be fulfilled. This transformation would be carried out on two fronts, economic and educational. Rousseau's maternal state would undertake economic planning on a vast scale. It would aim at both an egalitarian redistribution of wealth and a return of the means of production to the worker. It would seek to give men an independence and self-sufficiency which would eliminate the cruel necessity that forced them to compete and exploit each other or perish. Meanwhile, Rousseau's educational policy would work with a new generation, striving to make them independent psychologically, to give them a sense of themselves that did not depend on their performance in a competitive social system. The way to do this was to construct educational enclaves that would protect the young trees—the children—from the destructive pressures of the highway around them. Enclosed in a free and secure environment, they could be brought up to discover and to trust themselves, to develop identities that would be authentically their own. "All wickedness comes from weakness. Make man strong and he will be good." (*Emile*, I. 33) Once Rousseau's children of the future were grown up, grown into themselves, they would be strong enough to be good. Secure in their sense of who they were, they would have no need to prove themselves at one another's expense. They would be able to enter into human relationships based on sharing and giving, on genuine mutuality, a mutuality that overflowed from fullness of self. The overflow would lead them first into romantic love, and then, further outward, to a social contract. They would desire and support a political life in which they could all participate actively, a politics that would be a medium for self-expression. In such a society the power of the state and the sphere of political life would be vastly enlarged. At the same time, Rousseau insisted, the only sort of state that could be trusted with so much power would be one in whose affairs all the people participated fully, one whose policies and actions could be directly and strictly controlled from below. Rousseau's description of the communal festival evoked beautifully a vision of how private and public happiness could come together, how the road to individuality and the road to community could be one.

Taken together, these images and ideas provide a rich legacy for modern political thought, and form a sort of agenda for nearly all the radical movements of the past two centuries. The programs of nineteenth-century socialism and anarchism, of the twentieth-century welfare state and the contemporary New Left, can all be seen as further developments of the structure of thought whose foundations Montesquieu and Rousseau laid down. What these very different movements share is a way of defining the crucial political task at hand: to make modern liberal society keep the promises it has made, to reform it—or revolutionize it— in order to realize the ideals of modern liberalism itself. The agenda for radical liberalism which Montesquieu and Rousseau brought up two centuries ago is still pending today.

Montesquieu and Rousseau have given us an agenda, but no utopia. They point the way for a politics of authenticity, but they deliver no fully realized vision of what we should find at the end. Two hundred years later, radical critics of modern society still have no overall vision of a new world. Some see this as a sign that the utopian imagination of Western man has dried up. Perhaps they are right; but perhaps this is not so bad. It may be, as Judith Shklar has argued persuasively, that utopian thinking is an obsolescent survival of classical values. Insofar as utopian thought seeks to create a closed, homogenous, all-absorbing political *cosmos,* it is antithetical to the dynamism, heterogeneity and openness of modern life—modern life both as it is and as we should like it to be.[2] If this is so, it explains why Rousseau's most concrete representation of a community founded on authenticity, in the republic of Valais, should represent an escape from the modern city into a timeless void. The utopia of Valais, for all its beauty and decency, is a rigidly closed society, devoid of diversity; its members have no chance to change, to experiment in living. For a modern man, to enter this closed world would be to alienate himself from his need for novelty, growth and self-development—a need which Rousseau understood so well. Even if a society like this could exist, modern men could live in it only by killing themselves inside; this utopia would be a home for deadened souls. For the politics of authenticity, any final solution would be a dissolution.

Rousseau often moved toward precisely this sort of solution. His vision of how sweet modern life could be only sharpened his awareness of how bitter it was. So far as he could see, there was no way to translate the vision into fact; the politics of authenticity possessed great imaginative power, but no real power to change the world. This disparity deepened his despair, and plummeted him into very different visions, into a psychic underworld which I have called the politics of inauthenticity. There he tried to reconcile himself to an alienated reality by destroying his capacity to imagine any alternative modes of reality. Rousseau came to see that he could save himself (and other modern

2 Shklar, "The Political Theory of Utopia," *Daedalus* (Spring, 1965), 367–81.

men) from despair only by saving himself (and them) from hope. Since any man's sense of himself was in itself an alternative, and hence a source of hope, it would be necessary to blot out the sense of self entirely. His desperate need to blot out the self drove him to become the most original and brilliant theorist of totalitarianism. The closed cosmos of Clarens, the first and perhaps the most imaginative and terrifying of modern anti-utopias, brought this perverse project to a triumphant fulfillment. In Rousseau's description of Clarens, and throughout his other writings, he showed the actual and potential rulers of the modern world that the liberal institutions which modernity was engendering could be a blessing in disguise. The welfare-oriented maternal state turned out to contain the same ambiguous potentialities that every mother carries within herself: its power to nourish and sustain life could be used to weaken and destroy life; the source of basic trust could be turned—or could turn itself—into a source of basic anxiety and terror. If the rulers were shrewd, they could control their subjects more totally than ever through a rule of veils, masks, disguises that could captivate men's minds while infusing them with the illusion that they were free.

And yet, even when Rousseau was most deeply involved in the politics of inauthenticity, he left clues to let us know that he was not dissolved in it. As much as he loved the world of Clarens, he tore himself away from it in the end, and recognized how misguided his longing for such a life had been; that life, he knew, turned out to generate far more terror and anxiety than it was meant to avert. If he understood and unfolded all the totalitarian potentialities of modern life, and showed how they could be transformed into actualities, we must remember that in his old age he totally dropped out of modern life, and lived alone and forlorn "at

319

the bottom of the abyss" in desperate hope of keeping his sense of self alive. If his ideas of domination recall the darkest corners of the Machiavellian world, we must remember how Rousseau himself understood the ambiguities of that world. "Machiavelli pretended to instruct kings, but it was the people he really taught. His *Prince* is the book of republicans." (*Contract*, III.6, 409) Just as Machiavelli's recipes for repression could be transformed by the people themselves into weapons of popular liberation, so Rousseau's own insight into how the self may be alienated can be transformed into insight into how self-alienation may be conquered. Rousseau is telling us that the impulses and needs that lead modern man out of himself must be understood and overcome in order to lead him back to himself. Here, too, only the hand that made the wound can heal it. The politics of inauthenticity is an integral and indispensable part of the politics of authenticity.

In the end, as we have seen, Rousseau gave up and dropped out. He had lost all hope that the tree could flourish on the highway—that the self could thrive in modern society; he saw in that society only "the crushing force of social conventions." He withdrew as deep as he could go into the woods, far from men, hoping to keep the self barely, dully, narrowly—but distinctly—alive. Must we follow him? Maybe not so fast. It is important to remember that both Montesquieu and Rousseau were living in a pre-revolutionary age. Neither they nor anyone else in their time could imagine concretely how men might act purposively and in concert to transform the social system as a whole. Hence the political options and ideas available to them were strictly limited. Montesquieu showed how an oppressed group might arise, but only in heroic last-ditch resistance, not in a revolt planned and organized systematically to succeed.

Rousseau, devoid of political hopes, came to feel that men could be themselves only by going underground, withdrawing into the interstices of society, where they might hope to survive. But this ideal, too, was purely reactive and defensive. The age of Romanticism and of Revolution which began a generation later generated a new realm of possibility, and a new model of authenticity: *l'homme révolté*, the man who gains his freedom and becomes himself by striving to liberate both himself and his fellow-men from a social system that alienates them all. Since then, the underground has become a temporary, tactical enclave, where radicals can get themselves together and develop their forces for a frontal attack on their system's roots. The thick woods which protected Rousseau's solitary walker yesterday shield guerrilla bands today.

Montesquieu and Rousseau were sealed off from a whole dimension of hope in which all of us since 1789 have lived; at the same time, they were protected from a new dimension of despair. The fact that it seems concretely possible to realize the ideal of authenticity has made it that much harder to bear when self-realization does not arrive. A failed revolution can be far more destructive to those who live through it than no revolution at all. A constant alternation of enchantment and disenchantment, hope and despair, has made the search for authenticity almost unbearable; suffering souls in search of a way out of the anguish of themselves have formed a vast constituency for politicians of inauthenticity, for totalitarians both of the sword and of the veil, of the Right and of the Left—and, perhaps most insidious of all, for totalitarianism of the "liberal" Center. So many of the imaginative landmarks of modern literature—from Clarens to the Grand Inquisitor's Cell to the Penal Colony to the Balcony to wherever Naked Lunch is eaten—are laboratories for hideous "experiments on what can be done to the self"! Some of the greatest spirits of our age have followed Rousseau's example, taken trips into their own underworlds, and returned, more fully and honestly themselves. Others, martyrs to modernity, have never come back. Meanwhile, so much of the horror of twentieth-century history stems from a politics which has transformed the theory of inauthenticity into practice on a mass scale, and from the many experiments which the holders of total power have carried out on the selves of the people they control. Many of the victims have been killed in monstrous ways; but many others remain alive and happy in the suburbs and offices and classrooms and legislative halls of the modern world. There is only one genuine form of respect we can pay to this last class of victims: to try to learn how to bring them back to themselves.

In this last enterprise Montesquieu and Rousseau may be of special help to us; they may help us to renew our precarious hopes. It should be clear by now that the approach to modern society I have found in Montesquieu and Rousseau prefigures Marxism in many deep ways. It is particularly close to that contemporary "revisionist" form of Marxism which has tried to incorporate the psychological sensitivity and insight of Freud and the psychoanalytic tradition. This synthetic project has generally de-emphasized class polarities, and argued that advanced industrial society generates forms of consciousness—generally false consciousness—and alienation which are shared by all. The ablest thinkers in this tradition today—Herbert Marcuse and R. D. Laing, for instance—have used it to paint a monochromatically dismal picture of our society. If all classes are essentially alike, according to this view, it is because all are essentially conditioned, manipulated, *embourgeoisées*. No one in this system is autonomous—not even at the top. No one even has an ego or an id—indeed, these Freudian categories are obsolescent; the system builds and programs everyone to order. Hence only an "underclass" which is totally "outside" the system can even understand it, let alone work to change it. The chances that such an underclass will form are very dim; even if it should form, the chances are that it will be co-opted. Real reform is possible only if an intellectual and spiritual vanguard, who possess a "higher form of consciousness," can manipulate the oppressed but confused masses into action. But while possible, this prospect is very improbable. Hence the self can preserve itself only by totally dropping out—by withdrawing into the woods, or into madness, or into both —by living secret lives and creating invisible communities underground. Montesquieu and Rousseau suggest that even in a thoroughly repressive society, there may be alternatives to the polarities of total revolution or total retreat. They argue that even though everyone is indeed conditioned by an alienated social system, *this conditioning may include a capacity to criticize and transcend the system.* We can see such a capacity deeply entrenched in the character structure of urban men today. The metropolis infuses us with survival skills. Primary among these skills is an ability to tell faces from masks, truths from lies, realities from appearances: an essential skill in a system where everyone is always trying to deceive everyone else. Essential, too, is a highly developed sensibility, a capacity for deep feeling—which we must know how to manipulate, to turn on and off at will, in order to bend others to our purposes. However, the very powers which enable us to see through others can also enable us to see through ourselves—or rather, to see *into* ourselves, through the masks the system has made us wear. If we look into ourselves, we will see how completely our society cuts us

323

off from ourselves, from our deepest feelings and needs and sources of happiness. And "we" here means *everyone*—the upper as well as the underclass, the sultans as well as the slaves. Everyone is being cheated by the system. Everyone has the power to see when he is in a box, and to try to break out. It may take a long and bitter fight, but it is at least possible to begin. The system is a long way from destroying itself, but, as the *Communist Manifesto* says, it bears within it the seeds of its destruction. If this is so, then, the people do not need to be manipulated; they need only to be educated. Radical critics do not need to expound philosophy; we need only to point very intently to what is there. One of the most important things for radical critics to point to is all the powerful feeling which the system tries to repress—in particular, every man's sense of his own unique, irreducible self. But we cannot evoke this feeling in other people unless we are in touch with it in ourselves. It is with ourselves, then, that the politics of authenticity must begin.

Montesquieu and Rousseau can bring more hope to us than they could feel for themselves. The men of the Enlightenment could not foresee the rise of a revolutionary politics. Still, they understood how profoundly political the problem of personal authenticity was, how deeply interwoven were the destinies of the self, society, and the state in the modern age. They lived at a crucial moment in human history, on the eve of the French and Industrial Revolutions. At such a moment, just before the flood, two great streams of consciousness—self-consciousness and social consciousness—converged. For perhaps a century, they flowed and developed together, as one. After the catastrophes of 1848, their unity was split, and they went strictly separate ways. Nevertheless, their overflow formed and nourished the ground our culture still stands on today. And there are signs today that they may be coming together again. Our society is filled with people who are ardently yearning and consciously striving for authenticity: moral philosophers who are exploring the idea of "self-realization"; psychiatrists and their patients who are working to develop and strengthen "ego-identity"; artists and writers who gave the word "authenticity" the cultural force it has today—some consciously influenced by existentialism, others ignorant of it, but all bent on creating works and living lives in which their deepest, truest selves will somehow be expressed; young people, hip or straight, seeking to "get themselves together," determined above all to "do their own thing"; countless anonymous men and women all over who are fighting, desperately and against all odds, simply to preserve, to feel, to be themselves. All these seekers after authenticity are just beginning to learn a fact of life which our first seekers always knew: that whoever you are, or want to be, you may not be interested in politics, but politics is interested in you.

Marshall Berman

Marshall Berman was born in New York City in 1940. He is a graduate of Columbia College and holds advanced degrees from Oxford and Harvard. Currently, he teaches political theory at The City College of New York, where he is Assistant Professor of Political Science. Mr. Berman has contributed articles of a political and cultural nature to such journals as *Partisan Review* and *Dissent.*